Top Accounting and Auditing Issues for 2023 | CPE Course

Kelen Camehl, CPA, MBA
Lewis R. Fisher, CPA
Robert K. Minniti, CPA, CFE, CrFA, CVA, CFF, MAFF, CGMA, PI, DBA
Cecil Patterson, Jr., CPA, MBA

D1383231

 Wolters Kluwer

Contributors

Contributing Editor . . . . Kelen Camehl, CPA, MBA

Robert K. Minniti, CPA, CFE, CrFA, CVA, CFF, MAFF, CGMA, PI, DBA

Cecil Patterson, Jr., CPA, MBA

Production Coordinator . . . . Mariela de la Torre; Jennifer Schencker;

Gokiladevi Sashikumar; Anna Dougherty

Production . . . . Sharon Sofinski; Anbarasu Anbumani

ISBN: 978-0-8080-5933-2

2700 Lake Cook Road
Riverwoods, IL 60015
800 344 3734
CCHCPELink.com

SUSTAINABLE FORESTRY INITIATIVE

Certified Sourcing

www.sfiprogram.org

SFI-01681

Printed in the United States of America

Introduction

Top Accounting and Auditing Issues for 2023 CPE Course helps CPAs stay abreast of the most significant new accounting and auditing standards and important projects. It does so by identifying the events of the past year that have developed into hot issues and reviewing the opportunities and pitfalls presented by these changes. The topics reviewed in this course were selected because of their impact on financial reporting and because of the role they play in understanding the accounting and auditing landscape in the year ahead.

Module 1 of this course reviews top accounting issues.

Chapter 1 provides an overview of updates to U.S. generally accepted accounting principles (GAAP) impacting the 2022 calendar year-end reporting period. To ensure all recent pronouncements are captured, this chapter revisits standards issued in late 2021, to alert readers to changes that could impact their reporting. Discussion will also be provided on existing standards originating from the FASB's Private Company Council and how these can streamline reporting requirements.

Chapter 2 is designed to assist accountants and auditors who are working with small businesses. The chapter assumes that there will be a limited budget for implementing cybersecurity internal controls for a small business. It will also discuss working directly with small business owners and bookkeepers, and some of their resistance to formalized internal controls. Since an effective risk assessment is necessary to develop internal controls, cyber fraud risks specific to small businesses will also be covered.

Chapter 3 reviews real-world applications for blockchains. Many people have heard of blockchains but are not sure what they are or how they work. You might know that blockchains are used for cryptocurrency transactions, but are you aware of the other business and accounting uses for blockchain technology? This chapter explores current and possible future uses for blockchain technology in businesses, government entities, and in the accounting and auditing profession. Examples of how blockchains work will be provided.

Module 2 of this course reviews top auditing issues.

Chapter 4 reviews internal control and internal control systems from the auditor's point of view. It provides updates on internal controls and American Institute of Certified Public Accountants (AICPA) auditing standards, as well as internal control and audit reports. It also covers the new quality management standards approved by the AICPA Accounting Standards Board (ASB), discusses internal control and COVID-19 issues, along with other related matters.

Chapter 5 presents a basic overview of auditing crypto assets and liabilities. It discusses cryptocurrencies and tokens and how these assets and liabilities should be recorded on the books.

Chapter 6 presents a basic overview of the fraud risks auditors may encounter when conducting remote audits. It discusses the risks and provides auditing procedures that can help to mitigate the risks.

Chapter 7 gives an overview of environmental, social, and governance (ESG) reporting requirements and standards and ESG's impact on generally accepted auditing standards (GAAS) and attestation.

Module 3 of this course reviews SEC reporting issues.

Chapter 8 provides an overview of the rules and regulations with respect to the management's discussion and analysis (MD&A) section of an entity's consolidated financial statements filed with the U.S. Securities and Exchange Commission (SEC).

Chapter 9 provides an overview of non-GAAP financial measures with a particular emphasis on comments from the U.S. Securities and Exchange Commission (SEC) and the Financial Accounting Standards Board (FASB), as well as comment letter analysis from several of the Big 4 accounting firms.

Study Questions. Throughout the course you will find Study Questions to help you test your knowledge, and comments that are vital to understanding a particular strategy or idea. Answers to the Study Questions with feedback on both correct and incorrect responses are provided in a special section beginning at ¶ 10,100.

Final Exam. This course is divided into three Modules. Take your time and review all course Modules. When you feel confident that you thoroughly understand the material, turn to the Final Exam. Complete one or all three Final Exams for continuing professional education credit.

Go to **cchcpelink.com/printcpe** to complete your Final Exam online for immediate results. My Dashboard provides convenient storage for your CPE course Certificates. Further information is provided in the CPE Final Exam instructions at ¶ 10,300. **Please note, manual grading is no longer available for Top Accounting and Auditing Issues. All answer sheets must be submitted online for grading and processing.**

August 2022

PLEDGE TO QUALITY

Thank you for choosing this CCH® CPELink product. We will continue to produce high quality products that challenge your intellect and give you the best option for your Continuing Education requirements. Should you have a concern about this or any other Wolters Kluwer product, please call our Customer Service Department at 1-800-344-3734.

COURSE OBJECTIVES

This course provides an overview of important accounting and auditing developments. At the completion of this course, the reader will be able to:

- Recognize required GAAP reporting requirements for your company or clients
- Identify proper accounting treatment for cryptocurrencies
- Summarize recent SEC proposals
- Identify accounting issues related to Paycheck Protection Program (PPP) loan treatment and the Employee Retention Tax Credit
- Differentiate how various Accounting Standards Updates (ASUs) apply
- Recognize how to properly apply new accounting standards
- Identify risks for cyber fraud
- Develop cost-effective cybersecurity internal controls for small businesses

- Define what a blockchain is
- Identify how blockchains work
- Identify uses for blockchains
- Identify updates on internal controls and AICPA auditing standards
- Identify updates on internal control and audit reports
- Recognize internal control and COVID-19 issues
- Differentiate effective dates of Statements on Auditing Standards (SAS)
- Recognize the auditor's requirement relevant to understanding an entity's control activities
- Identify true statements regarding risk assessment procedures and internal controls
- Differentiate in what section of the auditor's report the auditor's opinion is under AU-C 700
- Describe the key audit matters paragraph in the auditor's report
- Recognize the changes included in SAS No. 142
- Identify financial reporting considerations related to subsequent events
- Identify the steps in an audit of crypto assets and liabilities
- Recognize audit procedures for auditing crypto assets and liabilities
- Define fraud and several fraud theories
- Recognize fraud risks that can arise when planning and conducting remote audits
- Identify audit procedures that can help to mitigate fraud risks
- Describe the basics of ESG for management and auditors in ESG engagements, including ESG requirements and standards
- Identify issues for present and future situations and engagements with ESG positions
- Recognize the impacts ESG has on generally accepted auditing standards (GAAS) and attestation
- Identify what an auditor needs to know about management's policies and procedures that are unique to climate-related matters
- Differentiate relevant AU-C sections and how they apply
- Describe examples of climate-related matters that could raise substantial doubt about an entity's ability to continue as a going concern
- Describe the requirements proposed by the Securities and Exchange Commission (SEC) for public companies
- Identify the SEC Regulation applicable to MD&A
- Recognize the primary objective and focus areas related to MD&A
- Identify key information that should be included within a company's MD&A
- Recognize the types of transactions that should be discussed in MD&A

- Identify methods to enhance the presentation of MD&A

- Differentiate between a GAAP financial measure and a non-GAAP financial measure

- Recognize examples of different types of non-GAAP financial measures

- Identify which SEC guidance is applicable to different types of non-GAAP financial measures

- Recognize disclosures within the scope of Regulation G

- Identify key requirements included within both Regulation G and Regulation S-K related to these measures

---

Additional copies of this course may be downloaded from **cchcpelink.com/printcpe**. Printed copies of the course are available for $8.00 by calling 1-800-344-3734 (ask for product 10024493-0010).

Contents

MODULE 1: TOP ACCOUNTING ISSUES— CHAPTER 1: 2022 GAAP Update

¶ 101 WELCOME

This chapter provides an overview of updates to U.S. generally accepted accounting principles (GAAP) impacting the 2022 calendar year-end reporting period. To ensure all recent pronouncements are captured, this chapter revisits standards issued in late 2021, to alert readers to changes that could impact their reporting. Discussion will also be provided on existing standards originating from the FASB's Private Company Council and how these can streamline reporting requirements.

¶ 102 LEARNING OBJECTIVES

Upon completion of this chapter, you will be able to:

- Recognize required GAAP reporting requirements for your company or clients
- Identify proper accounting treatment for cryptocurrencies
- Summarize recent SEC proposals
- Identify accounting issues related to Paycheck Protection Program (PPP) loan treatment and the Employee Retention Tax Credit
- Differentiate how various Accounting Standards Updates (ASUs) apply
- Recognize how to properly apply new accounting standards

¶ 103 ACCOUNTING FOR CRYPTOCURRENCIES

A cryptocurrency is "a medium of exchange that is built on distributed ledger technology." Cryptocurrency has no intrinsic value because its only purpose is to function as a medium of exchange. Unlike some other digital assets, cryptocurrency provides a holder with no contractual rights or obligations. Cryptocurrency is a digital asset that is not issued by a jurisdictional authority (sovereign government), and it is not considered a security under U.S. securities law. Examples of cryptocurrency include, but are not limited to, the following:

- Bitcoin
- Dogecoin
- Litecoin
- Ethereum

It is estimated that there are over 9,000 distinct cryptocurrencies, and that number is growing. Globally, cryptocurrencies have over $1.5 trillion in market value. Much of the current corporate media focus is on companies involved in the mining or trading of cryptocurrencies. That focus reflects the fact that most of the public companies holding cryptocurrencies engage in crypto mining companies or crypto exchanges.

Authoritative Guidance

Accountants looking for guidance on financial reporting issues related to the use of cryptocurrencies in business transactions will find limited guidance in the Financial Accounting Standards Board (FASB) Accounting Standards Codification (ASC). In fact, there is no specific guidance specific to digital assets in the GAAP codification.

To fill that void, the American Institute of Certified Public Accountants (AICPA) published a practice aid entitled "Accounting for and Auditing of Digital Assets" (https://www.aicpa.org/resources/download/accounting-for-and-auditing-of-digital-assets-practice-aid-pdf) that addresses several basic questions about the application of existing U.S. GAAP to cryptocurrencies. The practice aid offers a helpful framework that preparers and auditors can consult when faced with accounting questions regarding cryptocurrencies. Although the AICPA guidance is nonauthoritative, its analyses and recommendations are grounded in existing U.S. GAAP. For this reason, preparers and auditors have been applying it in practice. In January 2022, the AICPA added several Q&As to its practice aid. The FASB also recently added a research project on digital assets to its agenda. These developments are discussed in more detail later in this section.

Accounting for Cryptocurrencies: Current Practice

Under existing GAAP, cryptocurrencies are not considered cash or cash equivalents. For investment companies, cryptocurrency is measured at fair value net of costs, with subsequent remeasurement. Companies that do not meet the definition of an investment company account for cryptocurrencies as indefinite lived intangible assets. The purchase of cryptocurrency is recorded at cost.

Balance Sheet Classification for Cryptocurrency	
Cash or cash equivalent?	No, it is not legal tender.
Financial instrument?	No, it is just a medium of exchange.
Inventory?	No, it is not tangible personal property.
Foreign currency?	No, it is not backed by a government.

Impairment is evaluated annually or more frequently if a triggering event indicates that it is more likely than not that the asset is impaired. If an impairment indicator exists and the carrying value of the cryptocurrency exceeds its fair value, an impairment loss equal to the difference is recognized in income. The adjusted carrying amount becomes the new accounting basis for the cryptocurrency.

A subsequent recovery in value is not recognized until it is realized. Fair value is typically based on pricing data on various cryptocurrency exchanges. Although a cryptocurrency's price or value is always referenced using a fiat currency, such as the U.S. dollar or the Euro, the value of any cryptocurrency is independent of any country, fiat currency, or crypto exchange. Moreover, because cryptocurrency represents a decentralized digital currency, there is no standard price at any given time and prices for the same cryptocurrency often vary by small amounts on various exchanges. Entities should carefully assess the markets in which the cryptocurrency trades to determine the principal (or most advantageous) market, whether that market is active, whether trades are orderly, and whether the information produced by the market is reliable.

Financial Statement Disclosures

In addition to appropriately classifying cryptocurrency holdings as intangible assets on the balance sheet, companies should consider the appropriate presentation of cryptocurrency transactions in the cash flow statement and the classification of cryptocurrency-related gains and losses in the income statement. Relevant disclosures may include the following:

- Revenue contracts that involve the acceptance of noncash consideration
- Intangible assets with indefinite lives, including impairments
- Fair value measurements
- Significant noncash transactions that involve the exchange of noncash assets

Recent Developments

FASB. In October 2020, the FASB considered whether to add a project on cryptocurrencies to its agenda. Stakeholders had asked the FASB to consider whether the current practice of accounting for cryptocurrencies as indefinite-lived intangible assets is appropriate. At that time, the FASB decided not to add the topic to its agenda because the issues were not pervasive. Most companies were not holding material amounts of cryptocurrencies, and those that accepted Bitcoin and other cryptocurrency as payment for goods and services typically converted those digital assets immediately into cash.

During 2021, the FASB issued an Invitation to Comment (ITC) to obtain input on the development of its standards-setting agenda. Although the ITC addressed a long list of potential topics, more than half of the respondents listed digital assets as a high priority.

AICPA. In early 2022, the AICPA added the following three new cryptocurrency topics to its practice aid:

- *Contracts involving the future delivery of cryptocurrency.* This topic addresses the accounting for a contract to provide a customer with goods or services in exchange for a promise to receive a fixed quantity of cryptocurrency.

- *Cryptocurrency asset lending.* This topic applies to situations in which a company lends a fixed number of units of cryptocurrency to a borrower for a fixed term in exchange for a fee (i.e., interest) payable monthly in units of that same cryptocurrency. At the end of the term, the borrower must deliver the borrowed units of cryptocurrency to the lender. In this scenario, the ownership of the loaned cryptocurrency is transferred to the borrower and the borrower has the right to transfer, encumber, or pledge the cryptocurrency in any way it chooses. Further, the borrower is not required to post collateral.

- *Cryptocurrency mining.* The AICPA practice aid addresses two questions related to cryptocurrency mining. The first concerns how the mining company should account for transaction fees and block rewards. The second question involves an arrangement in which the mining company shares its computing infrastructure with a mining pool run by a third-party operator. Although each participant in the pool operates its own computing infrastructure, block rewards are collected by the operator and transferred to the pool participants in accordance with an agreed-upon formula.

Presidential Executive Order. Underscoring the heightened interest in cryptocurrencies, on March 9, 2022, President Biden issued an executive order setting forth a national policy for digital assets. The Executive Order lays out a framework to comprehensively consider opportunities for digital currencies, including central bank digital currencies, while simultaneously identifying and mitigating the risks these digital currencies present to consumers, investors, businesses, financial stability, and national security.

¶ 104 RECENT SEC PROPOSALS

Recent U.S. Securities and Exchange Commission (SEC) activity may be of interest to practitioners and those in reporting positions. This activity may signal future activity by the FASB. In the nine months ended February 28, 2022, the SEC issued more than 20 proposals, compared to the first six months of 2021, when it issued only one proposal. Although none of these recent proposals would change financial reporting related disclosures, some would impact the periodic reports and proxy filings of many public companies.

The four major proposals for consideration are as follows:

- Pay for Performance
- Rule 10b5/Insider Trading
- Share Repurchases
- Recovery of Executive Compensation

Pay for Performance

This proposal would require companies to disclose the relationship between executive compensation and financial performance, as mandated by the Dodd-Frank Act. The proposed rule would not apply to foreign registrants, registered investment companies, or emerging growth companies. While smaller reporting companies are within the scope of these disclosures, they would provide only scaled disclosures.

The SEC released this proposal in 2015 but did not finalize it. It has now reopened the comment period and suggested potential changes to the original proposal. Under the original proposal, companies would be required to provide a table disclosing compensation, cumulative total shareholder return, and peer group shareholder return for each of the most recent five years.

Compensation information would be disaggregated to disclose annual compensation to the chief executive officer separately from the average annual compensation to the other named executive officers. The other named executive officers would include the CEO and the other three most highly compensated executive officers.

The table would present two measures of compensation: summary compensation and compensation paid during the year. Summary compensation would be determined consistent with the existing executive compensation disclosure rules. A separate disclosure of compensation paid is proposed to comply with the legislative language referring to "executive compensation actually paid."

Cumulative total shareholder return was originally proposed as the sole measure of financial performance. This measure aligns with the legislative language that defines financial performance as incorporating changes in the value of the company's common stock as well as dividends and distributions. In addition, cumulative total shareholder return is already disclosed in the company's stock performance graph.

Based on the feedback for its original proposal, the SEC is now proposing that the table present three additional measures of financial performance: pre-tax income, net income, and a company-selected measure of performance. The company-selected measure of performance would be defined as the most important performance measure not already disclosed in the table that the company uses to link compensation to performance. The revised proposal would also require companies to separately list the five most important performance measures, in order of importance, that are used to set executive pay. Smaller reporting companies would report scaled information that would, among other things, exclude peer group total shareholder return information and be limited to the most recent three years.

Rule 10b5/Insider Trading

This proposal, which would affect both individuals and issuers, would add new conditions to the availability of the affirmative insider trading liability defense available to directors and corporate officers. Issuers would be required to disclose their insider trading policies and procedures and report equity compensation awards made shortly before or after the disclosure of material nonpublic information.

Rule 10b5-1, which was adopted in 2000, established several conditions which, if met, allow an insider who has access to material non-public information to assert an affirmative defense against insider trading liability. These conditions create a safe harbor for trading based on a plan that establishes a regular, predetermined program for buying or selling company securities. The proposal would address shortcomings in this rule that open the door to potential abuses. Specifically, it would add a cooling-off period before trading can begin under a newly adopted or modified trading arrangement. It would preclude an affirmative defense for multiple overlapping trading arrangements for open market trades in the same class of securities. In addition, officers and directors would have to certify that they are not aware of material nonpublic information when adopting a new or modified trading arrangement.

The proposal would require companies to disclose the following:

- The company's insider trading policies and procedures. (Companies that do not have such policies and procedures would be required to explain why they do not.)
- The company's policies and practices regarding the timing of equity awards and the release of material nonpublic information.
- Quantitative information, in tabular format, about equity compensation awards granted within 14 calendar days before or after the release of material nonpublic information.
- The adoption or termination of any Rule 10b5-1 trading arrangements by directors, officers, and issuers during the quarter. The terms of these arrangements would also be disclosed.

Share Repurchases

This proposal would require companies to provide more detailed and more frequent disclosures about purchases of their equity securities.

In the 1980s, the SEC adopted a rule addressing a company's purchase of its own shares of stock. Acknowledging the need to balance a company's legitimate business reasons for purchasing its shares against the potentially significant effect of those purchases on the market for those shares, the rule was intended to minimize the disruptive effect of share repurchases on a company's stock price. Companies that complied with the rule were offered protections from liability against allegations of stock price manipulation. The rule created a safe harbor for share repurchases by an issuer.

The rule did not impose any specific disclosure requirements on companies. Although companies often repurchase shares pursuant to a publicly announced share repurchase program, disclosure of a repurchase plan is not required to qualify for the safe harbor. The SEC amended its rules in 2003 to require quarterly disclosure of actual share repurchases executed in both open market and private transactions. The disclosure includes the number of shares purchased (regardless of whether the purchase was part of a publicly announced repurchase program) by month, the number of shares purchased as part of a publicly announced repurchase program, and the maximum shares that may yet be repurchased under that program.

In 2016, the SEC issued a concept release regarding Regulation S-K. One of the questions asked was whether investors found these disclosures useful. Some commentators requested expanded disclosures, but others did not. The proposal would expand both the frequency and the information content of share repurchase disclosures. Companies would disclose the following:

- Repurchase transactions one business day after the execution of a share repurchase order.
- Additional qualitative information about their share repurchases such as the objective of share repurchases, the criteria used to determine the amount of

repurchases, and any policies or restrictions relating to purchases and sales by officers and directors during a repurchase program. It would also indicate whether the purchases were made in reliance on the safe harbor.

This information would be incremental to the current quarterly disclosure of share repurchases by month.

Recovery of Executive Compensation

This proposal would direct national securities exchanges and national securities associations to establish listing standards requiring issuers to adopt a policy providing for the recovery of incentive-based compensation when an error in the financial statements results in a restatement. It would also require companies to disclose their policy and any recovery of incentive compensation resulting from a restatement. These proposed changes are mandated by the Dodd-Frank Act. The proposal would apply to all listed issuers, including smaller reporting companies, emerging growth companies and foreign registrants, except for certain registered investment companies that do not provide incentive-based compensation.

The SEC released this proposal in 2015 but did not finalize it soon after. In October 2021, the SEC reopened the comment period and asked for input on changes to its original proposal. The proposal would implement Congress's mandate that national securities exchanges and associations prohibit the listing of securities of companies that have not established a compensation recovery policy for situations in which executives received incentive-based compensation for financial results that were materially misstated. (These policies are commonly called "clawback policies.") Congress's mandate applies to all securities listings, not just those of domestic companies or larger companies. The proposal would direct national securities exchanges and associations to establish listing standards requiring companies to adopt and comply with a compensation recovery policy that:

- Requires recovery from current and former executive officers who received incentive-based compensation during the three fiscal years preceding the date on which the company is required to prepare an accounting restatement to correct a material error. The recovery policy must apply regardless of whether that executive engaged in misconduct or was responsible for the misstatement.
- Determines the amount of compensation to be recovered on the basis of the corrected financial information.
- Prohibits indemnifying executives against the loss of recoverable incentive-based compensation.

For this purpose, executive officers include the company's president, principal financial officer, principal accounting officer, and any vice president in charge of a principal business unit, division, or function. Incentive-based compensation includes compensation that is based in whole or in part on any measure that is derived from the company's financial statements, stock price, or total shareholder return. The proposal also would require companies to file their compensation recovery policy as an exhibit to the annual report and to make certain disclosures if the company were required to recover compensation under its policy due to a restatement of its historical financial statements.

In reopening the comment period, the SEC asked for input on the proposed definition of an accounting restatement. Specifically, the SEC is proposing that this term include restatements to correct errors that were not material to the previously issued financial statements but would result in a material misstatement if (1) the errors were left uncorrected in the current period or (2) the errors were corrected in the current period. The proposal would amend Regulation S-K and require the filing of an additional exhibit in connection with the filing of Form 10-K.

¶ 105 PPP LOAN TREATMENT AND EMPLOYEE RETENTION TAX CREDIT

Paycheck Protection Program (PPP) Loan Treatment

There currently is no specific authoritative guidance on properly disclosing and reporting PPP loan forgiveness in the financial statements from a GAAP standpoint. ASC Topic 470, *Debt*, provides general guidance for this issue. However, the AICPA Center for Plain English Accounting (CPEA) issued more specific discussion on this issue over one year ago. While the AICPA guidance is not authoritative, it is instructive and useful for ensuring adequate treatment.

According to the guidance, if the PPP loan is forgiven, if it is thought of as a subsequent event, it is a Type II event. Therefore, it would be disclosed in the financial statements, but it would not be recorded if it occurred subsequently. As required by the debt model, there must be a "legal" release. A legal release means that a company must have something from the lender that positively states that the loan has been forgiven. This is challenging for a PPP loan because there is diversity in the type of forgiveness notification companies have received. Every bank seems to have a different format for relaying that a loan has been forgiven, and in practice it does not appear that a formal SBA certificate noting forgiveness is received.

Each company should make a policy election as to how it will record the PPP loan and disclose where on the balance sheet the loan would reside if it has not been forgiven yet. It should also indicate where on the income statement the loan will reside once the forgiveness is received. Often it appears as a line item in "other income" when it has been forgiven.

PPP loan forgiveness does not impact an entity's operating expenses or its gross margin. Note that there is no language that prohibits the entity from having flexibility in the income statement. In some cases, it has been included as an operating expense because the entity said the PPP loan was used for rent and to offset employee expenses.

Regardless, the entity should ensure it has made a policy election and that it has properly disclosed it in the footnotes to the financial statements.

Employee Retention Credit/PPP Loan Interaction

The Employee Retention Credit (ERC) program was dramatically enhanced beginning January 1, 2021. The program originally offered a credit of up to $5,000 per employee for very small companies, that is, companies with fewer than 100 employees. The ERC program was expanded in 2021 to allow companies of up to 500 employees to meet the definition of a "small employer" and to then receive up to $7,000 per employee per quarter through Q3. That means if a company qualified, it could get an ERC of up to $21,000 per eligible employee during 2021.

Application for the ERC is administered by filing IRS Form 941. If a company determined it qualifies for the ERC but neglected to file, it can file an amended Form 941 and Form 941X for those applicable quarters to claim the ERC. In practice, many companies claimed the ERC in 2021 and the monies did not start arriving until 2022, a delay of almost 12 months in receiving the credit.

Because the IRS set up the ERC to be administered through the payroll tax form, there is not an effective way for the IRS to determine which companies qualified based on the new formula. This means a company qualifies without exception versus the subjective methodology, which is very rare. A limited pool of companies would qualify under that. As a result, some taxpayers abused the ERC program. From a reporting standpoint, this raises red flags.

Also, if a company received PPP loan forgiveness and utilized wages over a certain period, it cannot claim those same wages for the ERC (i.e., it cannot "double-dip"). The problem is that many companies haven't taken proper steps to ensure that they didn't double-dip. If a company has taken advantage of both programs, it would have a contingency where it would have to repay that money to the government. From a U.S. GAAP standpoint, if practitioners see a company has claimed both the ERC and the PPP, they should at least perform an inquiry in a review. From an audit standpoint, practitioners should obtain the populations of those two amounts to ensure that the client hasn't claimed credits for which it is not eligible.

¶ 106 FAIR VALUE OF EQUITY SECURITIES: PROPOSED CHANGES

The FASB has issued ASU 2022-03 in March of 2022 to consider the treatment of fair value of an equity security that is subject to a lock-up, market standoff, or similar agreement that restricts the sale of the security for a period. Under U.S. GAAP, the fair value of an asset must consider the asset's characteristics, including restrictions on the sale of the asset if a market participant would also take those characteristics into account.

Equity securities, particularly those issued by emerging companies, are occasionally subject to sale restrictions. Some sale restrictions arise because the equity security is unregistered and does not qualify for an exemption from registration. Other restrictions result from a contractual agreement, such as a lock-up or market standoff agreement, that prohibits the investor from selling the securities for a specific period of time.

Currently, many companies see a distinction between these types of restrictions. They view restrictions related to a security's registration status as a characteristic of the security. On the other hand, they consider a contractual sale restriction, such as a lock-up agreement, to be specific to the investor who holds the security. A contractual sale restriction is therefore not a characteristic of the security that is relevant to a market participant.

However, some companies, consider both types of sale restrictions to be characteristics of the equity security. Therefore, they factor the effect of contractual sale restrictions into the fair value of an equity security. Investment companies, which measure their holdings of equity securities at fair value under U.S. GAAP, often take this view. These alternative views have led to diversity in practice.

ASU *Fair Value Measurement (Topic 820)—Fair Value Measurement of Equity Securities Subject to Contractual Sale Restrictions*, eliminates this diversity by clarifying that a contractual restriction is not a characteristic of the equity security that is being measured. As a result, the fair value of an equity security that is subject to a lock-up, market standoff, or similar agreement would not be discounted to reflect the limitations on sale that result from that agreement.

Although the contractual restrictions would not be part of the "unit of account" that is being measured, ASU 2022-03 does not address whether or how to account for the separate contractual agreement.

For public business entities, the amendments in this Update are effective for fiscal years beginning after December 15, 2023, and interim periods within those fiscal years.

For all other entities, the amendments are effective for fiscal years beginning after December 15, 2024, and interim periods within those fiscal years. Early adoption is permitted for both interim and annual financial statements that have not yet been issued or made available for issuance. Transition would be prospective, with special transition provisions for investment companies. It makes this clarification by amending the following three sections of the current fair value measurement guidance:

- *Definition of a restricted security.* Add a definition of *restricted security* to the Master Glossary. Under the proposal, a security whose sale is restricted due to a lock-up, market standoff, or similar agreement would not meet the definition of a restricted security.

- *Discussion of general principles.* Add clarifying language to explain that a contractual restriction is a characteristic of the company that holds the security, not the security itself.

- *Example of the effect of a restriction on the sale of an equity security.* Modify the current example to distinguish between a restriction on sale that is specific to the equity security and thus relevant to a market participant and a contractual restriction that is not specific to the equity security and thus not considered in determining fair value.

It is a narrow issue, but with the proliferation of start-up companies and the use of equity instruments to entice investors, the matter could create complications for practitioners and/or those in charge of reporting for the related companies

STUDY QUESTIONS

---

1. Which of the following statements is incorrect with respect to cryptocurrency?

   a. It is a medium of exchange that is built on distributed ledger technology.

   b. It has no contractual rights.

   c. It is considered a security under U.S. securities law.

   d. It is not issued by a jurisdictional authority.

2. How is cryptocurrency accounted for by investment companies under current practice?

   a. It is accounted for as an indefinite lived intangible asset.

   b. It is measured at fair value net of costs.

   c. It is recorded at cost with subsequent consideration of impairment.

   d. There is recognition of subsequent increases in value only when realized.

3. Which of the following is one of the four major SEC proposals discussed in this chapter?

   a. Climate-change disclosures

   b. Asset retirement obligations

   c. Pay for performance

   d. Related-party leases

¶ 107 RECENT AUTHORITATIVE U.S. ACCOUNTING STANDARDS

This section covers Accounting Standards Updates (ASUs) issued in late 2021 through the first three months of 2022, in chronological order.

Financial Instruments – Credit Losses (Topic 326): *Discount Rates— Not Public Business Entities*

Number	Issue Date	Transition Guidance
ASU 2022-02	3-31-2022	326-10-65-5
Earliest Effective Annual Period (Years Beginning or Ending After)	12-15-2022	
Implementation Information Effective Date	ASU No. 2022-01 is effective for public business entities for fiscal years beginning after December 15, 2022, and interim periods within those fiscal years. For all other entities, ASU No. 2022-01 is effective for fiscal years beginning after December 15, 2023, and interim periods within those fiscal years. Early adoption is permitted on any date on or after the issuance of ASU No. 2022-01 for any entity that has adopted the amendments in ASU No. 2017-12 for the corresponding period. If an entity adopts the amendments in an interim period, the effect of adopting the amendments related to basis adjustments should be reflected as of the beginning of the fiscal year of adoption (i.e., the initial application date).	

These amendments eliminate the troubled debt restructuring (TDR) recognition and measurement guidance and instead require that an entity evaluate (consistent with the accounting for other loan modifications) whether the modification represents a new loan or a continuation of an existing loan. The amendments also enhance existing disclosure requirements and introduce new requirements related to certain modifications of receivables made to borrowers experiencing financial difficulty.

For public business entities, these amendments require that an entity disclose current-period gross write-offs by year of origination for financing receivables and net investment in leases within the scope of Subtopic 326-20.

Gross write-off information must be included in the vintage disclosures required for public business entities in accordance with paragraph 326-20-50-6, which requires that an entity disclose the amortized cost basis of financing receivables by credit quality indicator and class of financing receivable by year of origination.

Derivatives and Hedging (Topic 815): *Discount Rates—Not Public Business Entities*

In 2017, the FASB issued a new hedging standard to better align the economic results of risk management activities with hedge accounting. One of the major provisions of that standard was the addition of the last-of-layer hedging method. For a closed portfolio of fixed-rate prepayable financial assets or one or more beneficial interests secured by a portfolio of prepayable financial instruments, such as mortgages or mortgage-backed securities, the last-of-layer method allows an entity to hedge its exposure to fair value changes due to changes in interest rates for a portion of the portfolio that is not expected to be affected by prepayments, defaults, and other events affecting the timing and amount of cash flows.

Since issuing that standard, stakeholders have told the FASB that the ability to elect hedge accounting for a single layer is useful, but hedge accounting could better reflect risk management activities if expanded to allow multiple layers of a single closed portfolio to be hedged under the method.

The ASU expands the current single-layer method to allow multiple hedged layers of a single closed portfolio under the method. To reflect that expansion, the last-of-layer method is renamed the *portfolio layer method*.

Government Assistance (Topic 832): *Discount Rates—Not Public Business Entities*

Number	Issue Date	Transition Guidance
ASU 2021-10	11-17-2021	832-10-65-1
Earliest Effective Annual Period (Years Beginning or Ending After)	12/15/2021	
Implementation Information Effective Date	ASU No. 2021-10 is effective for financial statements issued for annual periods beginning after December 15, 2021, for all entities except not-for-profit entities and employee benefit plans within the scope of Topics 960, 962, and 965 on plan accounting. Early adoption is permitted. ASU No. 2021-10 should be applied: 1. Prospectively to all transactions within the scope of ASU No. 2021-10 that are reflected in financial statements at the date of initial application and to new transactions that are entered into after the date of initial application 2. Retrospectively.	

These amendments are expected to increase transparency in financial reporting by requiring business entities to disclose information about certain types of government assistance they receive.

The amendments require the following annual disclosures about transactions with a government that are accounted for by applying a grant or contribution accounting model by analogy to other accounting guidance such as a grant model within FASB Accounting Standards Codification (ASC) Topic 958, *Not-for-Profit Entities*, or International Accounting Standards (IAS) 20, *Accounting for Government Grants and Disclosure of Government Assistance*:

- Information about the nature of the transactions and the related accounting policy used to account for the transactions
- The line items on the balance sheet and income statement that are affected by the transactions, and the amounts applicable to each financial statement line item; and
- Significant terms and conditions of the transactions, including commitments and contingencies.

Leases (Topic 842): *Discount Rates—Not Public Business Entities*

Number	Issue Date	Transition Guidance
ASU 2021-09	11-11-2021	842-10-65-6
Earliest Effective Annual Period (Years Beginning or Ending After)	12-15-2021	
Implementation Information Effective Date	An entity that has not yet adopted Topic 842 as of November 11, 2021, should apply ASU No. 2021-09 to all new and existing leases when the entity first applies Topic 842. An entity that has adopted Topic 842 as of November 11, 2021, should apply ASU No. 2021-09 for financial statements issued for fiscal years beginning after December 15, 2021, and interim periods within fiscal years beginning after December 15, 2022. Earlier application is permitted as of the beginning of the fiscal year of adoption.	

Topic 842 currently provides lessees that are not public business entities with a practical expedient that allows them to make an accounting policy election to use a risk-free rate as the discount rate for all leases. The FASB originally provided this practical expedient to relieve those lessees from the cost and complexity of having to calculate an incremental borrowing rate.

Some private company stakeholders noted that a risk-free rate is low compared with their expected average incremental borrowing rates, and that using the risk-free rate election could increase an entity's lease liabilities and right-of-use assets.

To address these concerns, the amendments in the ASU allow lessees that are not public business entities to make the risk-free rate election by class of underlying asset, rather than at the entity-wide level. It also requires that, when the rate implicit in the lease is readily determinable for any individual lease, a lessee use that rate (rather than a risk-free rate or an incremental borrowing rate), regardless of whether it has made the risk-free rate election.

Business Combinations (Topic 805): *Accounting for Contract Assets/ Liabilities*

Number	Issue Date	Transition Guidance
ASU 2021-08	10-28-2021	805-20-65-3
Earliest Effective Annual Period (Years Beginning or Ending After)	12-15-2022	
Implementation Information Effective Date	The amendments are effective for public business entities for fiscal years, including interim periods within those fiscal years, beginning after December 15, 2022. For all other entities they are effective for fiscal years, including interim periods within those fiscal years, beginning after December 15, 2023. Entities should apply the amendments prospectively to business combinations that occur after the effective date. Early adoption is permitted, including in any interim period, for public business entities for periods for which financial statements have not yet been issued, and for all other entities for periods for which financial statements have not yet been made available for issuance.	

This ASU requires entities to apply Topic 606 to recognize and measure contract assets and contract liabilities in a business combination. The amendments improve comparability after the business combination by providing consistent recognition and measurement guidance for revenue contracts with customers acquired in a business combination and revenue contracts with customers not acquired in a business combination.

Compensation: *Stock Compensation*

Number	Issue Date	Transition Guidance
ASU 2021-07	10-25-2021	718-10-65-16
Earliest Effective Annual Period (Years Beginning or Ending After)	12-15-2021	
Implementation Information Effective Date	The amendments are effective prospectively for fiscal years beginning after December 15, 2021, and interim periods within fiscal years beginning after December 15, 2022. Early adoption, including application in an interim period, is permitted for financial statements that have not been issued or made available for issuance as of October 25, 2021.	

This ASU provides private companies the option to elect a practical expedient to determine the current price input of equity-classified share-based awards issued as compensation using the reasonable application of a reasonable valuation method. The characteristics of this method are the same as the characteristics used in the regulations of the U.S. Department of the Treasury related to Section 409A of the U.S. Internal Revenue Code (the Treasury Regulations) to describe the reasonable application of a reasonable valuation method for income tax purposes.

SEC Update (Various Topics)

Number	Issue Date	Transition Guidance
ASU 2021-06	8-9-2021	N/A
Earliest Effective Annual Period (Years Beginning or Ending After)	N/A	
Implementation Information Effective Date	Upon addition to the FASB Codification.	

Leases (Topic 842): *Certain Leases with Variable Lease Payments*

Number	Issue Date	Transition Guidance
ASU 2021-05	7-19-2021	842-10-65-5
Earliest Effective Annual Period (Years Beginning or Ending After)	12-15-2021	
Implementation Information Effective Date	An entity that has not yet adopted ASU No. 2016-02 as of July 19, 2021, should apply ASU No. 2021-05 when it first applies ASU No. 2016-02 and should apply the same transition method elected for ASU No. 2016-02. An entity within the scope of ASC paragraph 842-10-65-1(a) that has adopted ASU No. 2016-02 as of July 19, 2021, should apply ASU No. 2021-05 for fiscal years beginning after December 15, 2021, and interim periods within those fiscal years. Earlier application is permitted. An entity within the scope of ASC paragraph 842-10-65-1(b) that has adopted ASU No. 2016-02 as of July 19, 2021, should apply ASU No. 2021-05 for fiscal years beginning after December 15, 2021, and interim periods within fiscal years beginning after December 15, 2022. Earlier application is permitted. See a discussion of the transition methods available in ASU No. 2021-05.	

This ASU amends the lease classification requirements for lessors to align them with practice under ASC Topic 840. Lessors should classify and account for a lease with variable lease payments that do not depend on a reference index or a rate as an operating lease if both of the following criteria are met:

- The lease would have been classified as a sales-type lease or a direct financing lease in accordance with the classification criteria in ASC paragraphs 842-10-25-2 through 25-3; and
- The lessor would have otherwise recognized a day-one loss.

When a lease is classified as operating, the lessor does not recognize a net investment in the lease, does not derecognize the underlying asset, and therefore does not recognize a selling profit or loss.

(Topics 260, 470, 718, 815): Modifications to Equity Related Matters

Number	Issue Date	Transition Guidance
ASU 2021-04	5-3-2021	815-40-65-2
Earliest Effective Annual Period (Years Beginning or Ending After)	12-15-2021	
Implementation Information Effective Date	The amendments are effective for all entities for fiscal years beginning after December 15, 2021, including interim periods within those fiscal years. An entity should apply the amendments prospectively to modifications or exchanges occurring on or after the effective date of the amendments. Early adoption is permitted for all entities, including adoption in an interim period. If an entity elects to early adopt the amendments in an interim period, the guidance should be applied as of the beginning of the fiscal year that includes that interim period.	

This ASU provides guidance for a modification or an exchange of a freestanding equity-classified written call option that is not within the scope of another Topic. It specifically addresses:

- How an entity should treat a modification of the terms or conditions or an exchange of a freestanding equity-classified written call option that remains equity classified after modification or exchange
- How an entity should measure the effect of a modification or an exchange of a freestanding equity-classified written call option that remains equity classified after modification or exchange; and
- How an entity should recognize the effect of a modification or an exchange of a freestanding equity-classified written call option that remains equity classified after modification or exchange.

Intangibles–Goodwill and Other (Topic 350): *Accounting Alternative for Triggering Events*

Number	Issue Date	Transition Guidance
ASU 2021-03	3-30-2021	350-20—65-4
Earliest Effective Annual Period (Years Beginning or Ending After)	12-15-2019	
Implementation Information Effective Date	The amendments are effective on a prospective basis for fiscal years beginning after December 15, 2019. Early adoption is permitted for both interim and annual financial statements that have not yet been issued or made available for issuance as of March 30, 2021. An entity should not retroactively adopt the amendments for interim financial statements already issued in the year of adoption. The amendments also include an unconditional one-time option for entities to adopt the alternative prospectively after its effective date without assessing preferability under Topic 250, *Accounting Changes and Error Corrections.*	

This ASU provides an accounting alternative that allows private companies and not-for-profit organizations to perform a goodwill triggering event assessment, and any resulting test for goodwill impairment, as of the end of the reporting period, whether the reporting period is an interim or annual period. It eliminates the requirement for companies and organizations that elect this alternative to perform this assessment during the reporting period, limiting it to the reporting date only.

The scope of the alternative is limited to goodwill that is tested for impairment in accordance with Subtopic 350-20, *Intangibles—Goodwill and Other—Goodwill.*

Franchisors (Topic 952-606): *Revenue from Customers—Practical Expedient*

Number	Issue Date	Transition Guidance
ASU 2021-02	1-28-2021	952-606-10-65-1
Earliest Effective Annual Period (Years Beginning or Ending After)	12-15-2019	
Implementation Information Effective Date	If an entity has not yet adopted Topic 606, this guidance allows for an option of modified retrospective transition or full retrospective transition and an effective date of annual reporting periods beginning after December 15, 2019, and interim reporting periods within annual reporting periods beginning after December 15, 2020. If an entity has already adopted Topic 606, these amendments are effective in interim and annual periods beginning after December 15, 2020. Early application is permitted. For these entities, this guidance should be applied retrospectively to the date Topic 606 was adopted.	

This ASU introduces a new practical expedient that simplifies the application of the guidance about identifying performance obligations for certain franchisors. The practical expedient permits franchisors that are not public business entities to account for pre-opening services provided to a franchisee as distinct from the franchise license if the services are consistent with those included in a predefined list within the guidance. Additionally, it includes an accounting policy election to recognize the pre-opening services as a single performance obligation.

Reference Rate Reform (Topic 848): *Scope*

Number	Issue Date	Transition Guidance
ASU 2021-01	1-7-2021	848-10-65-2
Earliest Effective Annual Period (Years Beginning or Ending After)	1-7-2021	
Implementation Information Effective Date	An entity may elect to apply ASU No. 2021-01 on contract modifications that change the interest rate used for margining, discounting, or contract price alignment retrospectively as of any date from the beginning of the interim period that includes March 12, 2020, or prospectively to new modifications from any date within the interim period that includes or is subsequent to January 7, 2021, up to the date that financial statements are available to be issued. An entity may elect to apply ASU No. 2021-01 to eligible hedging relationships existing as of the beginning of the interim period that includes March 12, 2020, and to new eligible hedging relationships entered into after the beginning of the interim period that includes March 12, 2020.	

This ASU clarifies that certain optional expedients and exceptions in Topic 848 for contract modifications and hedge accounting apply to derivatives that are affected by the discounting transition. The ASU also amends the expedients and exceptions in Topic 848 to capture the incremental consequences of the scope clarification and to tailor the existing guidance to derivative instruments affected by the discounting transition.

Financial Services—Insurance (Topic 944): *Effective Date and Early Application*

Number	Issue Date	Transition Guidance
ASU 2020-11	11-5-2020	944-40-65-2
Earliest Effective Annual Period (Years Beginning or Ending After)	12-15-2022	
Implementation Information Effective Date	The amendments permit the delay of the implementation of ASU No. 2018-12, *Financial Services—Insurance (Topic 944): Targeted Improvements to the Accounting for Long-Duration Contracts (LDTI)*, by one year as follows: For SEC filers, excluding smaller reporting companies as defined by the SEC, LDTI is effective for fiscal years beginning after December 15, 2022, and interim periods within those fiscal years. For all other entities, LDTI is effective for fiscal years beginning after December 15, 2024, and interim periods within fiscal years beginning after December 15, 2025. Early adoption is permitted. If early adoption is elected, the transition date is either the beginning of the prior period presented, or the beginning of the earliest period presented. If early application is not elected, the transition date is the beginning of the earliest period presented.	

This ASU allows the delayed adoption date of ASU No. 2018-12, as noted in the "Effective Date" information above. And it allows insurance companies to restate only one previous period, rather than two, if they choose to early adopt LDTI.

¶107

Codification Improvements

Number	Issue Date	Transition Guidance
ASU 2020-10	10-29-2020	105-10-65-6
Earliest Effective Annual Period (Years Beginning or Ending After)	12-15-2020	
Implementation Information Effective Date	The amendments are effective for annual periods beginning after December 15, 2020, for public business entities. For all other entities, the amendments are effective for annual periods beginning after December 15, 2021, and interim periods within annual periods beginning after December 15, 2022. Early application of the amendments is permitted for and varies based on the entity. The amendments should be applied retrospectively and at the beginning of the period that includes the adoption date.	

This ASU affects a wide variety of Topics in the Codification. They apply to all reporting entities within the scope of the affected accounting guidance.

More specifically, this ASU, among other things, contains amendments that improve the consistency of the Codification by including all disclosure guidance in the appropriate Disclosure Section (Section 50). Many of the amendments arose because the FASB provided an option to give certain information either on the face of the financial statements or in the notes to financial statements and that option only was included in the Other Presentation Matters Section (Section 45) of the Codification. The option to disclose information in the notes to financial statements should have been codified in the Disclosure Section as well as the Other Presentation Matters Section (or other Section of the Codification in which the option to disclose in the notes to financial statements appears). Those amendments are not expected to change current practice.

Debt (Topic 470): *Amendments to SEC Paragraphs Pursuant to SEC Release No. 33-10762*

Number	Issue Date	Transition Guidance
ASU 2020-09	10-22-2020	470-10-S65-1
Earliest Effective Annual Period (Years Beginning or Ending After)	12-31-2020	
Implementation Information Effective Date	The final rules are effective on January 4, 2021. Voluntary compliance with the final amendments in advance of January 4, 2021, will be permitted. After voluntary compliance, subsequent Exchange Act or Regulation A periodic reports must comply with the final rules.	

This ASU amends and supersedes various SEC paragraphs to reflect SEC Release No. 33-10762, which includes amendments to the financial disclosure requirements applicable to registered debt offerings that include credit enhancements, such as subsidiary guarantees. These SEC changes are intended to both improve the quality of disclosure and increase the likelihood that issuers will conduct debt offerings on a registered basis.

¶107

Receivables (Topic 310): *Nonrefundable Fees and Other Costs*

Number	Issue Date	Transition Guidance
ASU 2020-08	10-15-2020	310-20-65-2
Earliest Effective Annual Period (Years Beginning or Ending After)	12-15-2020	
Implementation Information Effective Date	ASU No. 2020-08 is effective for public business entities for fiscal years, and interim periods within those fiscal years, beginning after December 15, 2020. Early application is not permitted. For all other entities, ASU No. 2020-08 is effective for fiscal years beginning after December 15, 2021, and interim periods within fiscal years beginning after December 15, 2022. Early application is permitted for all other entities for fiscal years, and interim periods within those fiscal years, beginning after December 15, 2020. All entities should apply ASU No. 2020-08 on a prospective basis as of the beginning of the period of adoption for existing or newly purchased callable debt securities.	

This ASU clarifies that an entity should reevaluate whether a callable debt security is within the scope of ASC paragraph 310-20-35-33 for each reporting period.

Not-for-Profit Entities (Topic 958): *Presentation and Disclosures by Not-for-Profit Entities for Contributed Nonfinancial Assets*

Number	Issue Date	Transition Guidance
ASU 2020-07	9-17-2020	958-10-65-4
Earliest Effective Annual Period (Years Beginning or Ending After)	6-15-2021	
Implementation Information Effective Date	ASU No. 2020-07 is effective retrospectively for annual reporting periods beginning after June 15, 2021, and interim periods with annual reporting periods beginning after June 15, 2022. Early adoption is permitted.	

This ASU requires a not-for-profit organization to present contributed nonfinancial assets as a separate line item in the statement of activities, apart from contributions of cash or other financial assets. It also requires a not-for-profit entity to disclose the following:

- Contributed nonfinancial assets recognized within the statement of activities disaggregated by category that depicts the type of contributed nonfinancial assets; and

- For each category of contributed nonfinancial assets recognized:

  — Qualitative information about whether the contributed nonfinancial assets were either monetized or utilized during the reporting period. If utilized, a description of the programs or other activities in which those assets were used.

  — The not-for-profit's policy (if any) about monetizing rather than utilizing contributed nonfinancial assets.

  — A description of any donor-imposed restrictions associated with the contributed nonfinancial assets.

— The valuation techniques and inputs used to arrive at a fair value measure, in accordance with the requirements in Topic 820, *Fair Value Measurement*, at initial recognition.

— The principal market (or most advantageous market) used to arrive at a fair value measure if it is a market in which the recipient not-for-profit entity is prohibited by a donor-imposed restriction from selling or using the contributed nonfinancial assets.

Debt and Derivatives (Topics 470 and 815): *Accounting for Convertible Instruments and Contracts in an Entity's Own Equity*

Number	Issue Date	Transition Guidance
ASU 2020-06	8-5-2020	260-10-65-4; 815-40-65-1
Earliest Effective Annual Period (Years Beginning or Ending After)	12-15-2021	
Implementation Information Effective Date	ASU No. 2020-06 is effective for public business entities that meet the definition of a SEC filer, excluding entities eligible to be smaller reporting companies as defined by the SEC, for fiscal years beginning after December 15, 2021, including interim periods within those fiscal years. For all other entities, the standard will be effective for fiscal years beginning after December 15, 2023, including interim periods within those fiscal years. Early adoption will be permitted.	

This ASU simplifies accounting for convertible instruments by removing major separation models required under current U.S. GAAP. Consequently, more convertible debt instruments will be reported as a single liability instrument and more convertible preferred stock will be reported as a single equity instrument with no separate accounting for embedded conversion features. The ASU removes certain settlement conditions that are required for equity contracts to qualify for the derivative scope exception, which will permit more equity contracts to qualify for it. The ASU also simplifies the diluted earnings per share (EPS) calculation in certain areas.

Revenue from Contracts with Customers (Topic 606) and Leases (Topic 842): *Effective Dates for Certain Entities*

Number	Issue Date	Transition Guidance
ASU 2020-05	6-3-2020	606-10-65-1; 842-10-65-1
Earliest Effective Annual Period (Years Beginning or Ending After)	Effective immediately	
Implementation Information Effective Date	ASU No. 2020-04 effective for all entities as of March 12, 2020, through December 31, 2022. See further discussion of the lengthy transition guidance in the ASU.	

This ASU permits private companies and not-for-profit organizations that have not yet applied the revenue recognition standard to do so for annual reporting periods beginning after December 15, 2019, and interim reporting periods within annual reporting periods beginning after December 15, 2020.

For leases, the ASU provides an effective date deferral to private companies, private not-for-profit organizations, and public not-for-profit organizations that have not yet issued (or made available) their financial statements reflecting the adoption of the guidance. It is intended to provide near-term relief for certain entities for whom the leases adoption is imminent.

¶107

Under the ASU, private companies and private not-for-profit organizations may apply the new leases standard for fiscal years beginning after December 15, 2021, and to interim periods within fiscal years beginning after December 15, 2022. Public not-for-profit organizations that have not yet issued (or made available to issue) financial statements reflecting the adoption of the lease's guidance may apply the standard for fiscal years beginning after December 15, 2019, including interim periods within those fiscal years.

Reference Rate Reform (Topic 848): *Facilitation of the Effects of Reference Rate Reform on Financial Reporting*

Number	Issue Date	Transition Guidance
ASU 2020-04	3-12-2020	848-10-65-1
Earliest Effective Annual Period (Years Beginning or Ending After)	3-12-2020	
Implementation Information Effective Date	ASU No. 2020-04 effective for all entities as of March 12, 2020, through December 31, 2022. See further discussion of the lengthy transition guidance in the ASU.	

This ASU provides temporary optional guidance to ease the potential burden in accounting for reference rate reform.

The new guidance provides optional expedients and exceptions for applying U.S. GAAP to contract modifications and hedging relationships, subject to meeting certain criteria, that reference LIBOR or another reference rate expected to be discontinued. The ASU is intended to help stakeholders during the global market-wide reference rate transition period. Therefore, it will be in effect for a limited time through December 31, 2022.

Financial Instruments: *Codification Improvements*

Number	Issue Date	Transition Guidance
ASU 2020-03	3-9-2020	825-10-65-7
Earliest Effective Annual Period (Years Beginning or Ending After)	Varies	
Implementation Information Effective Date	Varies. See ASU No. 2020-03 for specific effective dates as they pertain to each amendment.	

Credit Losses and Leases: *Amendments to SEC Paragraphs*

Number	Issue Date	Transition Guidance
ASU 2020-02	2-6-2020	N/A
Earliest Effective Annual Period (Years Beginning or Ending After)	Upon addition to FASB Codification	
Implementation Information Effective Date	N/A	

Investments and Derivatives: *Clarifying the Interactions between Topic 321, Topic 323, and Topic 815*

Number	Issue Date	Transition Guidance
ASU 2020-01	1-16-2020	825-10-65-6
Earliest Effective Annual Period (Years Beginning or Ending After)	12-15-2020	
Implementation Information Effective Date	ASU No. 2020-01 is effective for public business entities for fiscal years, and interim periods within those fiscal years, beginning after December 15, 2020. For all other entities, ASU No. 2020-01 is effective for fiscal years, and interim periods within those fiscal years, beginning after December 15, 2021. Early application is permitted, including early adoption in an interim period for (1) public business entities for periods for which financial statements have not yet been issued, and (2) all other entities for periods for which financial statements have not yet been made available for issuance. An entity should apply ASU No. 2020-01 prospectively at the beginning of the interim period that includes the adoption date.	

This ASU primarily clarifies that a company should consider observable transactions that require a company to either apply or discontinue the equity method of accounting under Topic 323, *Investments—Equity Method and Joint Ventures*, for the purposes of applying the measurement alternative in accordance with Topic 321 immediately before applying or upon discontinuing the equity method.

The ASU clarifies that, when determining the accounting for certain forward contracts and purchased options, a company should not consider, whether upon settlement or exercise, if the underlying securities would be accounted for under the equity method or fair value option.

STUDY QUESTIONS

4. Which of the following ASC Topics provides the disclosure requirements with respect to government assistance?

    a. ASC Topic 280

    b. ASC Topic 606

    c. ASC Topic 832

    d. ASC Topic 842

5. Which of the following ASUs requires entities to apply Topic 606 to recognize and measure contract assets and contract liabilities in a business combination?

    a. ASU 2021-07

    b. ASU 2021-08

    c. ASU 2021-10

    d. ASU 2022-02

6. ASU 2020-06 simplifies the accounting for _____ by removing major separation models required under current U.S. GAAP.

    a. Business combinations

    b. Revenue

    c. Leases

    d. Convertible instruments

MODULE 1: TOP ACCOUNTING ISSUES— CHAPTER 2: Cost-Effective Cybersecurity for Small Businesses

¶ 201 WELCOME

This chapter is designed to assist accountants and auditors who are working with small businesses. The chapter assumes that there will be a limited budget for implementing cybersecurity internal controls for a small business. It will also discuss working directly with small business owners and bookkeepers, and some of their resistance to formalized internal controls. Since an effective risk assessment is necessary to develop internal controls, cyber fraud risks specific to small businesses will also be covered.

¶ 202 LEARNING OBJECTIVES

Upon completion of this chapter, you will be able to:

- Identify risks for cyber fraud
- Develop cost-effective cybersecurity internal controls for small businesses

¶ 203 INTRODUCTION

Fraud can be defined simply as someone making a false statement that somebody else relied upon to their detriment. In the case of occupational fraud, the false statement is an employee's breach of his or her fiduciary responsibility to the employer. When a person accepts employment, they agree to work in their employer's best interest. If an employee breaches that fiduciary responsibility—for example, they embezzle funds or have a conflict of interest—that is a fraud, because the employee had promised to do what was best for the employer.

Dr. Edwin Sutherland was one of the first people in the United States to study fraud, and he came up with the term *white-collar crime* to differentiate crimes of trust, such as fraud, from other crimes like burglary, robbery, and so on. One of Dr. Sutherland's students, Dr. Donald Cressey, wanted to go a step further and find out what made people commit fraud. Dr. Cressey interviewed hundreds of convicted felons who were imprisoned for embezzlement and fraud to learn why they committed the crimes.

Dr. Cressey found that three factors were always present in the frauds: pressure, opportunity, and rationalization. These three factors constitute the fraud triangle. Dr. Cressey referred to pressure as an "unsharable financial need"—a need for funds that the fraud perpetrators could not obtain through their normal access to money, whether that was their paycheck, their savings account, or another source. He learned that there are many types of pressure to commit fraud. The pressure could come from the perpetrator's greed, desire to "keep up with the Joneses," overextension of credit card debt, unexpected home repair or medical bills, a spouse losing their job, and more.

At one point during the COVID-19 crisis, 53 million people in the United States[1] had been laid off, which put a great deal of pressure on many individuals. Other

---

[1] https://thecapitalist.com/fed-bank-predicts-53-million-americans-out-of-work-32-unemployment-rate/ https://www.forbes.com/sites/jackkelly/2020/07/09/

pressures came from COVID-19 medical bills or a breadwinner passing away from the virus. Unfortunately, the pandemic also caused spikes in gambling, alcoholism, drug addiction, and depression, which resulted in more pressures.

Rationalization refers to a fraudsters' ability to convince themselves that it is okay to commit the fraud. The third part of the fraud triangle is opportunity. Businesses can implement internal controls to reduce or eliminate the opportunities for employees to commit fraud. However, it has been difficult for many businesses to keep their internal controls up to date during times of rapid change, such as that experienced during the pandemic. Changes during the pandemic include some businesses shutting down and others having their employees work from home. In addition, the use of new technologies exploded, such as online/virtual meeting and collaboration platforms, using the cloud to transfer and save documents, and doing work like preparing tax returns remotely without ever meeting with clients in person.

These factors caused many issues for the accounting industry as well as their clients. These significant changes in how organizations conduct business allowed opportunity for criminals to creep in. Remember that change always comes with risk.

Several cybersecurity risks are related to the COVID-19 pandemic. One of those risks is civil litigation. If a company experiences a data breach that discloses its employees' information, those employees will likely sue the company. A recent appellate court ruling affirmed liability for employers who do not protect employees' confidential information.

According to one study conducted by Poneman[2], small businesses with fewer than 10,000 records compromised could have data breach costs of around $4 million. It is exceptionally expensive for a large organization to be a victim of a data breach, with resulting costs of billions of dollars. Companies whose data is breached also may be fined by the government for failing to provide proper internal controls and cybersecurity. They may also face damage to their reputation and loss of customers.

Usually, when the government settles on a data breach or other type of fraud lapse, it requires 20 years of ongoing audits for the company where, for example, the cybersecurity internal controls are audited by a third-party, independent auditor. In addition to paying these costs, the company also experiences a disruption to its business.

Many risks are associated with cyber fraud. A company that is a victim of ransomware might have to make major payments to retrieve its encrypted data. Baltimore and Atlanta are just two of the cities that were hit with ransomware in 2019.

¶ 204 FRAUD STATISTICS

The Association of Certified Fraud Examiners (ACFE) "Occupational Fraud 2022: A Report to the Nations" indicated that based on reports from certified fraud examiners (CFE), organizations lose approximately 5 percent of their revenue to fraud on an annual basis. The association documented the median loss per case at $117,000 and the average cost per case at $1,783,000. The report also suggests that a typical fraud case will cause $8,300 per month in losses for the victim organization and will last on average 12 months before the victim detects the fraud is occurring, or has occurred. A new piece of information in the 2022 report indicated that 8 percent of the fraud cases involved cryptocurrency. Since cryptocurrencies do not have a tangible aspect, all

---

(Footnote Continued)

nearly-50-million-americans-have-filed-for-unemployment-heres-whats-really-happening/?sh=2d2e0d6827d3

[2] https://www.ponemon.org/

frauds involving cryptocurrencies are cyber frauds. Of the cyber frauds involving cryptocurrencies, 48 percent involved bribery and kickback payments and 43 percent involved converting misappropriated assets.

As a reminder, the three basic elements of fraud, not to be confused with the Fraud Triangle, are the act of theft, concealment, and conversion. The act of theft means a perpetrator has to actually commit a fraudulent act. An individual can plan the most elaborate fraud, but if nothing is stolen and nobody is harmed, then there is no fraud. Once the fraudulent act occurs, there is a concealment. Criminals sometimes go to great lengths to conceal what they did, for various reasons. Usually, they don't want to lose their job, or don't want to go to jail. The third element of fraud is conversion. Fraudsters have to convert what they stole into something they can use. For example, if a criminal stole fixed assets or inventory, he will want to convert them into cash. Criminals who steal electronic data, Social Security numbers, or credit card numbers will need to sell them to get cash, or, in the case of credit card numbers, use them to make online purchases. Those who steal a large amount of money may need to launder it so that they can actually spend it without alerting the Internal Revenue Service (IRS) or the Financial Crimes Enforcement Network (FINCEN).

The ACFE also reported on information received from members as to what extent COVID-19 pandemic-related factors contributed to occupational frauds. The results are as follows:

	Significant Factor	Moderate Factor	Slight Factor	Not a Factor
Organizational Staffing Changes	12%	16%	14%	58%
Operational Process Changes	12%	14%	13%	60%
Internal Control Changes	13%	14%	12%	61%
Shift to Remote Work	15%	14%	9%	62%
Changes to Strategic Priorities	10%	12%	12%	65%
Technology Changes	9%	11%	10%	69%
Changes to Anti-Fraud Program	8%	11%	11%	70%
Supply Chain Disruptions	9%	11%	10%	71%

According to the Internet Crime Complaint Center (IC3) 2021 Annual Report (compiled from consumer and business complaints, the Federal Bureau of Investigation (FBI), the Federal Trade Commission (FTC), and state and local law enforcement agencies), there have been significant increases in cyber fraud over the last five years, and the number of cyber fraud cases continues to rise. In 2017, the IC3 reported 301,580 complaints with victim losses totaling $1.4 billion. In 2018, there were 351,937 complaints with $2.7 billion in losses. In 2019, the last non-pandemic year, the IC3 documented 467,361 complaints with $3.5 billion in losses for cybercrimes. In 2020, the first year of the COVID-19 pandemic, the IC3 reported 791,790 complaints with $4.2 billion in cyber fraud losses, and in 2021, the complaints increased to 847,376 and the losses to $6.9 billion.

The IC3 also documented increased growth in certain types of cyber frauds. Phishing, vishing, smishing, and pharming attacks increased from 25,344 complaints in 2017 to 323,972 complaints in 2021. Personal data breach complaints rose from 30,904 in 2017 to 51,829 in 2021, and identity theft complaints grew from 17,636 in 2017 to 51,629 in 2021. It is also important to remember that many cyber frauds are not reported to law enforcement authorities.

The IC3's 2021 report also detailed cyber fraud complaints from around the world, as shown in the following chart:

Country	Number of Complaints
United States	466,501
United Kingdom	303,949
Canada	5,788
India	3,131
Australia	2,204
France	1,972
South Africa	1,790
Germany	1,429
Mexico	1,326
Brazil	1,503
Philippines	1,051
Netherlands	673
Greece	585
China	571
Spain	560
Argentina	538
Pakistan	530
Italy	517
Malaysia	443
Turkey	422
Japan	419

The breakdown of the average weekly cyberattacks by industry in 2021 as reported by Check Point (www.checkpoint.com) is as follows:

Industry	Weekly Cyberattacks
Education and Research	1,605
Government and Military	1,136
Communications	1,079
ISP/MSP	1,068
Healthcare	830
SI/VAR/Distributor	778
Utilities	736
Manufacturing	704
Finance and Banking	703
Insurance and Legal	636
Leisure and Hospitality	595
Consultants	576
Software Vendor	536
Retail and Wholesale	526
Transportation	501

¶ 205 CYBERSECURITY AWARENESS

The Cybersecurity Hub has documented several steps toward cybersecurity awareness

- **Identify threats.** Understand the external cybersecurity threats to the organization and understand the internal cybersecurity threats posed by inappropriate use and lack of awareness.

- **Identify vulnerabilities.** Develop an inventory of information technology (IT) systems with direct and indirect communications links. Understand the consequences of a cybersecurity threat on these systems. Understand the capabilities and limitations of existing cybersecurity controls.

- **Assess risk exposure.** Determine the likelihood of vulnerabilities being exploited by external threats. Determine the likelihood of vulnerabilities being exploited by inappropriate use. Determine the security and safety impact of any individual, or combination of, vulnerabilities being exploited. (Similar to the COSO—Risk Assessment)

- **Develop protection and detection measures.** Reduce the likelihood of vulnerabilities being exploited through protection measures. Reduce the potential impact of a vulnerability being exploited. (COSO—Control Activities)

- **Establish contingency plans.** Develop a response plan to reduce the impact of threats that are realized.

- **Respond to cybersecurity incidents.** Respond to cybersecurity threats that are realized using the response plan. Assess the impact of the effectiveness of the response plan and reassess threats and vulnerabilities.

¶ 206 PHISHING

Phishing is a cybercrime in which the criminals contact the victim through email messages that appear to come from legitimate business or government sources. Social networking through phishing schemes is a common way to get around an organization's IT security. Often, the email headers are spoofed to make them look legitimate. One purpose of the phishing email is to obtain information such as names, addresses, Social Security numbers, phone numbers, dates of birth, credit card numbers, employer identification numbers (EINs), and other personal information from the victims. When the victim supplies the information, the criminals use the information to steal the victim's identity and assets. Criminals also send phishing emails containing links with the hope that the victim will click on the link and download the criminal's malware onto the victim's computer.

Criminals will often try to make you think a phishing email is coming from your bank, credit card company, or other financial institution. They may indicate there is a problem with your account or that your password is expiring. Either way, they ask you to click on the link in the email and enter your user ID and password. Once they have that information, they can use your user ID and password to access your real accounts and misappropriate all your funds. Criminals also use phishing emails to try to convince you there is an issue with your social media accounts, or that your accounts need to be updated. They will stress the fact that you will lose all your posts on accounts such as Facebook, Twitter, and LinkedIn if you don't immediately log in through the link in the email and update your account. Some criminals actually do their research before sending out a phishing email. This is known as *spear phishing*. They gather information on the prospective victim and tailor a phishing email directly to them. These emails can include the victim's name and the names of people the victim knows.

¶ 207 VISHING

Vishing is similar to phishing except the criminals use phone calls instead of emails. The criminals will call a new employee or newly promoted employee (they get the information from social media) pretending to be from the employer's IT department and telling them they need to finish setting up their computer for the access they will need. The criminals tell the employee they need to remote into their computer, and then once inside the system set up a backdoor so they have continued access to the company's computer systems.

Vishing calls are also made to alert individuals or businesses that fraud has been detected on their credit cards. The criminals used spoofed phone numbers to make it appear that the call is coming from a bank or financial institution. The criminals then ask the victim to verify information on the credit card, such as the account number, billing zip code, security code, or expiration date, in order to gain access to information that will allow them to use the credit card.

Other common vishing calls include calls that claim to be from the IRS trying to collect past due taxes, calls from collection agencies trying to collect past due bills, and calls from law enforcement or regulatory agencies trying to collect fines. A red flag for vishing calls is a request that payment be made with gift cards, with virtual currencies, or by sending money through a money transfer service. Fraudsters will also stress the urgency to pay immediately in order to avoid jail time or other penalties.

¶ 208 SMISHING

Smishing is similar to phishing and vishing but is done using text messages rather than phone calls or email. Criminals are still trying to obtain information or to get the victim to click on links so they can load malware onto the victim's devices. One smishing text claimed to be from the Federal Department of H&R Block, telling victims they needed to update their DBE Certification. It is unclear what that is, but this was obviously a fraud. Other common smishing texts spoof credit card processing platforms, banks, financial institutions, and government agencies.

¶ 209 QR CODE SCAMS

A newer type of cyber fraud involves QR codes. Many law enforcement agencies, including the State of New Jersey's Attorney General's Office, have posted warnings to businesses and consumers about the increased risk for QR code fraud. This is accomplished when the criminals place fraudulent QR codes at businesses, such as restaurants and bars, or affix fraudulent QR code stickers over the legitimate QR codes. The QR code often includes a message such as "New Menu" to entice victims to click on the website.

The Better Business Bureau (www.bbb.org) provides advice on how to avoid QR scams.

- **If someone you know sends you a QR code, confirm that it is legitimate before scanning it.** Whether you receive a text message from a friend or a message on social media from your workmate, contact that person directly before you scan the QR code to make sure they haven't been hacked.
- **Don't open links from strangers.** If you receive an unsolicited message from a stranger, don't scan the QR code, even if they promise you exciting gifts or investment opportunities.
- **Verify the source.** If a QR code appears to come from a reputable source, it's wise to double-check. If the correspondence appears to come from a government agency, call or visit its official website to confirm.
- **Be wary of short links.** If a URL-shortened link appears when you scan a QR code, understand that you can't know where the code is directing you. It could be hiding a malicious URL.

- **Watch out for advertising materials that have been tampered with.** Some scammers attempt to mislead consumers by altering legitimate business ads, such as placing stickers over the QR code. Keep an eye out for signs of tampering.
- **Install a QR scanner with added security.** Some antivirus companies have QR scanner apps that check the safety of a scanned link before you open it. They can identify phishing scams, forced app downloads, and other dangerous links.

STUDY QUESTION

1. Phishing is performed through which of the following communication channels?
   a. Social media
   b. Email
   c. Phone calls
   d. Text messaging

¶ 210 DENIAL OF SERVICE (DOS) ATTACKS

Denial of service (DoS) attacks occur when criminals use their own computer networks, or botnets, which are networks of infected computers, to bring down a website or computer system by overloading its capabilities, thereby crashing the system. In many instances, the criminals follow up on the DoS attack with an attempt to hack into the system and upload malware onto the victim's computer while the victim is busy trying to fix the damage being done by the DoS attack.

The most common and obvious type of DoS attack occurs when an attacker "floods" a network or website with large amounts of information or requests for access. When you type a URL for a particular website into your browser, you are sending a request to that site's computer server to view the webpage. The server can only process a certain number of requests at once, so if an attacker overloads the server with requests, it can't process your request. This is a "denial of service" because you can't access that site. In a distributed denial of service (DDoS) attack, an attacker may use your computer to attack another computer. By taking advantage of security vulnerabilities or weaknesses, an attacker could take control of your computer and then force it to send huge amounts of data to a website or send spam to particular email addresses. The attack is "distributed" because the attacker is using multiple computers, including yours, to launch the DoS attack.[3]

¶ 211 SPOOFING

Spoofing is a term used to describe fraudulent email activity in which the sender's address or other parts of the email header are altered to appear as though the email originated from a different source. Spoofing is also commonly used by spammers to hide the origin of an email. Fraudsters can also spoof websites and phone numbers. Spoofing phone numbers for vishing and smishing attacks is easy; there are even aps for that.

---

[3] Department of Homeland Security, www.us-cert.gov/ncas/tips/ST04-015.

¶ 212 RANSOMWARE

Another type of cyber fraud that has been on the rise in the last year is ransomware. Ransomware is a type of malware that is placed on a computer, which then encrypts all the files on the computer. The criminals then require that the victim pay a ransom to obtain the decryption key and have access to their files. The most well-known example of ransomware is CryptoLocker. Cryptowall 2.0 is a newer version of ransomware being used by cybercriminals. Another new type of ransomware, called Reveton, installs itself onto the computer without the user's knowledge. Then, the computer freezes. A bogus message from the FBI pops up on the screen saying the user violated federal law. To unlock their computer, the user must make a payment to the criminals.

For a single computer, cybercriminals will initially request a ransom ranging from $300 to $500. Larger ransoms are demanded when more computers are infected with the ransomware. Once the deadline for the payment has passed, the criminals raise the ransom demand to around $1,000 per infected computer.[4] Unfortunately, criminals are not always honest. When a victim makes a payment, sometimes the criminal gives them the decryption code, sometimes the criminal asks for more money, and sometimes the decryption code doesn't work, and the criminal refers the victim to a 900 number help desk where the victim pays by the minute for help decrypting their information. Governments have also been victims of ransomware. In the spring of 2018, the City of Atlanta was infected with ransomware that shut down city services for weeks.[5]

Typical ransomware software uses RSA 2048 encryption to encrypt files. To give you an idea of how strong this is, it is estimated it would take an average desktop computer approximately 6.4 quadrillion years to crack an RSA 2048 key.[6] One issue with ransomware is that it is a franchise type criminal activity. Criminals with no programming experience can contact ransomware developers on the dark net. The criminals pay an initial fee to get access to the ransomware, and the developer provides them with a link to send it out to all of their contacts. If victims click on the link, infect their systems with ransomware, and pay the ransom, the criminal gets 80 percent of the ransom and the developer gets 20 percent.

¶ 213 DATA BREACHES

The theft of information, also known as a *data breach*, is a crime that was virtually unknown two decades ago but is flourishing in the 21st century. A data breach is defined as the theft of personal information including names, Social Security Numbers, birth dates, medical information, driver's license numbers, usernames and passwords, and financial account information such as credit or debit card numbers. With an ever-increasing reliance on computers and information technology, organizations are increasingly susceptible to this type of fraud. Information thieves are misappropriating data and selling the stolen information on the dark net.

A data breach occurs when someone gains access to data that contains confidential information. Confidential information includes personally identifying information (PII) and personal health information (PHI). This breach can occur because of a lack of security, the bypassing of security, or the elimination of security. Data breaches occur when information is stolen from computers and other electronic devices. They can also occur when devices containing information are lost or misplaced. When a breach occurs, the organization is considered to be negligent in its duties to safeguard the

---

[4] https://www.knowbe4.com/.

[5] Kimberly Hutcherson, "Six Days After a Ransomware Cyberattack, Atlanta Officials Are Filling Out Forms by Hand." CNN, March 28, 2018, https://www.cnn.com/2018/03/27/us/atlanta-ransomware-computers/index.html.

[6] https://www.knowbe4.com/.

information provided to it by employees, customers, and others, and there is a significant cost associated with being a victim of a data breach. Approximately 62 percent of data breaches are caused by individuals outside the company such as hackers and other criminals. Insiders, such as disgruntled employees are responsible for around 11 percent of all data breaches. Twenty-five percent (25%) of data breaches are accidental loss or dissemination of data; and only 2 percent of data breaches are a direct result of state sponsored attacks.

Criminals breach the IT security of companies, not-for-profit organizations, and even governmental units and steal information from their computers. Often, the Human Resources department of an entity is targeted for payroll information, which includes Social Security numbers. Retail outlets are also targeted because they store customer information, including credit card numbers, on their computers. Not all data breaches are aimed at large organizations. Small businesses are also targeted, including tax providers, attorneys, medical offices, and insurance agents, because these professionals often have their clients' personal information stored on their computers.

One of the main reasons for stealing data is to profit from the data breach. Criminals can sell stolen user IDs and passwords for $5 to $20 each on the dark net. Criminals are aware that many people use the same passwords for multiple websites and computer systems. The purchased IDs and passwords are input into software that searches the Internet for websites where the stolen IDs and passwords work and then notifies a human operator that access has been gained so they can determine if there is any value in the website that was illegally accessed. This is known as *credential stuffing*. Another large market for information on the dark net is the sale of stolen credit card numbers. There are thousands of dark net sites selling stolen credit and debit card numbers. Prices range from $2 to $100 per credit or debit card number depending on the validity of the numbers. Some card brokers even offer guarantees that if you purchase a minimum number of credit or debit card numbers, should any of these numbers prove to be invalid, they will replace them for free; sort of a money-back guarantee for criminals.

In addition to credit card, debit card, and Social Security numbers, criminals also purchase names, addresses, dates of birth, phone numbers, driver's license numbers, health insurance ID numbers, union numbers, and other PII on the dark net. These purchases are usually done with virtual currencies, such as Bitcoin. There are even resources on the Internet for up-and-coming criminals, including books and videos on how to profit from stolen credit cards and how to do credential cramming. Stolen personal information is often used to commit identity theft.

Over the years, the theft of data has become a very profitable crime. In today's modern economy, businesses offer goods and services on credit to strangers based on the data in the buyer's credit history or through electronic means of payment such as credit and debit cards. With telecommunications and Internet technology, buyers and sellers do not need to meet in person to consummate their transaction. The Internet has made access to information almost instantaneous. Additionally, people's willingness to share personal information about themselves on social media has increased the risk of that information being misappropriated. Increased access to data on the Internet has provided criminals easier access to personal information from both inside and outside the United States. Identity thieves can use the Internet to gather an individual's identifying information without ever coming into personal contact with the victim.

As mentioned earlier, retail outlets are also targets of data breaches because they store customer information, including credit and debit card numbers on their computers. The cyberthieves targeted the point-of-sale (POS) cash registers in the Home Depot data breach, allowing them to obtain the credit and debit card information of every customer making a purchase at the stores. Data breaches allow criminals to obtain a substantial amount of information with a minimum risk of being caught. Many data breaches are initiated through phishing or other social networking attacks wherein the criminals email or otherwise contact an individual in the target company and include a virus or other form of malware in the communication.

One of the most well-known data breaches occurred in November and December of 2013, and the victim was Target. It was estimated that 70,000,000 debit and credit card numbers were stolen from Target's computers. In addition to the debit and credit card numbers, the criminals also misappropriated the customers' personal identification numbers (PINs), card verification value (CVV) codes, zip codes, and other personal information. The initial estimates of the costs to Target for this data breach were $3.6 billion. The Target data breach is important because of the litigation that followed. The banks that had to replace the 70 million stolen credit cards filed litigation against Target to recover their costs. The Federal District Court ruled in favor of the banks, and Target appealed the ruling. The Federal Appellate Court reaffirmed the lower court's ruling, and Target appealed to the Supreme Court. The Supreme Court declined to review the case, leaving the Appellate Court's ruling in place.

The courts have determined that companies have strict liability for lost information. In other words, the victims do not need to prove the stolen information was used in an identity theft. The fact that they need to pay to monitor their credit or take other actions to protect their identity creates sufficient grounds for damage awards. Businesses must use reasonable procedures to secure data in their possession. The procedures must be documented in writing and be tested or audited on a periodic basis.

There is no way to guarantee that an organization will not become a victim of a data breach, but good internal controls can reduce the risk of becoming a victim of this type of fraud.

STUDY QUESTION

2. Which of the following cyber frauds encrypts the data on your computer?

   a. Phishing

   b. Ransomware

   c. Spoofing

   d. Spyware

¶ 214 CREDENTIAL STUFFING

With regard to internal controls, it is extremely important to use complex passwords and update them on a regular basis. In fact, it is much better to use a complex passphrase consisting of a minimum of 24 characters including uppercase letters, lowercase letters, numbers, and special symbols. It is much harder for a criminal to hack a passphrase than to hack a short six-character password. The fact that many individuals use the same user ID and password for multiple sites is well known to criminals.

As mentioned earlier, credential stuffing is one of the ways criminals gain access to various systems. After criminals obtain user IDs and passwords through data breaches, phishing, or other means, they use software to test the acquired user IDs and passwords on various websites and computer systems. The criminal will attempt to access financial, social media, email, and other sites using the stolen information. Company and government websites are vulnerable because employees are not diligent in changing and protecting their passwords and often use the same password on multiple systems.

One common software for conducting credential stuffing is known as Sentry MBA. Although less than 1 percent of these attempts are successful, the successful attempts are very profitable for the criminals as they gain access to the victim's information and accounts. Remember that credential hacking is done at computer speeds, so a criminal can test the credentials millions of times an hour. If a criminal could obtain 1 million credentials by purchasing them in bulk on the dark net, they would be able to access approximately 10,000 accounts. Also, since a user ID and password is only attempted once per website, the user ID is not locked when it does not work, so the victim is unaware their information has been tested. The criminals also use botnets (hijacked computers) so that the requests all come from different IP addresses to prevent the tested website from recognizing the access attempt is coming from a single source.

Organizations need to monitor login failure rates as a detective control to determine if they are targets of a credential stuffing attack. Adding two-factor authentication to a website is a good preventive control to limit credential hacking. Another good internal control is requiring complex passwords that contain an uppercase letter, a lowercase letter, a number, and a symbol; requiring users to update passwords every 90 days; and prohibiting the reuse of passwords.

One way to determine if your organization is being attacked by a criminal using Sentry MBA is to Google "sentry mba [your company name]." Organizations can also search their web logs for some of the common user agent strings associated with Sentry MBA:

- Mozilla/4.0 (compatible; MSIE 7.0; Windows NT 6.0;.NET CLR 1.1.4322;.NET CLR 2.0.50727;.NET CLR 3.0.4506.2152;.NET CLR 3.5.30729)
- Mozilla/4.0 (compatible; MSIE 8.0; Windows NT 6.1;.NET CLR 1.1.4322;.NET CLR 2.0.50727;.NET CLR 3.0.4506.2152;.NET CLR 3.5.30729)
- Mozilla/5.0 (Windows; U; Windows NT 5.1; en-US; rv:1.9.0.11) Gecko/2009060215 Firefox/3.0.11
- Mozilla/5.0 (Windows; U; Windows NT 5.1; en) AppleWebKit/522.11.3 (KHTML, like Gecko) Version/3.0 Safari/522.11.3
- Opera/9.80 (Windows NT 6.0; U; en) Presto/2.2.0 Version/10.00

¶ 215 INTERNAL CONTROLS FOR CYBERSECURITY

As discussed earlier, internal controls help to prevent and detect both errors and fraud. Preventing errors supports quality. Preventing and detecting fraud protects not only a company's assets, but also its employees and owners. In discussing internal controls, organizations need to look at both preventive and detective controls. Preventive controls are put in place to stop errors or fraud from occurring. Detective controls—controls that help to detect—are put in place to help find errors or fraud after they have occurred.

In business, the controls over processes are known as internal controls. An internal control is defined as a process, effected by an entity's board of directors, management, and other personnel, designed to provide reasonable assurance regarding the achievement of objectives relating to operations, reporting, and compliance. Internal controls help to ensure the business is operating efficiently while minimizing errors and the opportunity for fraud. Management is ultimately responsible for designing effective internal controls and ensuring that they are monitored and operating effectively.

Although the ultimate responsibility for internal controls falls on owners or managers, it is the accountant who often is responsible for maintaining and monitoring them. A good accountant is a valued consultant to management or the business owner. The ability to recommend good internal controls to management or the business owner is a value-added service that many accountants provide. Additionally, management and business owners are generally grateful when an accountant detects an error or fraud and brings it to their attention. Remember that most small business owners are very good at their trade or profession, but many have limited experience with accounting or bookkeeping. These business owners rely on their accountants to protect them from fraud.

When developing internal controls for cybersecurity. the first step is to identify all the devices connected to the IT system and/or to the Internet. The Internet of things (IoT) includes many devices, such as cameras, microphones, cars, thermostats, appliances, copiers, scanners, office equipment, security systems, and more. It is also necessary to determine if the business is using any cloud computing services. Cloud computing is using the Internet to connect with remote servers to access data or software over the Internet. Companies increased their use of cloud computing during the pandemic because many employees were working from home.

The National Cyber Security Centre (www.ncsc.gov.uk) promotes the following 10 Steps to Cyber Security:

1. **Set up your risk management system.** Assess the risks to your company's information and systems.

2. **Network security.** Protect your networks from attack. Defend the network perimeter, filter out unauthorized access and malicious content. Monitor and test security controls.

3. **User education and awareness.** Produce user security policies covering acceptable and secure use of your system. Include staff training. Maintain awareness of cyberattacks.

4. **Malware prevention.** Produce relevant policies and establish anti-malware defenses across your company.

5. **Removable media controls.** Have a policy to control all access to removable media. Limit media types and use. Scan all media for malware before importing into the company system.

6. **Secure configuration.** Apply security patches and ensure the secure configuration of all systems is maintained. Create a system inventory and define a baseline build for all devices.

7. **Manage user privileges.** Establish effective management processes and limit the number of privileged accounts. Limit user privileges and monitor user activity. Control access to activity and audit logs.

8. **Incident management.** Establish an incident response and disaster recovery capability. Test your incident management plans. Provide specialist training. Report criminal incidents to law enforcement.

9. **Monitoring.** Establish a monitoring strategy and produce supporting policies. Continuously monitor all systems and networks. Analyze logs for unusual activity that could indicate an attack.

10. **Home and mobile working.** Develop a mobile working policy and train staff to follow the policy. Apply the secure baseline and build to all devices. Protect all data both in transit and at rest.

STUDY QUESTION

3. Applying security patches to ensure the secure configuration of all systems is maintained and creating a system inventory and defining a baseline build for all devices falls under the _____ step to cybersecurity.

    a. Security configuration

    b. Incident management

    c. Network security

    d. Monitoring

¶ 216 CYBERSECURITY FRAMEWORKS

The Committee of Sponsoring Organizations of the Treadway Commission (COSO), an advisory group that helps to combat fraud, released a Framework for Internal Controls that has five components:

- Control Environment
- Control Activities
- Risk Assessment
- Information and Communication
- Monitoring

The COSO requirements for IT include the following:

- Determines Dependency between the Use of Technology in Business Processes and Technology General Controls
- Establishes Relevant Technology Infrastructure Control Activities
- Establishes Relevant Security Management Process Control Activities
- Establishes Relevant Technology Acquisition, Development, and Maintenance Process Control Activities

Another cybersecurity framework is the COBIT framework, which was created and developed by the Information Systems Audit and Control Association (ISACA) and is used in conjunction with the COSO Framework. COBIT, which stands for Control Objectives for Information Technologies, is a best practices framework that has four main domains: plan and organize, acquire and implement, deliver and support, and monitor and evaluate. The framework is often used by public companies in the United States.

ISO 27001 was created and published by the International Organization for Standardization (ISO) and is probably the most well-known standard worldwide. It is most commonly used outside the United States and by multinational companies. The standard focuses on technology and assets and concentrates on risk mitigation.

NIST was created by the National Institute of Standards and Technology and is used for implementing the requirements contained in the Federal Information Security Act of 2002. It is used by government agencies and contractors and sets minimum requirements for IT security. The five components of the NIST Framework are: Identify, Protect, Detect, Respond, and Recover.

The Center for Internet Security (CIS) has recommended cybersecurity controls. Its Critical Security Controls provide specific ways to prevent attacks and prioritize actions with high payoff results. The 20 recommended controls are:

1. Inventory of authorized and unauthorized devices
2. Inventory of authorized and unauthorized software
3. Secure configurations for hardware and software on mobile devices, laptops, workstations, and servers
4. Continuous vulnerability assessment and remediation
5. Controlled use of administrative privileges
6. Maintenance, monitoring, and analysis of audit logs
7. Email and web browser protection
8. Malware defenses
9. Limitation and control of network ports, protocols, and services
10. Data recovery capability
11. Secure configuration for network devices such as firewalls, routers, and switches
12. Boundary defense
13. Data protection
14. Controlled access based on need to know
15. Wireless access control
16. Account monitoring and control
17. Security skills assessment and appropriate training to fill gaps
18. Application software security
19. Incident response and management
20. Penetration tests and reaction team exercises

HITRUST is a risk and compliance framework that is mostly used in the U.S. healthcare industry. HITRUST is designed to protect personal health information (PHI) and to maintain compliance with the Health Insurance Portability and Accountability Act (HIPAA). It defines a set of internal controls and is easily updated as regulations change. HITRUST is also easily modified for flexibility of scale (size, type, etc.).

STUDY QUESTION

4. Which of the following cybersecurity frameworks is used by government agencies and contractors?
   a. COBIT
   b. ISO 27001
   c. NIST
   d. HITRUST

¶ 217 INTERNAL CONTROLS FOR SMALL BUSINESSES

A primary and very cost-effective cybersecurity internal control for small businesses is limiting access to IT systems with user IDs and passphrases. As previously mentioned, businesses should require complex passphrases (see the following chart) and require employees and anyone else with access to update their passphrases every 90 days. Remember to reset the default local administrator passwords on all devices. When possible, businesses should also use multifactor authentication or biometrics. Multifactor authentication occurs when the user inputs their user ID and passphrase and a code, usually six digits, is sent to their company cell phone. Access is denied if the code is not input within two minutes to help prevent password spraying and credential stuffing. The most common biometric authentication currently in use is facial recognition, although fingerprints, palmprints, and retina scans are also used.

It is important to use passphrases that can't easily be hacked. Here is a chart showing how long it would take a cyber criminal to hack different types and lengths of passphrases.

Passphrase Security Chart				
Length of Passphrase in Characters	Only Numbers	Mixed lowercase and uppercase alphabet characters	Mixed numbers and lowercase and uppercase alphabet characters	Mixed numbers, lowercase and uppercase alphabet characters, and special symbols
3	Instantly	Instantly	Instantly	Instantly
4	Instantly	Instantly	Instantly	Instantly
5	Instantly	Instantly	3 seconds	10 seconds
6	Instantly	8 seconds	3 minutes	13 minutes
7	Instantly	5 minutes	3 hours	17 hours
8	Instantly	3 hours	10 days	57 days
9	4 seconds	4 days	153 days	12 years
10	40 seconds	169 days	1 year	928 years
11	6 minutes	16 years	106 years	71k years
12	1 hour	600 years	6k years	5m years
13	11 hours	21k years	108k years	423m years
14	4 days	778k years	25m years	5b years
15	46 days	28m years	1b years	2t years
16	1 year	1b years	97b years	193t years
17	12 years	36b years	6t years	14 qd years
18	126 years	1t years	374t years	1qt years

k = thousand

m = million

b = billion

t = trillion

qd = quadrillion

qt = quintillion

It is important for small businesses to have good internal controls to protect the organization from cyber-attacks. Some basic internal controls include the following:

- Router and switch controls
- Firewall (hardware and software)
- Virtual private network (VPN)
- Encryption
- Proxies
- Network intrusion prevention system (NIPS)
- Network intrusion detection system (NIDS)
- Security information and event management (SIEM)

- Spam filters
- SOC for cybersecurity (vendors and others with access)
- Encrypt all files that contain important or personal information

Business.org published an article ranking the best hardware firewalls for 2022.[7] The top four on the list are Cisco, Firewalla, Sonicwall, and Paloalto. According to the list of best software firewalls for 2022 published by Techradar (www.techradar.com), the following are the top five:

1. Bitdefender Total Security
2. Avast Premium Security
3. Norton 360 Deluxe
4. Panda Dome Essential
5. Webroot AntiVirus

A virtual private network (VPN) is an encrypted Internet connection for computers, cell phones, and other devices. An employee can work remotely and still connect to the company computers with a secure connection. A remote access VPN is used for employees who are working remotely or are working from home. A site-to-site VPN is used to link different fixed locations within the business.

PC Magazine rates VPNs on its website (https://www.pcmag.com/picks/the-best-vpn-services). For 2022, the top-rated VPNs include NordVPN, Surfshark, Private Internet Access, Proton VPN, and CyberGhost. The Techradar website included information on its top-rated encryption software for 2022:

1. Microsoft OneDrive (Personal Vault)
2. Folder Lock
3. AxCrypt
4. VeraCrypt
5. Secure IY 2000

Online marketplace vendor Capterra[8] provided the following rankings for top-rated file transferring software:

1. Smartsheet
2. MOVEit
3. Onehub
4. Cornerstone
5. Cerberus FTP
6. GoAnywhere
7. Globalscape
8. Biscom Secure
9. Bynder

---

[7] "Best Firewalls for Small Businesses 2022 Review." https://www.business.org/it/cyber-security/best-firewall-for-small-business/.

[8] https://www.capterra.com/sem-compare/file-sharing-software/?utm_source=bing&utm_medium=cpc.

In addition, Capterra[9] ranked its top-rated digital signature software as follows:

1. signNow
2. PandaDoc
3. ReadySign
4. DocuSign
5. OneSpan Sign
6. Foxit eSign
7. GetAccept
8. Drysign
9. Dotloop
10. Wesignature

The COVID-19 pandemic caused many businesses, including small businesses, to have employees work from home to maintain government mandated social distancing. Some key cybersecurity internal controls for employees working from home include:

- Conduct employee training
- Use multifactor authentication
- Install antivirus, ransomware, malware software
- Use email verifications for payments (CEO spoofing)
- Don't give information to unverified callers, emailers, or text messages
- Have an IT hotline for employee questions or issues
- No personal email, phones, or other devices
- Have a separate ISP for home and office
- Have separate routers for home and office
- Use WPA3 security (requires passwords to connect)
- Update firmware
- Disable remote access
- Disable universal plug-and-play
- Disable Wi-Fi protected setup (PINs are weak security)
- Have a guest network
- Use ethernet for work devices if possible
- Change the default SSID
- Conduct regular training for employees on how to protect company information
- Enroll in a backup or wiping program that backs up smartphones and will allow you to remotely erase the information on a lost or stolen phone
- Do not send company information over public Wi-Fi networks
- Do not reply to emails or click on links in emails from unknown sources
- Use a separate computer for bank and financial transactions
- Use external hard drives for data storage
- Have real-time monitoring of security events on your IT system

---

[9] https://www.capterra.com/sem-compare/file-sharing-software/?utm_source =bing&utm_medium=cpc.

- Update all software when vendor updates are made available
- Use multifactor authentication or biometrics
- Conduct regular penetration and phishing tests
- Unplug from the Internet
- Turn computers off
- Maintain an approved vendor list

Capterra[10] also provided rankings for its top-rated real-time IT monitoring software:

1. SolarWinds Service Desk
2. Freshservice
3. Splunk Enterprise
4. JumpCloud Directory Platform
5. Atera
6. ConnectWise Automate
7. xMatters
8. NinjaOne
9. ConnectWise RMM

Companies that accept credit, debit, or other payment cards need to be aware of the new PCI Data Security Standard v4.0[11]. Here are some highlights of what is new in version 4.0 (released March 31, 2022):

- Expanded multifactor authentication requirements
- Updated password requirements
- New e-commerce and phishing requirements
- Allowance of group, shared, and generic accounts
- Updated firewall terminology
- Added guidance for implementing and maintaining security
- New "areas for improvement" reporting
- Targeted risk analysis
- Customizable options

PCI v3.2.1 will remain active for two years to allow companies to adopt the new standards and will be discontinued on March 31, 2024. All businesses accepting credit or debit cards must implement PCI v. 4.0 before March 31, 2024 when PCI v 3.2.1 is discontinued.

In conclusion, we have identified cybersecurity risks for small businesses and have discussed various cybersecurity internal controls for small businesses. We reviewed cost effective internal controls that won't break the budget of a small business.

---

[10] "IT Management Software." https://www.capterra.com/sem-compare/it-management-software/?utm_source=bing&utm_medium=cpc.

[11] "At a Glance: PCI DSS v4.0." https://www.pcisecuritystandards.org/documents/PCI-DSS-v4-0-At-A-Glance.pdf?agreement=true&time=1650402657264.

STUDY QUESTIONS

---

5. Which of the following passphrases would take the longest for criminals to crack?

    a. A passphrase with 16 numbers

    b. A passphrase with 13 mixed lowercase and uppercase letters

    c. A passphrase with 12 mixed numbers, uppercase letters, and lowercase letters

    d. A passphrase with 11 mixed numbers, uppercase letters, lowercase letters, and special symbols

6. Which of the following creates an encrypted connection over the Internet?

    a. Virtual private network (VPN)

    b. Hardware firewall

    c. PCI data security

    d. Biometrics

MODULE 1: TOP ACCOUNTING ISSUES—
CHAPTER 3: Real-World Blockchain
Applications

¶ 301 WELCOME

This chapter will review real-world applications for blockchains. Many people have heard of blockchains but are not sure what they are or how they work. You might know that blockchains are used for cryptocurrency transactions, but are you aware of the other business and accounting uses for blockchain technology? This chapter explores current and possible future uses for blockchain technology in businesses, government entities, and in the accounting and auditing profession. Examples of how blockchains work will be provided.

¶ 302 LEARNING OBJECTIVES

Upon completion of this chapter, you will be able to:

- Define what a blockchain is
- Identify how blockchains work
- Identify uses for blockchains

¶ 303 INTRODUCTION

The world is becoming ever more reliant on technology. Gone are the days when we posted accounting transactions on green ledger sheets and used 10 keys to add up our numbers. Accountants, auditors, and businesses rely on technology on a daily basis, and technology continues to change. Other changes in technology include increased use of electronic data storage, increased use of electronic communications, increased access to data, larger databases, better tools for analyzing data, and the increased use of data in making business decisions. Examples of new and changing technologies include, but are not limited to, the following:

- Cloud computing, including cloud storage and software as a service
- Blockchains, which are discussed in this chapter
- Artificial intelligence, for robotics and also tied with data analytics
- Smart businesses and smart homes, voice and smartphone controlled
- Robotics for factories and delivery services
- Virtual reality for gaming and training
- Self-driving trucks and automated delivery systems
- Biometrics, such as facial recognition used for cybersecurity
- The Internet of things (IoT)
- Quantum computers (better, stronger, faster)
- Social media and digital communications
- Interactive TV
- On-demand services
- Internet sales (e.g., Amazon)

- Cryptocurrencies (based on blockchain technology)
- XBRL, used for financial reporting
- Streaming data
- Business intelligence (BI) and other uses of data analytics

Throughout history, there have been many advances to help businesses facilitate both business and financial transactions. Some of these are listed below:

- Money, which is a much better medium of exchange than barter
- Contracts that define obligations
- Banking systems—savings, checking, wires, Automated Clearing House (ACH), credit and debit cards, etc.
- Internet transactions—websites
- Mobile devices and applications
- Automatic teller machines (ATMs)
- Blockchains
- Cryptocurrencies
- Crypto tokens

¶ 304 BLOCKCHAIN BASICS

Blockchains are lists of records held on diverse computers, also known as *nodes*, that are used to record and verify data. Each node can send and receive transactions, and the data is synchronized throughout the network. Data is saved to multiple nodes so that it can be verified by seeking a consensus from the nodes. Each record is timestamped to record the date and time it was added to the blockchain.

Blockchain networks reduce the need for intermediaries like banks and credit card processors because they allow peer-to-peer transactions. You still need an intermediary, such as a crypto exchange, when you want to change a fiat currency, like U.S. dollars, into a cryptocurrency, or when you want to convert a cryptocurrency to a fiat currency.

Blockchains are used to track assets and transactions, including the following:

- Tangible assets such as real property, personal property, or cash
- Intangible assets such as patents or copyrights
- Digital assets such as cryptocurrencies and crypto tokens
- Accounting transactions
- Other transactions and events
- Smart contracts

All blockchain networks include the following characteristics:

- **Consensus.** All participants agree to the validity of the transaction or data on the blockchain.
- **Provenance.** Participants know where the asset, liability, or transaction comes from and how it has changed over time.
- **Immutability.** Recorded transactions cannot be changed. If an error occurs, a new transaction must be input to reverse the error.
- **Finality.** A single shared ledger gives all participants one place to go to determine the accuracy and validity of the information.

There are many benefits to using blockchains. Some of these advantages are detailed in the following list:

- **Saving time.** Transaction times are reduced because there are usually no intermediaries or separate registries. Most transactions are completed on a peer-to-peer basis.
- **Saving money.** Users save money by not duplicating efforts and by not using, and paying, intermediaries. For example, once a sale is recorded on a blockchain, both the buyer and seller have documentation of the transaction.
- **Increased security.** Because cryptography is used, there is more security against tampering with transactions, cybercrimes, and fraud.
- **Peer-to-peer transactions.** As mentioned above, transactions typically do not involve intermediaries.
- **Smart contracts.** The contract is built into the transaction.
- **Added privacy.** Using user IDs, permissions, encryption, and cryptography increases user privacy.
- **Auditability.** Because transactions are permanent and on a single shared ledger, they are easier to audit.
- **Operational efficiency.** Because all transactions are digital, the process for recording transactions is streamlined.
- **Data access.** Because all data is digital, it can be accessed, with appropriate permissions, anywhere in the world.

STUDY QUESTIONS

1. Which of the following identifies a node?

   a. Data on a blockchain

   b. A series of blocks

   c. A diverse computer

   d. The Internet

2. All participants agreeing to the validity of a transaction is known as which of the following?

   a. Consensus

   b. Provenance

   c. Immutability

   d. Finality

¶ 305 HOW BLOCKCHAINS WORK

The basic concept of a blockchain is to record and timestamp data, and to be able to verify the data that has been recorded on the blockchain. Data is stored on multiple nodes to increase reliability.

- Each and every transaction is recorded as a "block" of data, like a piece of a puzzle.
- Data blocks can record information such as who, what, where, when, and how.

- Data blocks can record conditions such as the temperature of food during shipment and storage, or the miles on a car's odometer when the title is transferred.
- Each block is connected to previous and subsequent blocks, just like the puzzle pieces. The more blocks in the chain, the stronger the blockchain.
- The blocks create a chain of data as an asset moves from one place to another, as conditions change, or when ownership changes. The blocks themselves do not move or change; the new blocks added to the blockchain record this information.
- The data blocks confirm the exact date and time an event occurs.
- The data blocks confirm the sequence of recorded events.
- The blocks are securely linked to prevent any block from being altered, and to prevent new blocks from being inserted between existing blocks; new blocks can only be added at the end of the chain.
- Each new data block strengthens the verifiability of the entire blockchain and helps to make the block chain tamper-evident, but not tamper-proof. Just like a puzzle, the more pieces that are connected, the clearer, or more accurate, the picture.

There are several types of blockchain platforms. A public blockchain, such as the one used to power Bitcoin and other cryptocurrencies, is on all kinds of computers all over the world. Anybody who is mining Bitcoins or other cryptocurrency is allowing the use of their computer to record these transactions. They are acting as a node, and they get paid in the cryptocurrency for allowing their computer to be used as a node. Public blockchains are all over the world. Nobody is controlling who is involved in the network; it is usually an open-source network.

Private blockchains, on the other hand, are held by organizations. For example, banking institutions might set up private blockchains for a companywide cryptocurrency or smart contracts. The blockchain works within the banking system, and all the data is stored on the bank's computers. Only the bank's employees and/or customers have access to the private blockchain.

Permissioned blockchains require user authentication and permission to access the data. This is accomplished with the use of electronic keys. There are two keys: a public key and a private key. When these two keys match up, users create a digital signature that allows them to view or add blocks to the chain—for example, to transfer the ownership of some or all data that they have stored on the blockchain. Note that the data doesn't transfer; it stays at the same place on the blockchain. Only the right to access the data is changed by adding a new block.

The public key is stored on the blockchain itself, so the public key is always available. The private key is what someone keeps in their wallet (discussed shortly). The private key allows them to access the information on the blockchain. One matches up the private key to the public key to create a digital signature. While the keys are not the same, the two of them together combine to allow someone to access the blockchain information. Because the private and public keys are a long string of alphanumeric characters, it is very difficult for anyone to guess it, even at computer speeds.

To look for, or verify, data on a blockchain, you use a blockchain explorer. Anybody can check the balance of any public address, and anyone can view any transaction details on any blockchain. Block explorer is a website or a tool that allows one to browse through blocks, viewing wallet addresses, network hashrate, transaction data, and other key information on the blockchain. Block explorer is simply a search tool. Every cryptocurrency that relies on its own blockchain will also have its own block explorer.

¶ 306 BLOCKCHAIN TERMINOLOGY

Take a few moments to review some basic blockchain terminology.

- **Blocks:** Blocks contain data for valid transactions that are hashed and encoded into the blockchain.

- **Block time:** Block time is the average time it takes the network to add an additional block to the blockchain. This can range from seconds to hours.

- **Decentralization:** Storing data across a peer-to-peer network.

- **Hard fork:** A hard fork refers to a radical change to the protocol of a blockchain network that effectively results in two branches, one that follows the previous protocol and one that follows the new version. In a hard fork, holders of tokens in the original blockchain will be granted tokens in the new fork as well, but miners must choose which blockchain to continue verifying. A hard fork can occur in any blockchain, and not only Bitcoin (where hard forks have created Bitcoin Cash and Bitcoin SV, among several others, for example).

- **Airdrop:** An airdrop occurs when you have free crypto coins sent to your wallet. You did not purchase or earn the coins.

- **Staking or farming:** A "proof of stake" is a consensus technique that allows blockchain networks to use less energy while retaining a reasonable level of decentralization on the internet.

- **Sign messages:** Sign messages, wallet signing, and digital signatures are digital ways to verify documents and digital messages. Sign messages is a kind of ID system to prove the ownership of Bitcoin or a cryptocurrency address. Without revealing your private keys, you can prove the ownership by sharing your wallet signature.

STUDY QUESTIONS

3. Storing data across a peer-to-peer network is known as which of the following?

   a. Blocks

   b. Decentralization

   c. Block time

   d. Digital signature

4. Having free crypto coins placed in a wallet is known as which of the following?

   a. Hard fork

   b. Staking

   c. Sign message

   d. Airdrop

¶ 307 USES FOR BLOCKCHAINS

One of the major uses for blockchains in the accounting and auditing professions is to store and manage audit evidence; verify the date audit evidence was obtained; verify who had care, custody, and control of audit evidence (especially valuable for forensic accountants); allow easy access to all audit evidence throughout the firm; and to provide a simple way for clients to provide documents for the auditors to review. Other business uses for blockchains include, but are not limited to the following:

- Transferring stocks, bonds, and financial assets (This could eliminate the need for stock exchanges and allow peer-to-peer purchases and sales.)
- Transferring title to assets (such as real estate, autos, etc.)
- Tracking contracts
- Tracking payments
- Regulatory reporting
- Supply chain management
- Tracking medical records (allowing people to access all their medical records anywhere in the world)
- Tracking insurance claims
- Energy trading (Blockchain is already being used to track solar and wind energy production.)
- Domain names (You can already register a domain name on a blockchain.)
- Payroll
- Data sharing
- Loyalty rewards programs
- Money transfers
- Debit, credit, or gift card transaction tracking
- ATM, electronic funds transfer (EFT), and other electronic payment tracking
- Copyright protection
- Patent protection
- Royalty payments
- Food safety
- Prescription drugs
- Insurance

Businesses can use blockchains in many different ways. For example, in the healthcare industry, "IoT-connected devices allow healthcare providers to monitor patient conditions remotely, in real time—an important advance. But what makes these IoT capabilities even more viable is an underlying blockchain infrastructure that can also verify the IoT sensors are producing valid, authentic information with which no one has tampered."[1] Employees can use blockchains to verify patient vitals, medication delivery, and more.

Many types of businesses can use smart contracts to automate the execution of an agreement. "Blockchain executes transactions using business processes that have been developed as software code and are referred to as smart contracts. Smart contracts can require that a specific contract term or milestone must be met before the next transaction can take place. They also make it possible to automate the monitoring and enforcement of contractual promises with minimal human intervention, resulting in greater efficiency and improved opportunities to scale up operations with less additional investment."[2] Blockchains can be used to verify performance objectives.

---

[1] Richard C. Kloch and Simon J. Little, "Blockchain and Internal Audit." 2019. https://theiia.fi/wp-content/uploads/2019/08/iaf-blockchain-internal-audit-july-2019-070119-2.pdf.

[2] Kloch and Little, 2019.

Blockchains also can be used in the payroll process. Payroll departments can use blockchains to track work time (billable hours), admin time (nonbillable hours), training time, travel time, sick time, vacation time, paid time off, and more. Blockchains are much more reliable than timecards and a time clock.

The insurance industry is another sector that is expanding its use of blockchains. "The insurance industry is exploring blockchain applications across a wide variety of operational functions, including claims handling, subrogation, and reinsurance."[3] Blockchains can be used to verify claims, payments, liens, recovery, and cost sharing.

Blockchains are also being used in the food industry. From production through distribution, blockchains can be used to track shipments of food and to verify temperatures of the food throughout the supply chain. Thermometers transfer temperatures and GPS locations to the blockchain via Wi-Fi connections.

Blockchains also have uses in government entities, including the following:
- Tracking documents
- Ensuring transparency of government information
- Tax payments and receipts
- IDs—passports, driver's license, professional licenses, etc.
- Tracking government services and government benefits
- Tracking court records, both civil and criminal
- Tracking criminal records and arrest records
- Digital voting
- Regulatory compliance
- Police and criminal records

One possible use for blockchains in governments is in the voting process. Blockchains can be used for voter registration and to verify the eligibility of individuals to vote. This includes verifying citizenship, verifying the proper voting district, verifying the individual is actually registered to vote, verifying the voter is alive at the time they vote, allowing for secure Internet voting, and verifying the accuracy of vote counts.

Blockchains will also be beneficial to individuals. Some uses include:
- Cryptocurrencies
- Wills and trusts (no need to fight over who gets what)
- Equity trading
- Monitoring IoT networks
- Keyless secure entry (to homes, autos, and businesses)
- Medical monitoring and records
- Prescription drug monitoring
- Asset ownership records

¶ 308 CRYPTOCURRENCIES

Cryptocurrencies are currently the biggest users of blockchain technologies. Virtual currency can be defined as virtual money. It is issued by its developers and used within a given virtual community. The European Banking Authority defines virtual currency as "a digital representation of value that is neither issued by a central bank or a public

---

[3] Kloch and Little, 2019.

authority, nor necessarily attached to a fiat currency, but is accepted by natural or legal persons as a means of payment and can be transferred, stored or traded electronically."

The definition of virtual currency from the Financial Crimes Enforcement Network (FinCEN) of the U.S. Department of the Treasury is similar: "a medium of exchange that operates like a currency in some environments, but does not have all the attributes of real currency." In particular, virtual currency does not have legal tender status in any jurisdiction. The IRS defines virtual currency as property, not as a currency. However, the American Institute of Certified Public Accountants (AICPA) considers cryptocurrencies to be long-lived intangible assets.

There are several different types of virtual currencies such as closed virtual currencies, single flow virtual currencies, and convertible virtual currencies. Closed virtual currencies are used in a closed community, most commonly multiplayer online games. The currency is fictional and has no value outside the game. Game rules often prohibit players from buying and selling the currency outside of the game.

Single flow virtual currencies are similar to coupons. Common examples are frequent flyer miles with airlines and Amazon Coin. The currency can be purchased, or provided with a purchase, and can be used to purchase goods and services from a provider but cannot be purchased or exchanged on an open market.

Convertible virtual currencies can be purchased and sold on exchanges and used to complete transactions with individuals, businesses, and governments. Bitcoin is currently the most well-known convertible virtual currency.

A cryptocurrency is a digital currency using cryptography to secure transactions and to control the creation of new currency units. Not all virtual currencies use cryptography, so cryptocurrencies are a subset of virtual currencies.

Although there are many advantages to using virtual currencies, there are disadvantages as well. These are listed in the following table.

Advantages and Disadvantages of Using Virtual Currencies	
Advantages	**Disadvantages**
No intermediary	Volatility and risk
Anonymity	Hacking and theft
Transparency	Growth industry (bugs)
Low fees	Wallets can be stolen
Irreversible transactions	No buyer protections
Worldwide use and access	No guarantee of value
No tracking	No physical form
No third-party seizure	

A newer type of crypto asset on the market is the crypto token. Crypto tokens are a type of virtual currency that represents fungible and tradable assets or utilities that reside on their own blockchains. Crypto tokens are new and are a very niche product. Examples of crypto tokens include copyrighted art, use of a vacation home, and green energy. Note that crypto tokens, like cryptocurrencies, are very volatile when it comes to price. Prices fluctuate like a roller coaster with no guarantee of a minimal value.

STUDY QUESTIONS

5. The IRS considers virtual currencies to be which of the following?

    a. Nontaxable

    b. Property

    c. Currency

    d. Securities

6. Airline frequent flyer miles are an example of which of the following?

    a. Closed virtual currency

    b. Single flow virtual currency

    c. Convertible virtual currency

    d. Public virtual currency

¶ 309 CRYPTO FRAUDS

Cryptojacking occurs when scammers use your computer or smartphone's processing power to "mine" cryptocurrency for their own benefit, and without your permission. Scammers can put malicious code onto your device simply by your visiting a website. Then they can help themselves to your device's processor and your electricity, without you knowing about it.

Hacking is also an issue for crypto assets. Hackers have been known to misappropriate large amounts of cryptocurrencies from exchanges and from individuals. Reports of hackers stealing crypto assets have been in the news.

¶ 310 VIRTUAL CURRENCY WALLETS

A virtual currency wallet is needed to buy, store, and use virtual currencies. A "wallet" is a software program that stores private and public keys and interacts with the virtual currencies' blockchain. The wallet doesn't store the virtual currencies or coins; it only maintains the information that allows the users to access the information for their transactions on the blockchain.

When a virtual currency transaction occurs, nothing is actually transferred. Rather, when an individual sends a virtual currency to someone, they are signing over the ownership of the Bitcoin. The public and private keys are compared, and if they match, the ownership is transferred and the transaction is recorded on the blockchain.

There are several types of virtual currency wallets. A user can create a paper wallet by printing a hard copy of the private key and the public key or by writing them down on paper. An advantage of a printed wallet is that it is safe from hackers. However, most people store the keys on their desktop or laptop, or on a mobile device like a cell phone. Other options include a jump drive, or a wallet stored on a CD or DVD, or on the web or in the cloud.

¶ 311 ACCOUNTING AND AUDITING FOR VIRTUAL CURRENCIES

There is currently a lack of official guidance for recording and auditing cryptocurrencies. Neither the Financial Accounting Standards Board (FASB), the Auditing Standards Board (ASB), nor the Public Company Accounting Oversight Board (PCAOB) have issued formal guidance for accounting or auditing cryptocurrency, although the FASB and PCAOB have projects in progress to develop official guidance.

In March 2019, the International Financial Reporting Interpretations Committee (IFRIC) issued "Holdings of Cryptocurrencies—Agenda Paper 4" (IFRIC 2019) stating that the accounting treatment for holding cryptocurrency follows the International Accounting Standard Board (IASB 38) on Intangible Assets (IASB 2004).

The Internal Revenue Service (IRS) issued guidance on the U.S. tax treatment of cryptocurrency transactions (IRS Notice 2014-21, 2014). The AICPA recommends recording crypto assets as long-lived intangible assets.

Crypto assets do not meet the definition of cash or cash equivalents, inventory, or financial instruments and therefore should not be recorded as such. All intangible assets, including crypto assets, should be initially recorded at cost/fair market value. Remember that it is necessary to conduct impairments, and, if necessary, to record impairment transactions if the value has fallen below book value on an other than temporary basis.

¶ 312 BLOCKCHAIN IN THE NEWS

Many articles discussing blockchain technology have been in the news recently. Here are just a few examples.

Global Blockchain in Manufacturing Market (2022 to 2027)— Industry Trends, Share, Size, Growth, Opportunity and Forecasts[4]

According to this May 2022 article on Yahoo! Finance, "The global blockchain in manufacturing market reached a value of US$ 717.6 million in 2021. Looking forward, the market is projected to reach a value of US$ 17,047.8 million by 2027, exhibiting a CAGR of 66.40% during 2022–2027."

3 Ways Blockchain Could Influence Web Design in the Future[5]

In this article, Sheba Karamat states: "Blockchain is a fresh upheaval in decentralized data storage. It uses cryptography to store data in discrete blocks. These blocks, once full, are linked to a chain of other blocks called a blockchain. Now, the genius of blockchain is that it is not centralized. Instead, all the data is spread throughout a whole network of nodes or users. This way, no one node can change the data in the shared database without being exposed. The whole network must vet all new data before it can be added to a block. And once added, you can't change the block data. This tech has had a great impact in sectors from business to production. Some claim that it may rival even that of the internet upheaval."

Blockchain Technology in the Food Industry[6]

This article from the Michigan State University Institute for Food Laws and Regulations explains how major food companies can use blockchain: "Global food supply chain failure has become a catch phrase for supply systems malfunction. Just look at the last two years to see the failure that supply chains have caused the food industry. Blockchain technology (BT) is one tool that could improve future food systems policies, traceability, and the flow and success of these supply chains. BT can enhance consumer trust, production speed, and product efficiency; things the food industry could use right now. BT can substantially improve global food supply chains by enabling faster and more cost-efficient delivery of products, improved supply chain transparency and tracea-

---

[4] "Global Blockchain in Manufacturing Market (2022 to 2027)—Industry Trends, Share, Size, Growth, Opportunity and Forecasts," May 4, 2022. https://finance.yahoo.com/news/global-blockchain-manufacturing-market-2022-114800345.html.

[5] Sheba Karamat, "3 Ways Blockchain Could Influence Web Design in the Future." May 2,

2022. https://finance.yahoo.com/news/3-ways-blockchain-could-influence-112139088.html.

[6] Scott Haskell, "Blockchain Technology in the Food Industry." April 21, 2022. https://www.canr.msu.edu/news/blockchain-technology-in-the-food-industry.

bility, upgrade the real-time coordination between trading partners, and substantially ameliorate record-keeping by all concerned parties."

Blockchain Technology Enables Fee Reduction, Anti-Corruption, and Smart Contracts: Trillions of Dollars of Opportunity[7]

This article discusses the rise of blockchain technology in the financial sector. Analyst Jamie Friedman states, "Cross-border e-commerce from a payments perspective is really complicated. Part of the complexity is that in a lot of the world, people don't pay with credit cards. They pay with some alternative payment mechanisms. If you're a big company and want to expand into an emerging market, you need to make sure that you enable that customer to pay the way they want to pay."

New Bill Establishes Group to Recommend Policies for Blockchain Tech in Washington State[8]

The use of blockchain in Washington State is highlighted in this article. Charlotte Schubert states: "Washington Gov. Jay Inslee signed legislation to establish a working group to evaluate blockchain technology in the state. The group will recommend policies to 'make Washington a favorable place to do business' and that 'facilitate the development of blockchain applications and the sector overall in Washington.' The group will also assess impacts on existing industries, evaluate racial equity in the sector, and assess electricity demand and environmental considerations of the technology, which supports the energy-intensive process of cryptocurrency 'mining.' Blockchain technology is commonly used as a ledger for transactions and has a variety of other uses. 'Mining' of cryptocurrencies has become increasingly popular in Washington state."

Global Blockchain in Healthcare Market Size to Grow USD 5.15 Bn By 2027[9]

This Digital Journal article from April 2022 notes: "As per our research report, the size of the global blockchain in the healthcare market is estimated to be growing at a CAGR of 72.98% from 2022 to 2027 and value USD 5.15 billion by 2027."

CPE NOTE: When you have completed your study and review of chapters 1-3, which comprise Module 1, you may wish to take the Final Exam for this Module. Go to **cchcpelink.com/printcpe** to take this Final Exam online.

---

[7] Jamie Friedman, "Blockchain Technology Enables Fee Reduction, Anti-Corruption, and Smart Contracts: Trillions of Dollars of Opportunity." May 4, 2022. https://www.twst.com/news/blockchain-technology-enables/.

[8] Charlotte Schubert, "New Bill Establishes Group to Recommend Policies for Blockchain Tech in Washington State." April 4, 2022. https://www.geekwire.com/2022/new-bill-establishes-group-to-recommend-policies-for-blockchain-tech-in-washington-state/.

[9] Newsmantraa, "Global Blockchain in Healthcare Market Size to Grow USD 5.15 Bn By 2027." April 5, 2022. https://www.digitaljournal.com/pr/global-blockchain-in-healthcare-market-size-to-grow-usd-5-15-bn-by-2027.

MODULE 2: TOP AUDITING ISSUES— CHAPTER 4: Auditing and Internal Control Issues

¶ 401 WELCOME

This chapter reviews internal control and internal control systems from the auditor's point of view. It provides updates on internal controls and American Institute of Certified Public Accountants (AICPA) auditing standards, as well as internal control and audit reports. It also covers the new quality management standards approved by the AICPA Accounting Standards Board (ASB), discusses internal control and COVID-19 issues, along with other related matters.

¶ 402 LEARNING OBJECTIVES

Upon completion of this chapter, you will be able to:

- Identify updates on internal controls and AICPA auditing standards
- Identify updates on internal control and audit reports
- Recognize internal control and COVID—19 issues
- Differentiate effective dates of Statements on Auditing Standards (SAS)
- Recognize the auditor's requirement relevant to understanding an entity's control activities
- Identify true statements regarding risk assessment procedures and internal controls
- Differentiate in what section of the auditor's report the auditor's opinion is under AU-C 700
- Describe the key audit matters paragraph in the auditor's report
- Recognize the changes included in SAS No. 142
- Identify financial reporting considerations related to subsequent events

¶ 403 INTRODUCTION

To obtain an adequate understanding of an internal control system to be tested, the auditor must first determine whether the audit is possible, and if yes, then determine the scope of the audit.

The coronavirus pandemic (COVID-19) has raised several questions about how to properly audit financial statements when internal controls have changed due to dramatic changes in an entity's business volume and activities.

Generally accepted auditing standards (GAAS) require the auditor to obtain an understanding of controls that are relevant to the audit and assess whether they are designed effectively to prevent or at least detect and correct material misstatements within the financial statements. Then the auditor is required to determine whether they've been implemented. Note that this chapter considers audits performed under GAAS and not audits under Public Company Accounting Oversight Board (PCAOB) standards with respect to public companies.

GAAS requires auditors to identify where and how the financial statements may include a higher risk of being materially misstated. The auditor uses that understanding to help design what further audit procedures might be effective in detecting any material misstatement that may exist. Those further audit procedures can either be tests of controls or substantive audit procedures.

While there are certainly standards and best practices with respect to audit approaches, it is important in this environment for auditors to also be creative and innovative in their audit approaches. This may involve performing procedures remotely, and it is predicated on understanding how the client is processing and controlling its financial accounting processes and working transactions through the financial statements. The auditor needs to understand the entity's internal control before determining whether procedures that might be performed remotely would truly be effective.

First, here is a review of some terms as defined in AU-C Section 200, *Overall Objectives of the Independent Auditor, and the Conduct of an Audit in Accordance with Generally Accepted Auditing Standards*. GAAS uses the following two categories of professional requirements, identified by specific terms, to describe the degree of responsibility it imposes on auditors:

- **Unconditional requirements.** The auditor must comply with an unconditional requirement in all cases in which such requirement is relevant. GAAS uses the word *must* to indicate an unconditional requirement.

- **Presumptively mandatory requirements.** The auditor must comply with a presumptively mandatory requirement in all cases in which such a requirement is relevant except in rare circumstances. GAAS uses the word *should* to indicate a presumptively mandatory requirement.

For Statements on Standards for Attestation Engagements (SSAEs) and Statements on Standards for Accounting and Review (SSARS), these terms have the same meaning.

¶ 404 AICPA AUDITING STANDARDS UPDATE

This section outlines a few relatively new audit standards. SAS No. 141, *Amendment to the Effective Dates of SAS Nos. 134–140*, issued in May 2020, delays the effective dates of SAS Nos. 134–140, and the amendments to other SASs made by SAS Nos. 134–140, from December 15, 2020, to December 15, 2021, to give firms more time to implement these SASs in light of the effect of the COVID-19 pandemic.

SAS Nos. 134, 136–137, and 139–140, as originally issued, do not permit early implementation. This statement amends these SASs to no longer preclude early implementation. SAS No. 141 and SAS Nos. 134 and 136–140 are interrelated because the ASB amended the auditor reporting model adopted in SAS No. 134 with the issuance of the subsequent SASs. The effective dates were aligned so that these SASs would be implemented as a suite, primarily to accommodate the amendments to the auditor reporting model. Accordingly, the ASB recommends that all of these SASs be implemented concurrently. SAS No. 141 is effective upon issuance.

AU-C Section 315B, *Understanding the Entity and its Environment and Assessing the Risks of Material Misstatement*, addresses the auditor's responsibility to identify and assess the risks of material misstatement in the financial statements through understanding the entity and its environment, including the entity's internal control. *Internal control* is defined in AU-C Section 315B as follows:

A process effected by those charged with governance, management, and other personnel that is designed to provide reasonable assurance about the achievement of the entity's objectives with regard to the reliability of financial reporting, effectiveness and efficiency of operations, and compliance with applicable laws and regulations. Internal control over safeguarding of assets against unauthorized acquisition, use, or disposition may include controls relating to financial reporting and operations objectives.

It is also important to know the definitions of the following terms related to internal control:

- **Assertions.** Representations by management, explicit or otherwise, that are embodied in the financial statements as used by the auditor to consider the different types of potential misstatements that may occur.

- **Business risk.** A risk resulting from significant conditions, events, circumstances, actions, or inactions that could adversely affect an entity's ability to achieve its objectives and execute its strategies or from the setting of inappropriate objectives and strategies.

- **Relevant assertion.** A financial statement assertion that has a reasonable possibility of containing a misstatement or misstatements that would cause the financial statements to be materially misstated. The determination of whether an assertion is a relevant assertion is made without regard to the effect of internal controls.

- **Risk assessment procedures.** The audit procedures performed to obtain an understanding of the entity and its environment, including the entity's internal control, to identify and assess the risks of material misstatement, whether due to fraud or error, at the financial statement and relevant assertion levels.

- **Significant risk.** An identified and assessed risk of material misstatement that, in the auditor's professional judgment, requires special audit consideration.

¶ 405 RISK ASSESSMENT PROCEDURES AND RELATED ACTIVITIES

The auditor should perform risk assessment procedures to provide a basis for the identification and assessment of risks of material misstatement at the financial statement and relevant assertion levels.

> **NOTE:** Risk assessment procedures by themselves, however, do not provide sufficient appropriate audit evidence on which to base the audit opinion.

The risk assessment procedures should include the following:

- Inquiries of management
- Analytical procedures
- Observation and inspection

The auditor should consider whether information obtained from the auditor's client acceptance or continuance process is relevant to identifying risks of material misstatement. If the engagement partner has performed other engagements for the entity, the engagement partner should consider whether the information obtained is relevant to identifying risks of material misstatement.

During the planning stage, the auditor should consider the results of the assessment of the risk of material misstatement due to fraud along with other information gathered in the process of identifying the risks of material misstatements. The engagement partner should do the following:

- Determine whether changes have occurred since the previous audit that may affect its relevance to the current audit.

- With other key engagement team members, discuss the susceptibility of the entity's financial statements to material misstatement and the application of the applicable financial reporting framework to the entity's facts and circumstances.
- Determine which matters are to be communicated to engagement team members who are not involved in the discussion.

¶ 406 THE ENTITY'S INTERNAL CONTROL

The auditor should obtain an understanding of the entity's components of internal control and its control environment, including relevant industry regulations and other external factors. The auditor must understand, among other things, the entity's operations, ownership, governance, the types of investments being made, the way the entity is structured, and how it is financed.

This will enable the auditor to understand the classes of transactions, balances, and disclosures to be expected in the financial statements. Part of that understanding involves the selection and application of accounting policies, including the changes and the reasons for them. Auditors should evaluate whether the entity's accounting policies are appropriate for its business and consistent with the applicable financial reporting frameworks and accounting policies used in the relevant industry. This includes the entity's objectives and strategies, related business risks that may result in the risk of material misstatement, and the measurement and review of financial performance.

As mentioned earlier, the auditor should obtain an understanding of internal control related to the audit. Keep in mind that most controls relevant to an audit are likely to relate to financial reporting, but not all controls that relate to financial reporting are relevant to the audit. The auditor should evaluate the design of the entity's internal controls and determine whether they have been implemented by the performing procedures.

In addition to communicating with the entity's personnel to evaluate its internal controls, the auditor should perform an inspection— a walkthrough—to ensure the controls are in place.

¶ 407 RISKS THAT REQUIRE SPECIAL AUDIT CONSIDERATION

As part of the risk assessment, the auditor should determine whether any of the risks identified are, in the auditor's professional judgment, significant risks. In exercising this judgment, the auditor should exclude the effects of identified controls related to the risk. In exercising professional judgment about which risks are significant risks, the auditor should consider at least the other risks.

Documentation

According to AU-C Section 315.33, the auditor should include the following in the audit documentation:

- Discussion among the engagement team required by paragraph .11, the significant decisions reached, how and when the discussion occurred, and the audit team members who participated
- Key elements of the understanding obtained regarding each of the aspects of the entity and its environment specified in paragraph .12 and each of the internal control components specified in paragraphs .15–.25, the sources of information from which the understanding was obtained, and the risk assessment procedures performed

- Identified and assessed risks of material misstatement at the financial statement level and at the relevant assertion level, as required by paragraph .26; and

- Risks identified and related controls about which the auditor has obtained an understanding as a result of the requirements in paragraphs .28–.31.

Risk Assessment Procedures and Related Activities

Obtaining an understanding of the entity and its environment, including the entity's internal control, is a continuous, dynamic process of gathering, updating, and analyzing information throughout the audit. The understanding of the entity establishes a frame of reference within which the auditor plans the audit and exercises professional judgment throughout the audit when certain points occur.

To understand the entity and its environment, the auditor must look at both industry factors and regulatory factors as outlined below:

- **Industry factors.** These include industry conditions such as the competitive environment, supplier and customer relationships, and technological developments.

- **Regulatory factors.** These factors include the regulatory environment, which encompasses, among other matters, the applicable financial reporting framework, and the legal and political environment.

  NOTE: The industry in which the entity operates may give rise to specific risks of material misstatement from the nature of the business or the degree of regulation.

¶ 408 THE ENTITY AND ITS ENVIRONMENT

AU-C Section 250, *Consideration of Laws and Regulations in an Audit of Financial Statements*, includes some specific requirements related to the legal and regulatory framework applicable to the entity and the industry or sector in which the entity operates.

Other External Factors

Examples of other external factors affecting the entity that the auditor may consider include, but are not limited to, the general economic conditions, interest rates and availability of financing, and inflation or currency revaluation.

Nature of the Entity

An understanding of the nature of an entity enables the auditor to comprehend matters such as:

- Whether the entity has a complex structure (e.g., with subsidiaries or other components in multiple locations). Complex structures often introduce issues that may give rise to risks of material misstatement. These issues may include whether goodwill, joint ventures, investments, or investments in entities formed to accomplish specific objectives are accounted for and disclosed appropriately.

- The ownership and relationships between owners and other people or entities.

This understanding helps in determining whether related-party transactions and balances have been appropriately identified, accounted for, and adequately disclosed in the financial statements.

The Entity's Internal Control

An understanding of internal control assists the auditor in identifying types of potential misstatements and factors that affect the risks of material misstatement and in designing the nature, timing, and extent of further audit procedures.

¶ 409 GENERAL NATURE AND CHARACTERISTICS OF INTERNAL CONTROL

Internal control is designed, implemented, and maintained to address identified business risks that threaten the achievement of any of the entity's objectives that concern the following:

- The reliability of the entity's financial reporting,
- The effectiveness and efficiency of its operations, and
- Its compliance with applicable laws and regulations.

At the risk of stating the obvious, the manner in which internal control is designed, implemented, and maintained varies with an entity's size and complexity. For example, smaller, less complex entities may use less structured means and simpler processes and procedures to achieve their objectives. More specifically, smaller entities with active management involvement in the financial reporting process may not have extensive descriptions of accounting procedures or detailed written policies.

For some entities, in particular very small entities, the owner-manager (the proprietor of an entity who is involved in running the entity on a day-to-day basis) may perform functions that in a larger entity would be regarded as belonging to several of the components of internal control. Therefore, the components of internal control may not be clearly distinguished within smaller entities, but their underlying purposes are equally valid.

Limitations of Internal Control

Internal control, no matter how effective, can only provide an entity with reasonable assurance about achieving its financial reporting objectives. Said another way, the likelihood of their achievement is affected by the inherent limitations of internal control. These include the realities that human judgment in decision-making can be faulty and that breakdowns in internal control can occur because of human error.

> **EXAMPLE:** Smaller, less complex entities often have fewer employees, which may limit the extent to which segregation of duties is practicable. However, in a small owner-managed entity, the owner-manager may be able to exercise more effective oversight than in a larger entity. This oversight may compensate for the generally more limited opportunities for segregation of duties.

Division of Internal Control into Components

The division of internal control into the following five components, for purposes of GAAS, provides a useful framework for auditors when considering how different aspects of an entity's internal control may affect the audit:

- The control environment
- The entity's risk assessment process
- The information system, including the related business processes relevant to financial reporting and communication
- Control activities
- Monitoring of controls

¶ 410 AU-C SECTION 700: *FORMING AN OPINION AND REPORTING ON FINANCIAL STATEMENTS*

AU-C Section 700 discusses the auditor's responsibility to form an opinion on the financial statements. It also outlines the form and content of the auditor's report.

> **NOTE:** AU-C Section 700 is not applicable when the auditor is forming an opinion and reporting on financial statements of employee benefit plans subject to the Employee Retirement Income Security Act of 1974 (ERISA). In such circumstances, SAS No. 136, *Forming an Opinion and Reporting on Financial Statements of Employee Benefit Plans Subject to ERISA*, applies.

AU-C Section 705, *Modifications to the Opinion in the Independent Auditor's Report*, and AU-C Section 706, *Emphasis-of-Matter Paragraphs and Other-Matter Paragraphs in the Independent Auditor's Report*, of this SAS address how the form and content of the auditor's report are affected when the auditor expresses a modified opinion (a qualified opinion, an adverse opinion, or a disclaimer of opinion) or includes an emphasis-of-matter paragraph or other-matter paragraph in the auditor's report.

This section does not require the communication of key audit matters. Rather, Section 701, *Communicating Key Audit Matters in the Independent Auditor's Report*, addresses the auditor's responsibility to communicate key audit matters when the auditor is engaged to do so.

AU-C Section 800, *Special Considerations—Audits of Financial Statements Prepared in Accordance with Special Purpose Frameworks*, addresses special considerations when financial statements are prepared in accordance with a special purpose framework. Section 805, *Special Considerations—Audits of Single Financial Statements and Specific Elements, Accounts, or Items of a Financial Statement*, addresses special considerations relevant to an audit of a single financial statement or of a specific element, account, or item of a financial statement.

Auditor's Objectives

The objectives of the auditor are to do the following:

- Form an opinion on the financial statements based on an evaluation of the audit evidence obtained, including evidence obtained about comparative financial statements or comparative financial information; and

- Express clearly the opinion on the financial statements through a written report.

¶ 411 AUDITOR'S REPORT

The auditor's report should be in writing and should have a title that clearly indicates that it is the report of an independent auditor. The auditor's report should be addressed, as appropriate, based on the circumstances of the engagement. The components of the report are outlined below.

Auditor's Opinion

The first section of the auditor's report should have the heading "Opinion" and include the auditor's opinion.

Basis for Opinion

Directly after the "Opinion" section should be a section with the heading "Basis for Opinion."

Going Concern

When applicable, the auditor should report in accordance with AU-C Section 570, *The Auditor's Consideration of an Entity's Ability to Continue as a Going Concern*.

Key Audit Matters

If the auditor is engaged to communicate key audit matters, the auditor should do so by following AU-C Section 701.

Responsibilities of Management for the Financial Statements

The "Responsibilities of Management for the Financial Statements" section of the auditor's report should describe management's responsibility for the following:

- The preparation and fair presentation of the financial statements in accordance with the applicable financial reporting framework, and for the design, implementation, and maintenance of internal control relevant to the preparation and fair presentation of financial statements that are free from material misstatement, whether due to fraud or error.

- When required by the applicable financial reporting framework, the evaluation of whether there are conditions or events, considered in the aggregate, that raise substantial doubt about the entity's ability to continue as a going concern (for the time period set by the applicable financial reporting framework, as applicable).

The description about management's responsibility for the financial statements in the auditor's report should not refer to a separate statement by management about such responsibilities, even if such a statement is included in a document containing the auditor's report.

Auditor's Responsibilities for the Audit of the Financial Statements

The "Auditor's Responsibilities for the Audit of the Financial Statements" section of the auditor's report should state that the objectives of the auditor are to:

- Obtain reasonable assurance about whether the financial statements as a whole are free from material misstatement, whether due to fraud or error, and

- Issue an auditor's report that includes the auditor's opinion.

Signature of the Auditor

The auditor's report should include the manual or printed signature of the auditor's firm and identify the city and state in which the auditor's report is issued.

Date of the Auditor's Report

The auditor's report should be dated no earlier than the date on which the auditor has obtained sufficient appropriate audit evidence on which to base the auditor's opinion on the financial statements, including evidence of the following:

- All the statements and disclosures that the financial statements comprise have been prepared.

- Management has asserted that it has taken responsibility for those financial statements.

¶ 412 AUDITOR'S REPORT ILLUSTRATIONS

Illustration No. 1: An Auditor's Report on Comparative Financial Statements Prepared in Accordance with Accounting Principles Generally Accepted in the United States of America

The following is an example of a general-purpose (not group audit) auditor's report on financial statements. Management is responsible for the preparation of the financial statements, and the terms reflect the description of management's responsibility. No key audit matters are included in this auditor's report.

Independent Auditor's Report

[Appropriate Addressee]

Report on the Audit of the Financial Statements

Opinion

We have audited the financial statements of ABC Company, which comprise the balance sheets as of December 31, 20X1 and 20X0, and the related statements of income, changes in stockholders' equity, and cash flows for the years then ended, and the related notes to the financial statements.

In our opinion, the accompanying financial statements present fairly, in all material respects, the financial position of ABC Company as of December 31, 20X1 and 20X0, and the results of its operations and its cash flows for the years then ended in accordance with accounting principles generally accepted in the United States of America.

Basis for Opinion

We conducted our audits in accordance with auditing standards generally accepted in the United States of America (GAAS). Our responsibilities under those standards are further described in the Auditor's Responsibilities for the Audit of the Financial Statements section of our report. We are required to be independent of ABC Company and to meet our other ethical responsibilities, in accordance with the relevant ethical requirements relating to our audits. We believe that the audit evidence we have obtained is sufficient and appropriate to provide a basis for our audit opinion.

Responsibilities of Management for the Financial Statements

Management is responsible for the preparation and fair presentation of the financial statements in accordance with accounting principles generally accepted in the United States of America, and for the design, implementation, and maintenance of internal control relevant to the preparation and fair presentation of financial statements that are free from material misstatement, whether due to fraud or error.

In preparing the financial statements, management is required to evaluate whether there are conditions or events, considered in the aggregate, that raise substantial doubt about ABC Company's ability to continue as a going concern for [insert the time period set by the applicable financial reporting framework].

Auditor's Responsibilities for the Audit of the Financial Statements
Our objectives are to obtain reasonable assurance about whether the financial statements as a whole are free from material misstatement, whether due to fraud or error, and to issue an auditor's report that includes our opinion. Reasonable assurance is a high level of assurance but is not absolute assurance and therefore is not a guarantee that an audit conducted in accordance with GAAS will always detect a material misstatement when it exists. The risk of not detecting a material misstatement resulting from fraud is higher than for one resulting from error, as fraud may involve collusion, forgery, intentional omissions, misrepresentations, or the override of internal control. Misstatements are considered material if, individually or in the aggregate, they could reasonably be expected to influence the economic decisions of users made on the basis of these financial statements.

In performing an audit in accordance with GAAS, we:
• Exercise professional judgment and maintain professional skepticism throughout the audit.
• Identify and assess the risks of material misstatement of the financial statements, whether due to fraud or error, and design and perform audit procedures responsive to those risks. Such procedures include examining, on a test basis, evidence regarding the amounts and disclosures in the financial statements.
• Obtain an understanding of internal control relevant to the audit in order to design audit procedures that are appropriate in the circumstances, but not for the purpose of expressing an opinion on the effectiveness of ABC Company's internal control. Accordingly, no such opinion is expressed.
• Evaluate the appropriateness of accounting policies used and the reasonableness of significant accounting estimates made by management, as well as evaluate the overall presentation of the financial statements.
• Conclude whether, in our judgment, there are conditions or events, considered in the aggregate, that raise substantial doubt about ABC Company's ability to continue as a going concern for a reasonable period of time.

We are required to communicate with those charged with governance regarding, among other matters, the planned scope and timing of the audit, significant audit findings, and certain internal control–related matters that we identified during the audit.

Report on Other Legal and Regulatory Requirements
[The form and content of this section of the auditor's report would vary depending on the nature of the auditor's other reporting responsibilities.]
[Signature of the auditor's firm]
[Auditor's city and state]
[Date of the auditor's report]

Illustration No. 2: An Auditor's Report on Comparative Financial Statements Prepared in Accordance With Accounting Principles Generally Accepted in the United States of America, Including Communication of Key Audit Matters

The following is an excerpt of the illustration from AU-C Section 700. This sample report does include a "Key Audit Matters" section.

Independent Auditor's Report

[Appropriate Addressee]

Report on the Audit of the Financial Statements

Opinion
We have audited the financial statements of ABC Company, which comprise the balance sheets as of December 31, 20X1 and 20X0, and the related statements of income, changes in stockholders' equity, and cash flows for the years then ended, and the related notes to the financial statements.

In our opinion, the accompanying financial statements present fairly, in all material respects, the financial position of ABC Company as of December 31, 20X1 and 20X0, and the results of its operations and its cash flows for the years then ended in accordance with accounting principles generally accepted in the United States of America.

Basis for Opinion

We conducted our audits in accordance with auditing standards generally accepted in the United States of America (GAAS). Our responsibilities under those standards are further described in the Auditor's Responsibilities for the Audit of the Financial Statements section of our report. We are required to be independent of ABC Company and to meet our other ethical responsibilities, in accordance with the relevant ethical requirements relating to our audits. We believe that the audit evidence we have obtained is sufficient and appropriate to provide a basis for our audit opinion.

Key Audit Matters

Key audit matters are those matters that were communicated with those charged with governance and, in our professional judgment, were of most significance in our audit of the financial statements of the current period. These matters were addressed in the context of our audit of the financial statements as a whole, and in forming our opinion thereon, and we do not provide a separate opinion on these matters.

[Description of each key audit matter in accordance with Section 701, *Communicating Key Audit Matters in the Independent Auditor's Report*]

STUDY QUESTIONS

1. Which of the following terms is used within GAAS to indicate that a requirement is unconditional?

    a. Should

    b. May

    c. Must

    d. Encouraged

2. Which of the following statements is correct with respect to the risk assessment process?

    a. The engagement partner should determine whether changes have occurred since the previous audit that may affect its relevance to the current audit.

    b. Risk assessment procedures by themselves can provide sufficient appropriate audit evidence on which to base the audit opinion.

    c. Risk assessment procedures only include inquiries and analytical procedures.

    d. During planning, the auditor need not consider the results of the assessment of the risk of material misstatement due to fraud.

3. As part of the risk assessment, the auditor should determine whether any of the risks identified are, in the auditor's professional judgment, a(n) _____ risk.

    a. Controllable

    b. Avoidable

    c. Significant

    d. Identifiable

¶413 NEW STATEMENTS ON AUDITING STANDARDS

Pre-SAS No. 134: Codification of GAAS Available Through 2021

To help auditors and firms that do not implement SAS Nos. 134–140 prior to December 15, 2021, a "Pre-SAS No. 134" edition of the auditing standards (the AU-C sections) in the AICPA Professional Standards is available. This edition contains SAS Nos. 122–133, as amended, and remains effective through 2021. It should be followed when SAS Nos. 134–140 have not been implemented.

Each AU-C section in this edition is designated with a B suffix (e.g., "AU-C Section 200B") to denote content that does not reflect the codification of SAS Nos. 134–140 or the amendments to other SASs made by SAS Nos. 134–140. Auditors and firms should no longer use this edition once SAS Nos. 134–140 are implemented.

SAS No. 142, Audit Evidence

In July 2020, the ASB issued SAS No. 142, *Audit Evidence*, which supersedes AU-C Section 500, *Audit Evidence*, and amends various other sections of SAS No. 122, *Statements on Auditing Standards: Clarification and Recodification*, as amended.

SAS No. 142 includes expanded guidance on evaluating whether sufficient appropriate audit evidence has been obtained. It expands the objective of the existing standard to be more broadly focused on considering the attributes of information to be used as audit evidence in assessing whether sufficient appropriate audit evidence has been obtained. Previously, the objective focused on the design and performance of audit procedures to obtain sufficient appropriate audit evidence, rather than evaluating the sufficiency and appropriateness of the audit evidence itself.

This change in focus is accomplished by establishing attributes of information to be used as audit evidence when evaluating whether sufficient appropriate audit evidence has been obtained by the auditor. Attributes of reliable information include its accuracy, completeness, authenticity, and susceptibility to bias. SAS No. 142 is effective for periods ending on or after December 15, 2022.

SAS No. 143, Auditing Accounting Estimates and Related Disclosures

SAS No. 143, issued in July 2020, supersedes SAS No. 122, *Statements on Auditing Standards: Clarification and Recodification*, as amended, and Section 540, *Auditing Accounting Estimates, Including Fair Value Accounting Estimates, and Related Disclosures*, and amends various other AU-C sections in the AICPA Professional Standards. Some of the fundamental aspects of SAS No. 143 that enhance the auditing standards relating to auditing accounting estimates and the auditor's focus on factors driving estimation uncertainty and potential management bias are listed. SAS No. 143 is effective for audits of financial statements for periods ending on or after December 15, 2023.

SAS No. 144, Amendments to AU-C Sections 501, 540, and 620 Related to the Use of Specialists and the Use of Pricing Information Obtained From External Information Sources

SAS No. 144 addresses certain comments that were received on the exposure draft that resulted in the issuance of SAS No. 143, *Auditing Accounting Estimates and Related Disclosures*.

Among other things, the SAS provides guidance in AU-C Section 501, *Audit Evidence—Specific Considerations for Selected Items*, on applying SAS No. 143 when management has used the work of a specialist in developing accounting estimates, as well as other amendments to enhance guidance about evaluating the work of the management's specialist; adds a new appendix to AU-C Section 540, *Auditing Accounting Estimates, Including Fair Value Accounting Estimates, and Related Disclosures*, that provides guidance on the use of pricing information from pricing services when evaluating management's estimates related to the fair value of financial instruments; and enhances the guidance in AU-C Section 620, *Using the Work of an Auditor's Specialist*, related to using the work of an auditor's specialist.

SAS No. 144 becomes effective for audits of financial statements for periods ending on or after December 15, 2023.

SAS No. 145, Understanding the Entity and Its Environment and Assessing the Risks of Material Misstatement

SAS No. 145 enhances the requirements and guidance on identifying and assessing the risks of material misstatement, in particular the areas of understanding the entity's system of internal control and assessing control risk. The SAS also includes extensive guidance regarding the use of information technology (IT) and the consideration of IT general controls. Finally, the SAS revises the definition of significant risks, includes new guidance on maintaining professional skepticism, and includes a new "stand-back" requirement intended to drive an evaluation of the completeness of the identification of significant classes of transactions, account balances, and disclosures by the auditor.

SAS No. 145 becomes effective for audits of financial statements for periods ending on or after December 15, 2023.

SAS No. 146, Quality Management for an Engagement Conducted in Accordance With Generally Accepted Auditing Standards

SAS No. 146 addresses public interest considerations by encouraging proactive management of quality at the engagement level, emphasizing the importance of the exercise of professional skepticism, enhancing the documentation of the auditor's judgments, and reinforcing the need for robust communications during the audit. The SAS makes clear that the engagement partner has overall responsibility for managing and achieving quality.

SAS No. 146 becomes effective for audits of financial statements for periods beginning on or after December 15, 2025.

¶ 414 COVID-19: GOING CONCERN, EMPHASIS OF MATTER, AND SCOPE LIMITATIONS

Going Concern

The COVID-19 pandemic has caused the financial position of many organizations to deteriorate. For clients in certain industries (e.g., restaurants, hospitality, etc.) and in certain geographical areas, an entity's ability to continue as a going concern may be questioned. In this case, the auditor should start by assessing whether there are any events or conditions (e.g., the pandemic) that raise substantial doubt that the entity can continue as a going concern. Note that management is also required to evaluate the entity's ability to continue as a going concern.

"Substantial doubt" means that in management's judgment, it is probable that the client will not continue as a going concern. When substantial doubt exists, disclosure in the financial statement notes is required, regardless of whether the doubt is alleviated by management's plans.

After determining whether there is substantial doubt, the auditor should consider management's plans to alleviate that doubt and then assess the impact on the auditor's report as follows:

- If management's plan alleviates substantial doubt, an unmodified opinion may be issued.
- If the going concern basis of accounting is appropriate but substantial doubt remains, an emphasis-of-matter paragraph is required.
- If the going concern basis of accounting is not appropriate, an adverse opinion should be issued.

The steps for auditor consideration of going concern are as follows:

- Consider whether there are any conditions or events that cause substantial doubt about the entity to continue.

- Inquire with management as to whether a going concern analysis has been performed.

- Consider the evaluation that management has performed (if applicable). Do you agree with it? How did management conduct the evaluation?

- Evaluate management's plans. Can management execute these plans? What should be the process if they cannot execute them? If management uses cash flows to make an evaluation, the auditor must consider those projections and evaluate the data.

- Determine whether the entity has the ability to access funding from an external third party, such as a parent entity, an owner-manager, or another source.

Risks and Uncertainties Plus COVID-19

Financial Accounting Standards Board (FASB) Accounting Standards Codification (ASC) 275, *Risks and Uncertainties*, requires disclosures that focus primarily on risks and uncertainties that could significantly affect the amounts reported in the financial statements in the near term or the near—term functioning of the reporting entity.

The risks and uncertainties addressed can stem from the nature of an entity's operations, the use of significant estimates, and current vulnerabilities due to certain concentrations. The effects of the COVID—19 pandemic may negatively impact significant estimates and exacerbate a vulnerability due to certain concentrations (e.g., business concentration in a market or geographical area severely affected by the effects of COVID—19). COVID—19 also may pose risks to the actual functioning of entities in certain industries (e.g., restaurants, hotels, and airlines).

Due to the effects of COVID—19, for entities with year—ends that fall after the declaration of the state of emergency, the necessity for and robustness of the disclosures may require additional scrutiny by the auditor.

¶ 415 NEW STANDARDS APPROVED BY THE AICPA

On May 12, 2022, the AICPA ASB voted to approve three standards, and the Accounting and Review Services Committee (ARSC) is expected to soon approve another standard, all designed to improve a firm's risk assessment efforts and audit quality. Under these standards, firms must assess their individual risks to audit quality and customize their quality management approaches to address the risks. The four standards, listed below, are expected to be released in June 2022:

- Statement on Quality Management Standards (SQMS) No. 1, *A Firm's System of Quality Management*

- SQMS No. 2, *Engagement Quality Reviews*

- SAS No. 146, *Quality Management for an Engagement Conducted in Accordance with Generally Accepted Auditing Standards*

- Statement on Standards for Accounting and Review Services (SSARS) No. 26, *Quality Management for an Engagement Conducted in Accordance With SSARS*

The standards' effective dates are periods ending on or after December 15, 2025.

STUDY QUESTIONS

4. Which of the following AU-C sections includes specific requirements related to the legal and regulatory framework applicable to the entity and the industry or sector in which the entity operates?

    a. AU-C Section 250

    b. AU-C Section 260

    c. AU-C Section 265

    d. AU-C Section 300

5. Internal control is designed, implemented, and maintained to address identified business risks that threaten the achievement of any of the entity's objectives that concern each of the following, *except?*

    a. The reliability of the entity's financial reporting

    b. The effectiveness and efficiency of its operations

    c. Its compliance with applicable laws and regulation

    d. Its ability to continue as a going concern

6. Which of the following AU-C sections was superseded by SAS No. 142?

    a. AU-C Section 250

    b. AU-C Section 500

    c. AU-C Section 530

    d. AU-C Section 580

MODULE 2: TOP AUDITING ISSUES— CHAPTER 5: Crypto Basics and Audit Considerations

¶ 501 WELCOME

This chapter presents a basic overview of auditing crypto assets and liabilities. It discusses cryptocurrencies and tokens and how these assets and liabilities should be recorded on the books.

¶ 502 LEARNING OBJECTIVES

Upon completion of this chapter, you will be able to:

- Identify the steps in an audit of crypto assets and liabilities
- Recognize audit procedures for auditing crypto assets and liabilities

¶ 503 INTRODUCTION

Companies, not-for-profits, and governments are increasingly accepting payments in cryptocurrencies and other crypto assets. This chapter will be helpful for auditors who are planning to perform an audit on crypto assets and liabilities. It reviews the steps for planning the audit, testing internal controls over crypto assets and liabilities, conducting analytical procedures, and performing substantive testing.

This chapter will also focus on the techniques and documentation requirements that an auditor needs to know to effectively audit crypto assets and offers practical advice for conducting an audit of crypto assets and liabilities. Please review Chapter 3, "Real-World Blockchain Applications," for a discussion of crypto terminology.

¶ 504 BLOCKCHAIN TERMINOLOGY

Virtual currencies are based on a technology known as *blockchain*. Blockchains are lists of records held on diverse computers (nodes) that are used to record and verify data. There are two types of blockchain platforms, *public* and *private*.

A public blockchain, such as the one used to power Bitcoin and other cryptocurrencies, is on all kinds of computers all over the world. Anybody who is mining Bitcoins or other cryptocurrency is allowing the use of their computer to record these transactions. They are acting as a node, and they get paid in the cryptocurrency for allowing their computer to be used as a node. Public blockchains are all over the world. Nobody is controlling who is involved in the network; it is usually an open-source network.

Private blockchains, on the other hand, are held and administered by organizations. For example, banking institutions might set up private blockchains for a company-wide cryptocurrency. The blockchain works within the banking system, and all the data is stored on the bank's computers.

Blockchain transactions are recorded on nodes all over the world, and virtually anybody can see them. If the transactions are encrypted, criminals may be able to see the data but may not be able to decrypt it and see what is in the file itself. How is cryptocurrency transferred? There are two keys: a public key and a private key. When these two keys match up, users get a digital signature that allows them to transfer the ownership of some or all of the cryptocurrency that they have stored on the blockchain. Note that the cryptocurrency doesn't transfer; it stays at the same place on the blockchain. Only the right to access the cryptocurrency transfers.

The public key is stored on the blockchain itself, so the public key is always available. The private key is what someone keeps in their wallet. The private key allows them to access the cryptocurrency. You match up the private key to the public key. And they're not the same, obviously, but the two of them together combine to allow someone to complete a transaction with that cryptocurrency. Because the public key is a long string of alphanumeric characters, it is very difficult for anyone to guess it, even using computer speeds. It is not easy to circumvent that piece of security.

Let's take a few moments to review some basic blockchain terminology included below:

- **Blocks:** Blocks contain data for valid transactions that are hashed and encoded into the blockchain.

- **Block time:** Block time is the average time it takes the network to add an additional block to the blockchain. This can range from seconds to hours.

- **Decentralization:** Storing data across a peer-to-peer network.

- **Hard fork:** A hard fork refers to a radical change to the protocol of a blockchain network that effectively results in two branches, one that follows the previous protocol and one that follows the new version. In a hard fork, holders of tokens in the original blockchain will be granted tokens in the new fork as well, but miners must choose which blockchain to continue verifying. A hard fork can occur in any blockchain, and not only Bitcoin (where hard forks have created Bitcoin Cash and Bitcoin SV, among several others, for example).

- **Airdrop:** An airdrop occurs when you have free crypto coins sent to your wallet. In this type of situation, you did not purchase or earn the coins.

- **Staking or farming:** A "proof of stake" is a consensus technique that allows blockchain networks to use less energy while retaining a reasonable level of decentralization on the Internet.

- **Sign messages:** Sign messages, wallet signing, and digital signatures are digital ways to verify documents and digital messages. Sign messages is a kind of ID system to prove the ownership of Bitcoin or a cryptocurrency address. Without revealing your private keys, you can prove the ownership by sharing your wallet signature.

To look for, or verify, data on an a blockchain, you use a blockchain explorer. Anybody can check the balance of any public address, and anyone can view any transaction details on any blockchain. Block explorer is a website or a tool that allows one to browse through blocks, viewing wallet addresses, network hash rate, transaction data, and other key information on the blockchain. Block explorer is simply a search tool. Every cryptocurrency that relies on its own blockchain will also have its own block explorer.

Virtual currency wallets are used to store cryptocurrency; see Chapter 3 for a review on how virtual currency wallets work.

In addition to cryptocurrencies. blockchains can be used to track tangible and intangible assets, as well as business and accounting transactions. Examples of the use of blockchains include, but are not limited to, the following:

- Tangible assets such as real property, personal property, or cash
- Intangible assets such as patents or copyrights

- Inventory and fixed assets
- Digital assets such as cryptocurrencies
- Accounting transactions
- Other transactions and events
- Smart contracts
- Transferring stocks, bonds, and financial assets
- Transferring title to assets
- Tracking contracts
- Tracking payments
- Regulatory reporting
- Supply chain management
- Tracking medical records
- Tracking insurance claims
- Energy trading
- Domain names
- Payroll
- Data sharing
- Loyalty rewards programs
- Money transfers
- Debit, credit, and gift card transaction tracking
- Automatic teller machine (ATM), electronic funds transfer (EFT), and other electronic payments
- Copyright protection
- Patent protection
- Royalty payments
- Food safety
- Prescription drugs
- Insurance

Blockchains can also be used by auditors for:

- Storing and managing audit evidence
- Verifying the date evidence was obtained
- Verifying the care, custody, and control of evidence
- Providing access to audit evidence throughout the firm
- Making it easy for clients to provide documents for review

¶ 505 CASH VERSUS ACCRUAL

When the word *cash* is mentioned, most people think of the currency and coins they have in their possession. In accounting, the term also includes checks not yet deposited into bank accounts, credit card payments waiting to clear, and other on demand deposits. Therefore, cash includes both cash on hand and cash deposited in demand accounts, such as a checking account, at financial institutions.

Cash equivalents include short-term highly liquid investments that are easily converted into a known amount of cash and are so near to their maturity that they have an insignificant risk to a change in their value. According to the Financial Accounting Standards Board (FASB), only investments with an original maturity of three months or less qualify as cash equivalents. Common examples of cash equivalents include, but are not limited to, treasury bills, commercial paper, and money market accounts.

> **NOTE:** At the time of this writing, the FASB has not issued formal statements for accounting for cryptocurrencies. The IRS considers cryptocurrencies to be property and not a currency. Therefore, when using the cash basis and following the IRS rules, cryptocurrencies should be recorded as investments. When compiling the balance sheet, most companies combine cash and cash equivalents together for presentation, rather than separating them into two different line items.

In the United States, the Securities and Exchange Commission (SEC) requires public companies to use accrual basis accounting; there is no option for a public company. Private companies can use the accrual basis or the cash basis, although the IRS puts limits on who can use the cash basis for tax accounting. Under the Tax Cuts and Jobs Act (TCJA) passed in 2017, the IRS allows small businesses with average annual gross receipts of $25 million or less in the prior three-year period to use the cash basis of accounting. The TCJA also exempts these small businesses from certain accounting rules for inventories, cost capitalization, and long-term contracts. As a result, more small businesses are now allowed to use cash basis accounting.

Accrual-based accounting relies on several generally accepted accounting principles (GAAP).

- **Matching principle.** The matching principle requires companies to match expenses with the revenue they generate. The matching principle is important for accrual-based accounting.

- **Periodicity assumption.** The periodicity assumption allows accountants to post transactions in time periods, even if the transaction extends beyond the end of the period. Accountants usually use months, quarters, and years to report accounting information. When a transaction extends past the cutoff for a period, an adjustment, known as an *accrual entry* or *adjusting entry*, is posted.

- **Revenue recognition principle.** The revenue recognition principle requires companies to recognize revenue when a product has been sold or a service has been performed. It does not matter when the payment for the product or service is received. The revenue recognition principle is important for accrual-based accounting. Using the revenue recognition principle, a company could recognize revenue for a period even though it received no payments or cash during the period.

There are five steps that should be applied for purposes of revenue recognition:[1]

1. Identify the contract(s) with a customer.

2. Identify the performance obligations in the contract.

3. Determine the transaction price.

4. Allocate the transaction price to the performance obligations in the contract.

5. Recognize revenue when (or as) the entity satisfies a performance obligation.

---

[1] FASB. "Revenue Recognition." https://fasb.org/page/PageContent/%2Fstandards%2Fimplementing%2Frevrec.html.

Constructive Receipt Doctrine

The constructive receipt doctrine is not in accordance with Generally Accepted Accounting Principles, but the Internal Revenue Service[2] (IRS) requires its use for cash-based accounting for tax purposes. Income although not actually reduced to a taxpayer's possession is constructively received by him in the taxable year during which it is credited to his account, set apart for him, or otherwise made available so that he may draw upon it at any time, or so that he could have drawn upon it during the taxable year if notice of intention to withdraw had been given. However, income is not constructively received if the taxpayer's control of its receipt is subject to substantial limitations or restrictions. Thus, if a corporation credits its employees with bonus stock, but the stock is not available to such employees until some future date, the mere crediting on the books of the corporation does not constitute receipt.

STUDY QUESTIONS

1. Which of the following allows someone to browse through key information on a blockchain?

    a. Public key

    b. Block explorer

    c. Virtual currency wallet

    d. Node

2. Having free crypto coins placed in a wallet is known as which of the following?

    a. Hard fork

    b. Staking

    c. Sign message

    d. Airdrop

3. Which of the following requires revenue to be recognized when the funds are available to the recipient?

    a. Matching principle

    b. Constructive receipt

    c. Revenue recognition principle

    d. Periodicity

¶ 506 GENERALLY ACCEPTED AUDITING STANDARDS

Before discussing audit procedures, let's review the generally accepted auditing standards (GAAS).

General Standards

- The auditor must have adequate technical training and proficiency to perform the audit.
- The auditor must maintain independence in mental attitude in all matters relating to the audit.
- The auditor must exercise due professional care in the performance of the audit and the preparation of the report.

---

[2] 26 CFR § 1.451-2.

Standards of Field Work

- The auditor must adequately plan the work and must properly supervise any assistants.
- The auditor must obtain a sufficient understanding of the entity and its environment, including its internal control, to assess the risk of material misstatement of the financial statements whether due to error or fraud, and to design the nature, timing, and extent of further audit procedures.
- The auditor must obtain sufficient appropriate audit evidence by performing audit procedures to afford a reasonable basis for an opinion regarding the financial statements under audit.

  NOTE: Factors that demonstrate the persuasiveness of audit evidence include:

  - Appropriateness of audit evidence
  - Relevance of audit evidence
  - Reliability of audit evidence
  - Sufficiency of audit evidence

Standards of Reporting

- The auditor must state in the auditor's report whether the financial statements are presented in accordance with GAAP.
- The auditor must identify in the auditor's report those circumstances in which such principles have not been consistently observed in the current period in relation to the preceding period.
- When the auditor determines that informative disclosures are not reasonably adequate, the auditor must state that in the auditor's report.
- The auditor must either express an opinion regarding the financial statements, taken as a whole, or state that an opinion cannot be expressed, in the auditor's report. When the auditor cannot express an overall opinion, the auditor should state the reasons therefor in the auditor's report. In all cases where an auditor's name is associated with financial statements, the auditor should clearly indicate the character of the auditor's work, if any, and the degree of responsibility the auditor is taking, in the auditor's report.

¶ 507 FINANCIAL STATEMENT ASSERTIONS

The following lists present a review of financial statement assertions:

Transactions and Events

- Occurrence
- Completeness
- Accuracy
- Cutoff
- Classification

Account Balances

- Existence
- Rights and obligations

- Completeness
- Valuation and allocation

Presentation and Disclosure

- Occurrence
- Rights and obligations
- Completeness
- Classification
- Accuracy and valuation

¶ 508 AUDIT PLANNING

Auditing standards require that an audit be designed to provide a reasonable assurance of detecting both material errors and fraud in the financial statements. To accomplish this, the audit must be planned and performed with an attitude of professional skepticism.

Planning the audit, per AS 2101, includes establishing the overall audit strategy for the engagement and developing an audit plan, which includes planned risk assessment procedures and planned responses to the risks of material misstatement. Planning is not a discrete phase of an audit, but rather a continual and iterative process that might begin shortly after (or in connection with) the completion of the previous audit and continues until the completion of the current audit.

The auditor should develop and document an audit plan that includes a description of:

- The planned nature, timing, and extent of the risk assessment procedures;
- The planned nature, timing, and extent of tests of controls and substantive procedures; and
- Other planned audit procedures required to be performed so that the engagement complies with PCAOB standards.

The auditor should modify the overall audit strategy and the audit plan as necessary if circumstances change significantly during the course of the audit, including changes due to a revised assessment of the risks of material misstatement or the discovery of a previously unidentified risk of material misstatement.

¶ 509 AUDIT GUIDANCE

At the time of this writing, there is a lack of official guidance for recording and auditing cryptocurrencies. The FASB and Public Company Accounting Oversight Board (PCAOB) have projects in progress to develop official guidance.

In March 2019, the International Financial Reporting Interpretations Committee (IFRIC) issued *Holdings of Cryptocurrencies—Agenda Paper 4* (IFRIC 2019), stating that the accounting treatment for holding cryptocurrency follows the International Accounting Standard (IASB 38) on Intangible Assets (IASB 2004). Neither the FASB, the Auditing Standards Board (ASB), nor the PCAOB have issued formal guidance for accounting or auditing cryptocurrency.

The Internal Revenue Service (IRS) issued guidance on the U.S. tax treatment of cryptocurrency transactions (IRS Notice 2014-21, 2014).

The AICPA has issued nonauthoritative guidance for crypto transactions. It recommends recording crypto assets as long-lived intangible assets. Crypto assets do not meet the definition of cash or cash equivalents, inventory, or financial instruments, and therefore should not be recorded as such. All intangible assets, including crypto assets, should be initially recorded at cost/fair market value.

¶ 510 CRYPTO ASSET DISCLOSURES

On March 31, 2022, the SEC released SEC Staff Accounting Bulletin No. 121,[3] which provided the SEC's interpretation regarding the financial statement disclosures required by public companies that hold crypto assets. It states the following:

> The interpretations in this SAB express views of the staff regarding the accounting for entities that have obligations to safeguard crypto-assets held for their platform users. In recent years, the staff has observed an increase in the number of entities that provide platform users with the ability to transact in crypto-assets. In connection with these services, these entities and/or their agents may safeguard the platform user's crypto-asset(s) and also maintain the cryptographic key information necessary to access the crypto-asset. The obligations associated with these arrangements involve unique risks and uncertainties not present in arrangements to safeguard assets that are not crypto-assets, including technological, legal, and regulatory risks and uncertainties. Specifically:
>
> **Technological risks** –there are risks with respect to both safeguarding of assets and rapidly-changing crypto-assets in the market that are not present with other arrangements to safeguard assets for third parties;
>
> **Legal risks** –due to the unique characteristics of the assets and the lack of legal precedent, there are significant legal questions surrounding how such arrangements would be treated in a court proceeding arising from an adverse event (e.g., fraud, loss, theft, or bankruptcy); and
>
> **Regulatory risks** –as compared to many common arrangements to safeguard assets for third parties, there are significantly fewer regulatory requirements for holding crypto-assets for platform users or entities may not be complying with regulatory requirements that do apply, which results in increased risks to investors in these entities.
>
> These risks can have a significant impact on the entity's operations and financial condition. The staff believes that the recognition, measurement, and disclosure guidance in this SAB will enhance the information received by investors and other users of financial statements about these risks, thereby assisting them in making investment and other capital allocation decisions.

¶ 511 INTERNAL CONTROLS

Internal controls help to prevent and detect both errors and fraud. Preventing errors supports quality. Preventing and detecting fraud protects not only a company's assets, but also the company's employees and owners. When discussing internal controls, one needs to look at both preventive and detective controls. Preventive controls are put in place to stop errors or fraud from occurring. Detective controls—controls that help to detect—are put in place to help find errors or fraud.

In business, the controls over processes are known as internal controls. An *internal control* is defined as a process, effected by an entity's board of directors, management, and other personnel, designed to provide reasonable assurance regarding the achieve-

---

[3] SEC. Staff Accounting Bulletin No. 121. https://www.sec.gov/oca/staff-accounting-bulletin-121.

ment of objectives relating to operations, reporting, and compliance. Internal controls help to ensure the business is operating efficiently while minimizing errors and the opportunity for fraud. The ultimate responsibility for internal controls falls on owners, the board of directors, or managers.

The Foreign Corrupt Practices Act of 1977 was the first federal law to require companies to have internal controls over financial transactions. The Sarbanes-Oxley Act of 2002 requires public companies to document and test their internal controls over financial reporting. The SEC also issued regulations requiring public companies to certify and disclose internal control information in periodic filings.

In October 1987, the Treadway Commission released its report titled "Report of the National Commission on Fraudulent Financial Reporting," which led to the Committee of Sponsoring Organizations (COSO) releasing a Framework for Internal Control. The COSO Framework was originally developed in 1992 and revised in 2013. A COSO Framework for small and medium sized entities was published in 2006. The COSO Framework for internal controls includes five components: the control environment, risk assessment, control activities, information and communication, and monitoring.

Auditors must obtain an understanding of the internal controls over crypto assets and liabilities, and should therefore consider the following questions:

- What crypto risks has the company identified in its risk assessment?
- Which employees have authority to conduct crypto transactions?
- How many crypto wallets does the company have?
- What is the security for crypto wallets?
- How is fair market value (FMV) determined?
- What cybersecurity is in place?
- How are capital gains and losses determined and tracked?
- How are impairment tests conducted?
- How are impairments, if any, recorded?
- How are deferred tax assets and deferred tax labilities related to crypto determined and recorded?
- If a crypto exchange was used, did the company get a Service Organization Control (SOC) report?
- How are private/public keys stored?
- Is there a segregation of duties between authorization, custody, and recording of cryptocurrency transactions?

¶ 512 SUBSTANTIVE TESTING

Substantive testing is designed to allow the auditor to test against the financial statement assertions provided by management. Basic substantive tests for crypto transactions include the following:

Existence

- Obtain evidence of crypto assets.
- Review exchange transactions for fiat currencies.
- Verify public and private keys.
- Review contractual documents for crypto payments.
  - Crypto held by a crypto exchange
  - Crypto held by a financial institution
- Verify transactions with a block explorer.

Rights and Obligations

- Who is the legal owner of the cryptocurrency held by the client?
- Is the cryptocurrency of the client held by an exchange segregated from the exchange's other holdings?
- What happens to the asset if the exchange goes out of business or loses the cryptocurrency assets?
- What are the internal controls at the exchange to protect the security of the asset?

Completeness

- Are all cryptocurrency transactions recorded on the blockchain?
- Are all cryptocurrency transactions recorded in the accounting system?

Occurrence

- Examine evidence verifying ownership of private keys.
- Vouch, on a sample basis, transactions recorded in the wallets to supporting documents.
- Vouch, on a sample basis, transactions in the accounting system to the wallet.

Presentation and Disclosure

- Nature of the asset or liability
- Fair value
- Accounting policies
- Contingencies
- Valuation
- Risks associated with crypto assets and liabilities

Valuation and Accuracy

- How was the historical cost determined and recorded?
- Was impairment testing done?
- Auditors should examine the client's data entry integrity controls, access controls, and storage controls to ensure the accuracy of the cryptocurrency transactions.

¶ 513 AUDITING CRYPTOCURRENCIES

When auditing cryptocurrencies, several questions should be considered:

- Are payments, revenue, or expenses, in dollar amounts paid using cryptocurrencies at the FMV on the date of payment (cash basis) or at the time of accrual, or are payments, revenue or expenses, in crypto amounts regardless of the dollar amount on the date of payment (cash basis) or at the time of accrual?
- How does the company adjust for crypto volatility between the accrual date and the payment date?
- Did the company convert the cryptocurrency into a fiat currency (proof of existence)?
- Were Forms 1099-K or 1099-MISC received and/or issued for cryptocurrency transactions (over $600)?

Remember that according to FASB ASC 606-10-32-23, any changes in the fair value of noncash consideration (e.g., a digital asset such as crypto) after contract inception due to the form of the consideration would not affect the transaction price for the revenue contract. The company should apply the relevant accounting guidance for the form of noncash consideration to determine how any change in fair market value of the digital asset should be recognized after contract inception.

¶ 514 RISK ASSESSMENT

This is where the auditor asks the "What could go wrong questions." These include: What are the risks for errors? and What is the risk for fraud? There are four principles relating to risk assessment in the COSO Framework:

1. The organization specifies objectives with sufficient clarity to enable the identification and assessment of risks relating to objectives.

2. The organization identifies risks to the achievement of its objectives across the entity and analyzes risks as a basis for determining how the risks should be managed.

3. The organization considers the potential for fraud in assessing risks to the achievement of objectives.

4. The organization identifies and assesses changes that could significantly impact the system of internal control.

¶ 515 FRAUD REVIEW

Fraud is a crime that can be committed by individuals, businesses, government entities, and even not-for-profits. Generally, fraud is a nonviolent crime. Fraud is considered a white-color crime; therefore, the theories as to why people commit crime will apply to why they commit various types of frauds. Organizations can limit the opportunity criminals have to commit fraud by establishing effective anti-fraud internal controls. To study fraud, we have to start with a definition. Fraud is:

> An intentional perversion of truth for the purpose of inducing another in reliance upon it to part with some valuable thing belonging to him or to surrender a legal right. A false representation of a matter of fact, whether by words or conduct, by false or misleading allegations, or by concealment of that which should have been disclosed, which deceives and is intended to deceive another so that he shall act upon it to his legal injury. Anything calculated to deceive, whether by a single act or combination, or by suppression of the truth, or suggestion of what is false, whether it be by direct falsehood or innuendo, by speech or silence, word of mouth, or look or gesture. A generic term, embracing all multifarious means which human ingenuity can devise, and which are resorted to by one individual to get advantage over another by false suggestions or by suppression of truth, and includes all surprise, trick, cunning, dissembling, and any unfair way by which another is cheated.[4]

AS 2301.08 states that "the auditor should design and perform audit procedures in a manner that addresses the assessed risks of material misstatement due to error or fraud for each relevant assertion of each significant account and disclosure." Questions to consider include: Did you participate in the fraud brainstorming session? Are there any opportunities for fraud you believe are not adequately covered in the audit plan?

---

[4] Black, Henry. *Black's Law Dictionary*, Sixth Edition. St. Paul, MN: West Publishing Co., 1990.

Regardless of the materiality threshold set for the audit, there is no materiality threshold for fraud. Fraud, in any amount, by management is a material weakness in the internal controls.

¶ 516 DISTRIBUTION OF DATA

When auditors and accountants look at data, typically it is normally distributed. In a *normal distribution*, 99.7 percent of data points are within three standard deviations from the mean, 95 percent are within two standard deviations, and 68 percent are within one standard deviation. Any anomalies—that is, items that are more than three standard deviations from the mean—must be investigated as potential errors or fraud. A *binomial distribution* of data occurs when a series of tests are conducted with two possible answers, such as yes/no, true/false, or correct/incorrect. In accounting and auditing, this type of testing is usually conducted to determine if internal controls are effective. *Random distribution* occurs when the data does not have a discrete pattern.

¶ 517 SAMPLING

Sampling allows practitioners to take a subset of the population and test it, and then extrapolate the characteristics of the sample to the whole population. The margin of error is the level of precision one requires for the sample. This is the plus or minus number that is often reported with an estimated proportion and is also called the *confidence interval*. It is the range in which the true population proportion is estimated to be, and it is often expressed in percentage points (e.g., ±2%).

The *confidence level* is the probability that the margin of error contains the true proportion. If the study was repeated and the range calculated each time, one would expect the true value to lie within these ranges on 95 percent of occasions. The higher the confidence level, the more certain one can be that the interval contains the true proportion.

Binomial distribution occurs when a series of tests are conducted with two possible answers such as yes/no, true/false, or correct/incorrect. In accounting and auditing, this type of testing is usually conducted to determine if internal controls are effective. *Random distribution* occurs when the data does not have a discrete pattern.

Sampling Risk

Auditors should apply professional judgment in assessing sampling risk. In performing substantive tests of details, the auditor is concerned with two aspects of sampling risk:

- The *risk of incorrect acceptance* is the risk that the sample supports the conclusion that the recorded account balance is not materially misstated when it is materially misstated.

- The *risk of incorrect rejection* is the risk that the sample supports the conclusion that the recorded account balance is materially misstated when it is not materially misstated.

The auditor is also concerned with two aspects of sampling risk in performing tests of controls when sampling is used:

- The *risk of assessing control risk too low* is the risk that the assessed level of control risk based on the sample is less than the true operating effectiveness of the control.

- The *risk of assessing control risk too high* is the risk that the assessed level of control risk based on the sample is greater than the true operating effectiveness of the control.

Sampling Methods

Methods appropriate for both statistical and nonstatistical sampling include *random sampling* and *systematic sampling*. In random sampling, all items have an equal chance of selection. Systematic sampling, which was commonly used before random number generators were available, selects every *n* th item with random start within the *n* interval. Methods for nonstatistical sampling include the following:

- **Haphazard selection.** The auditor selects sample items without intentional bias.
- **Block selection.** This is an audit of a group of contiguous transactions, such as invoices for May, invoices in a sequence, or invoices in a date range.
- **Block amount.** Everything is audited.

With regard to sampling internal controls, it is not possible to provide absolute assurance that the internal controls are effective. Auditors cannot determine if the controls are always working, so they use hypothesis testing to test internal controls. This involves developing a hypothesis (H0) and a null hypothesis (H1), for example:

- H0—All checks are properly approved prior to being signed.
- H1—All checks are not approved prior to being signed.

The auditor tests the null hypothesis, and if the sample doesn't have any data points supporting the null hypothesis, then the null hypothesis is rejected and the hypothesis is accepted.

¶ 518 AUDIT RISK MODEL

The audit risk model states that the audit risk is equal to the inherent risk times the control risk times the detection risk, or AR = IR × CR × DR. The inherent risk depends on the types of accounts the client has, and the control risk is determined by the auditor's evaluation of the design and the effectiveness of the client's internal controls. Again, this is an area where auditors can use data analytics to help determine the effectiveness of the controls. Many approvals, such as the approval to make a purchase or the approval to cut a check, are done in the accounting system. But the auditor can also use data analytics to tie out the invoice numbers from the PDF copies of the invoice by making sure the invoice number, the vendor name, and the amounts match so that the invoice details reflect what is on the accounting system. The auditor can run a data analytics process using artificial intelligence (AI) to look at every invoice the company has and compare each to the data in the accounting system. This can reveal duplicate invoices or invoices that are not reflected in the accounting system.

Procedures for reviewing financial statement transactions include the following:

- **Tracing.** Starting with a source document and verifying the transaction is recorded in the financial records.
- **Vouching.** Starting with the transaction record and verifying there is a corresponding source document.
- **Data analytics or data mining.** Using data analytics to test populations and identify items to test.

¶ 519 DATA ANALYTICS

Auditors can use several types of data analytics tools in the audit process. *Trend analysis* involves looking at trends such as sales trends, return trends, trends in write-offs, and trends for travel and office expenses. This type of analysis can uncover major changes or changes that are occurring faster than normal for the companies the auditor benchmarks for the client.

Most auditors are familiar with *ratio analysis*, which is typically addressed in college-level accounting courses. *Nonstatistical predictive modeling* is a method auditors can use to predict where things should be and then compare that to what is actually booked in the client's system to identify if there are any variances. For example, an auditor can use nonstatistical predictive modeling to predict patterns in rent for property management companies or to predict electrical usage or water usage for utility companies. *Descriptive statistics* involves concepts such as the mean, mode, median, and standard deviation, with which auditors should be familiar.

Regression analysis is the most complex type of analytical procedure auditors use and is performed using software. With this method, auditors can identify the accuracy of a client's estimates. Regression analysis can be used to determine various statistical measures, such as R2 (coefficient of determination), T-statistics, and standard error. It can also be used for correlations. For an electric company, for example, one would expect a spike in temperatures to cause a spike in electric usage. In addition, regression analysis is often applied for hypothesis testing, which is used to test internal controls.

There are two basic types of analytical procedures. One is *quantitative analysis*, which is performed on numerical data such as operational data. This information might include performance data, such as the number of widgets manufactured in one month and how many widgets were defective in each batch. Accounting data, such as payments, invoices, and receipts, is another form of quantitative information. Quantitative analysis involves things that we can define using numbers.

Qualitative analysis, on the other hand, involves things other than numbers, or unstructured data. This type of analysis can be performed on the results of questionnaires, such as customer, employee, or vendor surveys. Emails, text messages, contracts, and other such items can be qualitatively analyzed.

Descriptive analytics allows auditors to look at past performance, whereas diagnostic analytics uncovers causes. Predictive analytics allows auditors to predict the future and help an organization choose the best options for proceeding with a project.

Designing Audit Procedures for Data Analysis

In the planning stage of the audit, when designing the audit procedures for data analysis, the auditor must consider the following:

- Is the data complete? Has all the data been input into the system? Do we have all the data that the company has? Are there any contracts or payments that were not put into the accounting system?

- Is the data accurate? Does the data on the source documents match the data in the accounting system? Tracing and vouching must be built into the data analytics.

- Is data conversion necessary? For example, if one company acquired another and they are running on different accounting systems or different types of software, that data might need to be converted.

- Does the data need to be normalized? For example, dates such as 1/1/20, 1/1/2020, January 1, 2020, and 1 January 20 might need to be normalized so that all reflect the same format.

- Does the data need to be cleansed? This might be the case if errors, fraud, and duplications exist.

Auditors must look for these situations to determine what to add or remove from the system when designing their audit procedures.

When performing data analysis, auditors can employ statistical analysis, descriptive statistics, and inferential statistics (samples). Data mining is another tool auditors can use. Data mining software uses algorithms to identify data in large databases. There are many types of algorithms. One of the more common types are *classification algorithms*, which allow the auditor to gather all the transactions that belong to one account. *Regression algorithms* can be used to determine where things should be based on past data. Auditors can use *segmentation algorithms* to break up transactions, such as those that are outside three standard deviations or between two and three standard deviations of the mean for testing. *Association algorithms* allow auditors to bring together items that are associated. *Sequence analysis algorithms* can look for things such as duplicate invoices, duplicate receipt numbers, missing invoice numbers, and missing check numbers.

Electronic data analysis enables auditors to do the following:

- Retrieve values
- Filter data
- Compute derived values
- Find extremes
- Sort data
- Determine ranges
- Characterize ranges
- Find anomalies and outliers
- Cluster data
- Correlate data
- Provide contextualization (relevance to the user)

Impairments

Because crypto assets are long-lived intangible assets, they are subject to impairment testing. Auditors should review the company's conclusion based on the indicators of impairment. As a reminder, those indicators include:

- Obsolescence due to new technological changes
- Decline in performance (i.e., net cash flows of the asset or cash generating unit)
- Decline in market value of the asset
- Changes in economy such as an increase in labor cost, raw materials, etc., that would shrink the net cash flows of the asset
- Physical damage to the asset such as fire or other accident
- Major restructuring (reshuffling of products, segments, acquisition of new assets, etc.)

Future cash flow estimates used in an impairment analysis should include:

- All cash inflows expected from the use of the long-lived asset (asset group) over its remaining useful life, based on its existing service potential
- Any cash outflows necessary to obtain those cash inflows, including future expenditures to maintain (but not improve) the long-lived asset (asset group)
- Cash flows associated with the eventual disposition, including selling costs, of the long-lived asset (asset group)

To calculate the impairment, if any, a company would apply the two-step process outlined in ASC 360-10:

- Step 1: Test for recoverability by comparing the sum of all undiscounted net cash flows that the asset is expected to generate with the carrying value of the asset. If the carrying value is lower than the sum of cash flow, it indicates impairment, and vice versa.
- Step 2: Measure the impairment, once it is established that impairment has occurred, by determining the amount of impairment expense which is the difference between the carrying value of the asset and its fair value.

STUDY QUESTIONS

4. Which of the following standards requires an auditor to have adequate technical training and proficiency to perform the audit?

- **a.** General Standards
- **b.** Standards of Field Work
- **c.** Standards of Reporting
- **d.** Standards of Training

5. In a normal distribution, 95 percent of all data falls within ___ standard deviations of the mean.

- **a.** 1
- **b.** 2
- **c.** 3
- **d.** 4

6. Which of the following starts with the transaction record and verifies there is a corresponding source document?

- **a.** Vouching
- **b.** Tracing
- **c.** Data mining
- **d.** Control testing

MODULE 2: TOP AUDITING ISSUES— CHAPTER 6: Fraud Risks When Conducting Remote Audits

¶ 601 WELCOME

This chapter presents a basic overview of the fraud risks auditors may encounter when conducting remote audits. It discusses the risks and provides auditing procedures that can help to mitigate the risks.

¶ 602 LEARNING OBJECTIVES

Upon completion of this chapter, you will be able to:

- Define fraud and several fraud theories
- Recognize fraud risks that can arise when planning and conducting remote audits
- Identify audit procedures that can help to mitigate fraud risks

¶ 603 INTRODUCTION

With the COVID-19 pandemic, government shutdowns of businesses, employees working from home, inability to conduct site visits, and social distancing, what fraud risks should auditors consider when planning and conducting an audit in today's world? What additional fraud risks exist for observing inventory and verifying fixed assets? What are the additional risks when you cannot be on-site for the audit? What are the risks when employees are working from home? How do you conduct walk-throughs and interviews in a COVID-19 environment? This chapter explores these issues and discusses audit procedures that can help to mitigate these fraud risks. It will also discuss possible disclosures that may need to be added to the audit report for workarounds or scope limitations.

¶ 604 FRAUD REVIEW

The basic definition of fraud was discussed in Chapter 5; please refer to that definition for a refresher. White-collar crimes, like fraud, are illegal and/or unethical actions taken by employees or other agents of an organization.[1] The term *white-collar crime* is attributed to Dr. Edwin Sutherland, who first used the term in 1939. He pointed out the difference between crimes of trust, such as fraud, and blue-collar crimes such as murder and robbery. Dr. Sutherland was one of the early criminologists in the United States, and his works are widely accepted.[2] White-collar crimes are often viewed as being less severe than violent crimes despite the financial damage done by white-collar criminals.[3] Dr. Sutherland went on to note that the penalties for white-collar criminals

---

[1] Vadera, A., and Aguilera, R. (2015). The evolution of vocabularies and its relation to investigation of white-collar crimes: An institutional work perspective. *Journal of Business Ethics*, 128, 21–23.

[2] Alalehto, T., and Persson, O. (2013). The Sutherland tradition in criminology: A bibliometric

story. *Criminal Justice Studies: A Critical Journal of Crime, Law and Society*, 26, 1–18.

[3] Leshem, E., and Ne'eman-Haviv, V. (2013). Perception of white-collar crime among immigrants from the former Soviet Union in Israel. *Crime, Law & Social Change*, 59, 555–576.

tend to be less severe than the penalties imposed on violent criminals.[4] Court ordered restitution and voluntary restitution agreements are common punishments for white-collar criminals.[5] However, a study by the Association of Certified Fraud Examiners indicated that 53 percent of victims recover nothing after a fraud, 32 percent make a partial recovery, and only 15 percent make a full recovery of losses.[6]

¶ 605 FRAUD THEORIES

Theory of Differential Reinforcement

Gabriel Tarde was a 19th-century French criminologist who developed the theory of differential reinforcement in the 1880s and 1890s. The major components of the theory of differential reinforcement are that people are most likely to imitate the actions of those with whom they are in close contact and that individuals will imitate the actions of superiors. The concept of individuals imitating the actions of their superiors is a grounding principle in the Committee of Sponsoring Organizations (COSO) control environment or, as it is often referred to, the "Tone at the Top." Ethics flows from the top of an organization down through the ranks. Gabriel Tarde was also the first to recognize a criminal's tendency to return to the scene of the crime and to be a repeat offender.

Theory of Differential Association

The field of criminology has accepted Dr. Edwin Sutherland's (1947) theory of differential association and Ronald Akers's (1985) social learning theory.[7] There is empirical evidence to support the social learning theory's concepts that white-collar criminals anticipate the rewards they will obtain have greater value than the consequences they will suffer if caught, and that criminals learn their behavior from other criminals.[8]

Fraud researchers categorize fraudsters into one of three criminal categories: situational offenders, routine offenders, and professional offenders. Situational offenders are individuals who happen upon the opportunity and commit the crime. Routine offenders look for and take advantage of opportunities as a type of continuous criminal enterprise. Unlike most street criminals, professional fraudsters learn their trade from research and participation in the legitimate and illegitimate economy and from association with other criminal offenders.[9]

The Social Learning Theory

Akers's (1998) social learning theory postulates that individuals learn criminal activity and rationalize the acceptability of criminal activities based on their social networks.[10] One quantitative study using regression models to compare the variables supported the social learning theory as it relates to online criminal activity by linking peer offending to

[4] Dorminey, J., Fleming, A. S., Kranacher, M., and Riley Jr., R. (2012). The evolution of fraud theory. *Issues in Accounting Education*, 27, 555–579.

[5] Faichney, D. (2014). Autocorrect? A proposal to encourage voluntary restitution through the white-collar sentencing calculus. *Journal of Criminal Law & Criminology*, 104, 389-420.

[6] Association of Certified Fraud Examiners. 2018 Report to the Nation on Occupational Fraud and Abuse.

[7] Durrant, R., and Ward, T. (2012). The role of evolutionary explanations in criminology. *Journal*

of *Theoretical and Philosophical Criminology*, 4(1), 1–37.

[8] Moore, M. (2011). Psychological theories of crime and delinquency. *Journal of Human Behavior in the Social Environment*, 21, 226–239.

[9] Vieraitis, L., Copes, H., Powell, Z., and Pike, A. (2015). A little information goes a long way: Expertise and identity theft. *Aggression and Violent Behavior*, 20, 10–18.

[10] Akers, R. L. (1998). *Social learning and social structure: A general theory of crime and deviance*. Boston, MA: Northeastern University Press.

online criminal activities in juveniles.[11] Allen and Jacques (2013) conducted a qualitative study of 16 campus police officers of a large university and in their findings indicated a link between criminal activity and opportunity, social learning, peer pressure, supervision, and culture.[12] Another study indicated that virtual peers are just as influential to online criminals as traditional peers are to offline offenders.[13] Another mixed-methods cross-sectional study of 1,674 participants indicated that the social learning theory was valid despite the debate about the effects of self-control on criminal behavior.[14]

The social learning theory is a combination of the differential reinforcement theory and the theory of differential association (Akers, 1998). The theory of differential reinforcement postulates that criminal behavior occurs when individuals experience positive reinforcement, such as obtaining something they desire, either actual or anticipated, and the adverse consequences of their action are minor and do not control or prevent further criminal behavior.[15] The theory of differential association postulates that individuals learn criminal behavior by associating with other criminals, the same way law-abiding citizens learn to behave by associating with other individuals who obey the law.[16] Dr. Donald Cressey conducted a review of the critics' issues with Dr. Sutherland's differential association theory and stated that many of the critics' issues derived from misinterpretation by the critics.[17] The social learning theory also contains variables from other criminology theories, including deterrence, social bonding, and neutralization theories.[18]

Dr. Akers indicated that the probability persons will engage in criminal and deviant behavior increases (and the probability of conforming to the norm decreases) when those persons meet the following conditions: (a) they differentially associate with others who commit criminal behavior and espouse definitions favorable to it, (b) they are relatively more exposed in-person or symbolically to salient criminal/deviant models, (c) they define it as desirable or justified in a situation discriminative for the behavior, and (d) they have received in the past and anticipate in current or future situations a relatively greater reward than punishment for the behavior. Akers's social learning theory has received significant empirical support in explaining criminal behavior and is regarded as one of the leading theories in criminology.[19]

According to the social learning theory, it is possible that when fraudsters perceive that the potential benefits outweigh the risk of punishment associated with the criminal

---

[11] Holt, T., Bossler, A., and May, D. (2012). Low self-control, deviant peer associations, and juvenile cyberdeviance. *American Journal of Criminal Justice*, 17, 378–395.

[12] Allen, A., and Jacques, S. (2013). Police officer's theories of crime. *American Journal of Criminal Justice*, 39, 206–227. doi:10.107/s12103-013-9219-1.

[13] Miller, B., and Morris, R. (2014). Virtual peer effects in social learning theory. *Crime & Delinquency*, 1–27.

[14] Yarbrough, A., Jones, S., Sullivan, C., Sellers, C., and Cochran, J. (2012). Social learning and self-control: Assessing the moderating potential of criminal propensity. *International Journal of Offender Therapy and Comparative Criminology*, 56, 191–202.

[15] Megens, K., and Weerman, F. (2012). The social transmission of delinquency: Effects of peer attitudes and behavior revisited. *Journal of Research in Crime & Delinquency*, 49, 420–443.

[16] Moore, M. (2011). Psychological theories of crime and delinquency. *Journal of Human Behavior in the Social Environment*, 21, 226–239.

[17] Cressey, D. (1952). Application and verification of the differential association theory. *Journal of Criminal Law, Criminology & Police Science*, 43(1), 43–52.

[18] Capece, M., and Lanza-Kaduce, L. (2013). Binge drinking among college students: A partial test of Akers's social-structure-social learning theory. *American Journal of Criminal Justice*, 38, 503–519.

[19] Tittle, C. R., Antonaccio, O., and Botchkovar, E. (2012). Social learning, reinforcement and crime: Evidence from three European cities. *Social Forces*, 90, 863–890.

act of fraud, they will commit the crime.[20] The benefits received by the fraudsters include employment, health care, social status, purchasing power, and access to credit facilities. Because individuals with similar demographics and perhaps geographic locations can be grouped together, it is feasible that individuals observing others in the same demographic or geographic group receiving benefits from fraud would want to learn the skill from those who were successfully committing the crime.

The Fraud Triangle

The theoretical framework supporting fraud investigations and internal controls is the fraud triangle theory. The seminal work about why people commit fraud, including occupational fraud, is the fraud triangle developed by Dr. Donald Cressey in 1952. The fraud triangle has three main points: (1) pressure or needs, (2) rationalization, and (3) opportunity. Pressure comes from the need for something, such as cash to pay bills. Rationalization is how individuals find ways to believe actions they know are wrong are acceptable under the circumstances, such as convincing themselves they are only borrowing the money rather than stealing the money. Finally, opportunity occurs when the victim allows the fraudster access to the victim's assets. Kassem and Higson proposed a new fraud triangle theory adding a new dimension: (1) motivation, (2) capability, (3) opportunity, and (4) personal integrity.[21] There is currently insufficient research to support this expansion of the fraud triangle theory.

While Dr. Donald Cressey originally developed what researchers came to call the fraud triangle, he did not refer to it as such. Instead, the first use of the term *fraud triangle* to describe the idea came from the Association of Certified Fraud Examiners.[22] The American Institute of Certified Public Accountants (AICPA) integrated the fraud triangle into Statement on Auditing Standards No. 99.

Studies such as Dellaportas's 2013 study on why accountants commit fraud have continued to show the validity of Dr. Cressey's fraud triangle theory.[23] The cognitive dissonance theory indicates fraudsters commit the crime and then rationalize their behavior to improve their own self-worth.[24] The author of this chapter believes the cognitive dissonance theory supports the rationalization component of the fraud triangle theory. Other researchers have claimed the professional development of the fraud triangle as a criminology theory concentrates on limiting opportunity and an individual's lack of ethics to the exclusion of other factors such as the role of society and political agendas in combatting crimes such as fraud.[25]

Sykes and Matza studied how perpetrators of crimes rationalized their behavior by using neutralizing language.[26] There are five basic ways to use neutralizing language to rationalize criminal behavior: (1) denial of responsibility, (2) denial of victim, (3) denial

---

[20] Maskaly, J., and Donner, C. (2015). A theoretical integration of social learning theory with terror management theory: Towards an explanation of police shootings of unarmed suspects. *American Journal of Criminal Justice*, 40, 205–224.

[21] Kassem, R., and Higson, A. (2012). The new fraud triangle model. *Journal of Emerging Trends in Economics & Management Sciences*, 3(3), 191–195.

[22] Morales, J., Gendron, Y., and Guenin-Paracini, H. (2014). The construction of the risky individual and vigilant organization: A genealogy of the fraud triangle. *Accounting, Organizations & Society*, 39, 170–194.

[23] Dellaportas, S. (2013). Conversations with inmate accountants: Motivation, opportunity and the fraud triangle. *Accounting Forum*, 37(1), 29-39.

[24] Trompeter, G., Carpenter, T., Jones, K., and Riley, R. (2014). Insights for research and practice: What we learned about fraud from other disciplines. *Accounting Horizons, 28,* 769–804.

[25] Morales, J., Gendron, Y., and Guenin-Paracini, H. (2014). The construction of the risky individual and vigilant organization: A genealogy of the fraud triangle. *Accounting, Organizations & Society*, 39, 170–194.

[26] Sykes, G., and Matza, D. (1957). Techniques of neutralization: A theory of delinquency. *American Sociological Review*, 22, 664–670.

of injury, (4) condemnation of the condemners, and (5) appeal to higher loyalties.[27] By rationalizing their behavior, most white-collar criminals do not consider themselves to be criminals and deny they had intent when committing their crimes.[28] Except for their ability to rationalize their behavior and resistance to considering their activities as crimes, white-collar criminals have been assumed to be basically normal people.[29] Historically, white-collar crime, including identity theft, was considered to be a civil dispute under common law rather than a criminal act.[30]

The Elements of Fraud

There is another theory that explains how individuals commit white-collar crimes, such as fraud, which is known as the *elements of fraud*.[31] In this theory, Dorminey et al. stated there are three elements of fraud: (1) the act, (2) concealment, and (3) conversion. *The act* consists of the actual theft or misappropriation of assets. *Concealment* represents the perpetrator's attempts to hide the act from others. *Conversion* is the process of turning the ill-gotten gains into something the perpetrator can use. Criminals use other people's identities in order to conceal their illegal activities. Internal controls help to limit the opportunity fraudsters have to commit the act or crime.

The elements of fraud are used by managers to help identify the risk of fraud in a business.[32] Internal controls can be used to help prevent or detect the act, which is the first element in the elements of fraud theory. Managers and those with responsibility for governance must implement controls to restrict a perpetrator's access to assets and deny them the opportunity to commit the act of fraud. Based on the elements of fraud theory, managers and those charged with governance concentrate on developing internal controls for the theft or misappropriations of assets (Power, 2013).

¶ 606 PREDICATION OF FRAUD

It is necessary to determine if there is a predication of fraud before starting a fraud investigation. Sometimes red flags for fraud, upon examination, are nothing more than human error, with no intent to deceive or commit fraud. Predication of fraud is the sum total of the direct and circumstantial evidence that would lead a reasonable person, trained in law enforcement or fraud investigations, to believe that a fraud has occurred, is occurring, or will occur in the future. Suspicion alone, without any objective direct or circumstantial evidence, is an insufficient basis for conducting a fraud investigation. Because fraud investigations can be costly, it is necessary to determine that a predication of fraud exists prior to commencing a fraud investigation.

This should not be taken to indicate that suspicions of fraud should not be reported. Employees who suspect fraud should report their concerns to their supervisors, managers, human resources, or the company's audit committee. The Association of Certified Fraud Examiner's "2020 Report to the Nations on Occupational Fraud and

---

[27] Klenowski, P. (2012). "Learning the good with the bad": Are occupational white-collar offenders taught how to neutralize their crimes? *Criminal Justice Review*, 37, 461–477.

[28] Stadler, W., and Benson, M. (2012). Revisiting the guilty mind: The neutralization of white-collar crime. *Criminal Justice Review*, 37, 494–511.

[29] Benson, M. (2013). Editor's introduction—White-collar crime: bringing the offender back in. *Journal of Contemporary Criminal Justice*, 29, 324–330.

[30] Bennett, R., LoCicero, H., and Hanner, B. (2013). From regulation to prosecution to cooperation: Trends in corporate white collar crime enforcement and evolving role of the white collar criminal defense attorney. *Business Lawyer*, 68(2), 411.

[31] Dorminey, J., Fleming, A. S., Kranacher, M., and Riley, Jr., R. (2012). The evolution of fraud theory. *Issues in Accounting Education*, 27, 555–579.

[32] Power, M. (2013). The apparatus of fraud. *Accounting, Organizations and Society*, 38, 525–543.

Abuse" indicated that a majority of frauds are discovered by receiving tips, and over half of the tips reporting fraud come from employees.

¶ 607 OCCUPATIONAL FRAUDS

Frauds that affect the workplace are considered to be occupational frauds. There are three basic types of occupational frauds: asset misappropriation, corruption, and financial statement fraud. Asset misappropriation is the theft of assets, either tangible or intangible; these could be fixed assets, inventory, or data. Corruption is the misuse of an individual's position for personal gain, and financial statement fraud is commonly referred to as "cooking the books." According to the Association of Certified Fraud Examiners "2018 Report to the Nation's on Occupational Fraud and Abuse,"[33] asset misappropriation is the most common type of occupational fraud, followed by corruption and financial statement fraud. Many times, these types of fraud occur together because criminals cook the books to cover up corruption and theft of assets.

Asset misappropriations start with the basic theft of an organization's assets. Thefts of inventory, fixed assets, financial assets, data, and other intangible assets are common in today's world. Securing both tangible and intangible assets is important for all organizations. Cash and financial assets are frequently stolen by fraudsters.

¶ 608 GENERALLY ACCEPTED AUDITING STANDARDS (GAAS)

In order to have a good discussion about audit procedures let's take a moment to review the Generally Accepted Auditing Standards (GAAS) that were discussed in Chapter 5.

The requirement to supervise any assistants can pose additional difficulties during remote audits. When team members are working together in the office, they develop a rapport, ask questions, and assist each other. This type of team mentorship and assistance is harder to develop when employees are working remotely or from home. Team leaders need to develop good communications channels between all team members, remembering to draw the "wallflowers" into the conversations and discussions.

Historically, Public Company Accounting Oversight Board (PCAOB) and Peer Review auditors have documented deficiencies in audits for having insufficient appropriate audit evidence to support the audit opinion. This risk is exacerbated when conducting remote audits because team member observations of the sites, desks, and workflows of the client are limited to camera views.

STUDY QUESTIONS

1. Which statement about white-collar crime is true?
    a. White-collar crimes include robbery and murder.
    b. The term *white-collar crime* was coined by Gabriel Tarde.
    c. More than half of the victims of white-collar crime fully recover their losses.
    d. Court-ordered restitution is a common punishment for white-collar crimes.

2. Who developed the Social Learning Theory?
    a. Gabriel Tarde
    b. Ronald Akers
    c. Edwin Sutherland
    d. Donald Cressey

---

[33] Available at www.acfe.com.

3. Which of the following types of occupational fraud occurs most frequently?

    a. Corruption

    b. Financial statement fraud

    c. Tax fraud

    d. Asset misappropriation

¶ 609 FINANCIAL STATEMENT ASSERTIONS

In order to have a good discussion about remote audit risks, let's take a moment to review the financial statement assertions that were outlined in Chapter 5. Remember, audit procedures must be designed to obtain a reasonable assurance that management's financial statement assertions are legitimate.

Transactions and Events

- Occurrence
- Completeness
- Accuracy
- Cutoff
- Classification

Account Balances

- Existence
- Rights and Obligations
- Completeness
- Valuation and Allocation

Presentation and Disclosure

- Occurrence
- Rights and obligations
- Completeness
- Classification
- Accuracy and Valuation

¶ 610 AUDIT PLANNING

Auditing standards require that an audit be designed to provide a reasonable assurance of detecting both material errors and fraud in the financial statements. Please review the Audit Planning section in Chapter 5, "Crypto Basics and Audit Considerations."

In addition to the audit planning previously discussed, as part of planning a remote audit, the auditor must gain a proper understanding of the entity and document this in the workpapers. Some items to consider include the following:

- Industry factors
- Regulatory factors
- Legal factors
- Competition

- External factors
- Internal factors
- Nature of the entity
- History of the entity
- Entity's internal controls
- Management structure
- Employee competencies
- Financial performance
- Business risks
- Cybersecurity risks
- Insurance coverage
- Business strategies
- Entity's objectives
- COVID-19 risks
- Fraud risks

¶ 611 SPECIFIC FRAUD RISKS

The following sections describe a variety of fraud risks that can arise in an audit.

Skimming

Skimming is a fraud where employees or volunteers steal cash or checks before transactions are entered into the accounting system. They provide the customer with products or services and instead of entering the transaction into the cash register, they pocket the payment and don't record a sale. This is a common fraud when employees are working alone, in drive-through retail outlets, and at fundraising events for not-for-profit organizations. Governments are also susceptible because many taxpayers prefer to pay taxes and fines in cash or by check. Skimming can be difficult to detect because nothing has been entered into the accounting system so there is no audit trail or transaction to review.

Common internal controls that are effective in preventing and detecting skimming include using cameras to record cash registers and cash collection points. Many businesses post signs at the cash registers asking customers to report to management any time they don't receive a receipt for their transaction. Often customers are offered a reward, such as a free coffee or gift card, for taking the time to make the report. This brings the customer into the internal control process and makes it difficult for employees to process transactions without receipts.

Employees can also use coupons and discounts to conduct skimming schemes. An example of this would be ringing up a customer who doesn't have a coupon at the cash register and then voiding the transaction after the customer leaves and reinputting the transaction with the coupon. The employee can then pocket the cash. The explanation for the transaction is that the customer remembered the coupon or discount after the original transaction was processed and asked to have the coupon or discount applied.

Skimming is also done by business owners in order to reduce their tax burden. By removing receipts from the business, they can reduce both their sales tax and income tax liabilities. A common red flag for owner skimming is owners offering discounts for cash payments. The owners pocket the cash payments and don't include them in the company financials or on their tax returns. This type of fraud can be difficult to detect and is usually discovered during a tax audit when the auditors do a lifestyle audit to show the business owner is living well beyond their means based on the reported tax income. Receipts skimming is also done to reduce alimony and child support payments, which are based on income. Another common reason for owner skimming is to qualify for government benefits or to qualify for needs-based scholarships and government-backed student loans for their children's college education.

Skimming can be difficult to detect under normal circumstances but is especially difficult to detect with remote audits. Since the auditors are not observing the day-to-day operations of the client while conducting the audit, the risk of missing a skimming fraud is increased. To mitigate this, the auditors should ask the client to install webcams throughout the business at the beginning of the year so auditors can review the recordings on a sample basis.

Lapping

Lapping is a fraud scheme where employees "rob Peter to pay Paul." Lapping most commonly occurs in organizations that have many customers who have similar payments. A typical lapping plan works in this pattern: An employee steals a payment from "Customer A" and pockets the money. Before "Customer A" gets a late notice or late fee, the employee steals a payment from "Customer B" and posts it to "Customer A's" account. Then the employee steals funds from "Customer C" to cover the theft from "Customer B." At this point "Customer A" and "Customer B" are current on their payments and the employee only needs to worry about covering the payment for "Customer C." It can be difficult for employees to track all the payments they have stolen and to cover them before they become past due, making lapping one of the easier frauds to detect.

Auditors performing remote audits should perform additional data mining procedures to detect unusual transactions or patterns in payment applications.

Asset Misappropriations

Asset misappropriation is usually tied to items of value that can be easily monetized. Cash is one of the most frequently stolen assets because once the criminal has the cash in their possession, it is difficult to prove they stole the cash, and it wasn't theirs to start with. This is another reason to have cameras as part of a business's internal controls. Cash can be stolen from cash registers, from safes and vaults, from the mail room, and from deposits. Asset misappropriation can also include the theft of inventory and fixed assets. Criminals are usually trying to steal small expensive items that are easily converted into cash. An organization missing inventory or fixed assets should search online sales sites such as eBay and Craigslist as the thieves often try to sell the items they have pilfered.

When considering the fraud risk for misappropriation of assets, don't forget the risk of data theft. Data breaches are a type of cyber fraud where the criminals steal information with the intent to use or sell that information. A data breach occurs when someone gains access to information that contains confidential information. Confidential information includes personally identifying information (PII) and personal health information (PHI). A breach can occur because of a lack of security, the bypassing of security, or the elimination of security. Data breaches happen when information is stolen from computers and other electronic devices. They can also occur when devices containing information are lost or misplaced. Because an organization is considered to be negligent in its duties to safeguard the information provided to it by employees, customers, and others, there is a significant cost to being a victim of a data breach.

Criminals breach the information technology (IT) security of companies, not-for-profit organizations, and even governmental units and steal information from their computers. Often, the Human Resources department of an entity is targeted for payroll information, which includes Social Security numbers. Retail outlets are also targeted because they store customer information, including credit card numbers, on their computers. Not all data breaches are aimed at large organizations. Small businesses are also targeted, including tax providers, attorneys, medical offices, and insurance agents, because these professionals often have their clients' personal information stored on their computers.

Once again, auditors should perform additional data analytics to discover unusual transactions or activities that could be a red flag for asset misappropriations.

Accounts Payable Frauds

There are numerous ways to commit accounts payable fraud. The most basic accounts payable fraud scheme is to submit multiple invoices for the same transactions. The extra invoice will be sent with a different invoice number or a slightly altered invoice such as a "-A" at the end to attempt to circumvent the automated controls in the victim's accounting software. Sometimes statements are generated by the criminal after a payment is received but before it is posted to the system, in order to obtain a duplicate payment. If the victim questions the statement, they are told it "crossed in the mail."

Criminals will also generate fake invoices, or documents that look like invoices, in order to obtain payments. The classic example of this was invoices for the "Yellow Book," which were made to look like invoices for Yellow Pages ads. Today we see fake invoices for website optimization and search engine optimization (SEO), services that were never ordered or provided, but the fraudsters hope the victim will process the invoice. There was an interesting fake invoice scheme in Arizona a few years ago. The fraudsters sent out fake invoices for $300 to limited liability companies in Arizona claiming that they had not filed their annual corporate reports. It should be noted that limited liability companies in Arizona are not required to file corporate reports. The invoices contained the logo for the Arizona Corporation Commission and were written to look like official correspondence from the Corporation Commission. The Attorney General for the State of Arizona sent out a warning because thousands of businesses fell victim to this fake invoice scheme.

Another type of accounts payable fraud is payment splitting. Payment splitting occurs when an employee gets an invoice, either real or fake, that is over their approval limit. To avoid review by a supervisor, the employee splits the invoice into two payments, both of which fall into the employee's approval limit. Sometimes employees collude with vendors to have them reissue multiple invoices when the original payment is over their approval limit.

Shell companies are often created in order to create and submit fake invoices. A shell company is a company in name only. It is properly registered with the state, has an employer identification number (EIN), PO Box address, and usually has a bank account, but it provides no actual goods or services and has no operations other than generating invoices and receiving payments. Form W-9s are generated and the shell companies are set up as vendors in the victim's accounting system. Fake invoices are sent out, and the payments are processed through the shell company's bank account.

It isn't always necessary to go to all the trouble of setting up a shell company in order to commit a disbursement fraud. Employees can find a stale vendor (a vendor that hasn't been used in a while) and process a change of address for that vendor. Since the vendor is already in the system and approved, there is no need for a new W-9 or approval. The employee then creates and approves invoices for the vendor and misappropriates and cashes the checks.

Altering a check is also a common type of disbursement fraud. Accounting personnel can print a check and then alter the payee in the accounting system. It is also possible to steal a check from the check run and then to negotiate the check, making it look like a legitimate cashed check on the bank reconciliation.

Escheated funds are another area that are ripe for disbursement fraud. Sometimes recipients fail to cash the checks they are sent. These checks have been issued but they are variances on the bank reconciliation. At a certain point, depending on the state, the funds should be turned over to the government. Employees can reissue the checks, usually having them sent to a new address controlled by the employee, and then cash the checks. From the company's perspective it appears that the check was reissued and cashed by the intended recipient.

Remotely accessing accounting and bank records should be a normal process in a remote audit. It is still necessary to verify source documents for the accounting transactions.

Inventory Frauds

Businesses that maintain inventory are susceptible to various inventory frauds. The most common issue with inventory is the theft of inventory, either by employees or by shoplifters using the old "five-fingered discount." Inventory is stolen and the criminals either use the items themselves or sell them for cash or virtual currencies. The stolen inventory can also be bartered for drugs, prostitutes, or other illegal items. It is important to have good internal controls in place to keep the inventory secure. This can include using barcodes, RFID chips, cameras, locked display cases, and alarm systems.

One type of inventory theft scheme involves having an employee who works at a cash register collude with an outside party. The accomplice brings several items to the checkout point, including one high-priced item. The employee rings up the items but places their hand over the barcode of the high-priced item while passing it over the scanner, thus preventing it from being recorded. The accomplice then pays for the lower priced items and walks out with all of the items, including the items not recorded by the cash register. If a supervisor is watching or even if cameras are present, this can look like a legitimate sale and no red flags are raised until the inventory is counted, and shortages are detected.

Another inventory fraud scheme starts with an employee removing inventory from the store or warehouse and passing it off to an accomplice. The accomplice brings the item back to the store and requests a refund. There is usually an excuse for not having an original receipt, such as "It was a gift." The employee then processes a refund by paying the accomplice and returning the stolen item into the store's inventory.

Criminals also commit inventory fraud in manufacturing companies. In addition to pilfering finished goods, they steal scrap. A classic example occurs at home builders. Subcontractors order more materials, such as drywall, countertops, or wiring, and they cut the items down to size or keep the extra. Sometimes subcontractors use the stolen goods to fix up the properties they purchased to flip. They have a good profit margin when all their materials are free.

Failing to remove inventory from the books once it is sold is another classic inventory fraud scheme. This was easier to do when companies used periodic inventory tracking rather than perpetual inventory tracking. Since the inventory isn't removed from the books, the cost of goods sold is lower and the profits are higher. The Phar-Mor fraud is a classic case study for this type of fraud. Phar-Mor even moved inventory from store to store so every day when the auditors arrived to count the inventory, the stores were full of inventory. The auditors didn't know they were counting the same inventory over and over again.

Shell companies are also used in inventory frauds. A shell company is a company in name only; it doesn't have any actual operations. In this fraud the purchasing manager orders inventory from a shell that he or she set up, or had a relative or friend set up. The shell company then orders the merchandise from legitimate vendors, repackages it, and sends it to the victim company. The shell company will then invoice the victim, typically for 10 percent to 20 percent over what they purchased the merchandise for from the legitimate vendor, and the difference is all profit. A good internal control to prevent this type of inventory fraud is to do periodic Internet price checks on all the goods and services purchased to make sure the prices being paid are in line with the market.

It is not uncommon for owners, managers, and employees to temporarily use items from inventory for personal purposes. The items are removed from the packaging and used by the fraudsters. The items are then repackaged and sold as new. The unsuspecting customer believes they are purchasing a new product when in fact they are purchasing a used product.

Merchandise inventory fraud also occurs through short shipping. This fraud can be conducted by either management or employees. When a customer places an order for 100 items, the company short-ships 98 items hoping the victim doesn't count the items upon receipt. Should the customer count the items, the company claims it is an error and immediately offers to ship the missing items or to issue a credit memo. Employees commit this type of fraud by stealing items prior to shipping, and if a shortage is reported, they will claim it was an error.

Manufacturers can commit inventory fraud by incorrectly recording overhead and other indirect costs as direct inventory costs that are then capitalized with the inventory rather than being expenses in the period in which the expense was made. For large construction projects like buildings or airplanes, companies can manipulate the percentage of completion in order to manipulate the costs of construction.

It is always necessary to commit financial statement fraud, or cook the books, to explain the inventory shortages when a physical inventory count is done. Commonly, transactions are entered to record the stolen inventory as breakage, shrinkage, spoilage, or obsolescence. Other ways to conceal inventory frauds include altering inventory counts, altering inventory values, recording phantom inventory, recording intercompany sales as final sales, failing to record inventory at the lower of cost or market, and using improper cutoffs for recording inventory purchases and sales.

Additional types of inventory frauds to consider include the following:

- Round tripping
- Channel stuffing
- Inventory misappropriation
- False return schemes
- Scrap schemes
- Phantom inventory scheme
- Inventory purchase schemes
- Personal use scheme
- Capitalized cost schemes
- Spoilage frauds

¶611

- Breakage frauds
- Miscounting inventory
- Cutoff issues
- False purchases
- Excessive orders

Since remote auditors are not on-site, there is an increased risk of missing the signs of an inventory fraud. Auditors are using the client's personnel and cameras to help reduce this risk, but cameras can fool the viewer and do not offer the same assurance as observing the inventory count in person. Always remember the classic Phar-Mor inventory fraud. Additional review of inventory purchases and sales documents could help to mitigate this risk. Additional procedures may be necessary to validate items in transit, including having shipping and receiving personnel take photos of the items shipped and received, making sure the photos are date and time stamped. Having the client provide photos of items written off for spoilage, breakage, and scrap can also add to the audit evidence.

Payroll Frauds

There are numerous types of payroll fraud schemes. Payroll fraud schemes can be conducted by employees, the accounting department, or by owners and managers. The most basic payroll fraud scheme conducted by employees is to improperly record hours on a time sheet, thereby getting paid for hours that are not worked. Workers have been known to ask their fellow employees to "Clock me out because I need to leave early," or to ask someone to "Punch me in" if they know they are going to be late. The unwritten agreement is a quid pro quo that if you help me out now, I will do the same for you in the future. This is an example of combining asset misappropriation and corruption into one fraud scheme. Another common employee fraud scheme is slow work for overtime. This works because the employee deliberately works slowly knowing the work needs to be done by a certain deadline, then the employee works overtime to get the job done.

Employees have another scheme that applies to fire departments, police departments, and other essential service personnel. Employees usually have sick days or personal time off that they can use, and they take those days when friends who need some extra cash are on call. They get the day off and the friend gets overtime for the shift. There is an understanding that the favor will be returned when the employee who took the day off needs some overtime. Paperwork requirements can also be used to create overtime: leaving all of the paperwork until the end of the shift and then working overtime to get caught up. Audits of government entities have shown many first responders receive half of their W-2 income from overtime. This is a difficult area to control because the work needs to be done and many times there are legitimate reasons for the overtime.

Many payroll frauds can be conducted by employees in the accounting department. Accounting personnel can enter ghost employees or ghost independent contractors into the accounting system. Ghost employees are fictitious employees who do not exist except on the books. Remote auditors have a difficult time identifying ghost employees or payroll diversions because they are not on-site to meet with and talk to employees. Remote meetings are a mitigating factor but don't completely eliminate the increased risk for payroll fraud. Auditor's also must take care in years where a client received a Paycheck Protection Program (PPP) loan or an employee retention tax credit.

Tax Frauds

There are numerous types of tax frauds available to criminals willing to break the law. Some of the more common types include income tax fraud, sales and use tax fraud, excise tax fraud, payroll tax fraud, property tax fraud, and estate and gift tax fraud.

Income tax fraud is unfortunately fairly common. It is usually done in conjunction with financial statement fraud. When most people first think of financial statement fraud, they think of large companies like Enron and WorldCom, and individuals like Bernie Madoff, who cooked the books to increase revenue and/or decrease expenses to make the company look more profitable and drive up the stock price. However, it should be noted that the vast number of financial statement frauds in the United States work in the opposite direction. Small and midsized businesses reduce revenue and inflate expenses in order to make the company look less profitable, thereby reducing the tax burden on the business owners. This is particularly common for sole proprietorships and pass-through entities. The ultimate goal is to reduce the income and sales taxes paid by the owners to allow them to keep more money in their pockets.

Business owners do this by skimming revenue out of the business. They might even offer customers discounts for paying in cash, so they don't have to record the transaction on the books or deposit the funds in a bank, which leaves a paper trail. Business owners can also record personal expenses as business expenses to reduce the taxable income of the business. The new big-screen TV for the house is recorded as a computer monitor for the business or the family vacation is recorded as a business trip.

Not recording sales in the accounting system also allows the business owner to avoid paying sales and use taxes on those transactions. Business owners can also misuse their sales tax exemption certificates, which allow the business to avoid paying sales taxes on items the business purchases for resale in the business, to make personal purchases. The most common place this author has seen this done is restaurants, where the owners purchase the family groceries at a restaurant supply store and use the business's sales tax exemption certificate to avoid paying sales taxes on those purchases. Many businesses make purchases on the Internet or from out of state and fail to report and pay the use taxes on those transactions. The recent *Wayfair* decision by the Supreme Court that overturned the previous *Quill* decision will probably make it harder to avoid paying sales and use taxes on internet and out-of-state purchases.

Business owners have been known to borrow money from payroll withholdings, including an employee's payroll tax withholdings, 401(k) withholdings, or other items withheld from the employee's paycheck. These monies are often used to fund operations or to pay the owners. Businesses sometimes misclassify employees as independent contractors in order to avoid paying the business's half of the employees' payroll taxes.

Remote auditors should perform additional procedures to verify taxes are accurately calculated, reported, and paid, reconciling the tax filings with the books as well as verifying deferred tax assets and deferred tax liabilities. Auditors should determine if a client took advantage of the payroll tax deferral in 2020 or the employee retention credit in 2020 or 2021.

Unemployment Frauds

Due to the effects of the COVID-19 pandemic, in a matter of months, the United States went from having the lowest level of unemployment in years to having 50 million people unemployed. State unemployment agencies were not ready for that type of expansion, and to complicate matters, the federal government changed the rules, increasing who was eligible for unemployment benefits.

Moreover, states had outdated computer systems for unemployment claims that could not handle the increased numbers of people applying for aid. In addition, sole proprietors, gig workers, and independent contractors were suddenly eligible for unemployment benefits.

Unemployment programs also now covered people who had a breadwinner in their family who died from COVID-19, even if they had never worked. For example, consider a scenario where a husband was staying home, taking care of the kids, and the wife was employed. The wife contracted the coronavirus and died. Even though the husband was not employed, he could now get unemployment benefits due to changes to the program to help individuals from suffering from the virus.

All these factors resulted in unemployment frauds skyrocketing in 2020, and this type of fraud continued to be an issue in 2021. Unemployment fraud affected many states, from Hawaii to Texas to New York. California had billions of dollars in unemployment fraud.

One example of unemployment fraud centers around people who received debit cards for unemployment benefits from a state they do not live or work in. This type of fraud should be immediately reported to the bank that issued the card, as well as to the local police department, the Federal Trade Commission, and the Internet Crime Complaint Center (IC3).

Scammers frequently applied for unemployment in another person's name, and often in another state, which makes it difficult for the victim to track and correct the fraud. In one case, a California Employment Development Department worker filed multiple phony unemployment claims, including one in the name of U.S. Senator Dianne Feinstein. Often, victims are unaware of these crimes and only discover them later, when they get an audit notice from the IRS for failing to report all the unemployment payments they never received and never applied for.

Many businesses had their unemployment insurance premiums rise to super-high levels because fraudsters used the business's information to apply for fraudulent unemployment benefits for individuals. The fraudster had to steal an individual's identity but also had to claim an employer.

Remote auditors should obtain a sample of the documents received from the state's unemployment office and verify that the client accurately and timely responded to all claim notifications.

Fixed Asset Frauds

Fixed assets are the assets that are used to operate a business or used to generate revenue. The term *property, plant, and equipment* has historically been used to describe fixed assets. However, in today's economy, property, plant, and equipment is better defined as a subset of fixed assets. In the 21st century, businesses increasingly rely on intangible assets—for example, websites and streaming services—to generate revenue. When accounting for the assets necessary to operate a business and generate revenue, one needs to consider both tangible and intangible assets. Tangible assets have a physical substance, such as furniture or a building, and you can "reach out and touch them." Intangible assets, such as a website or patent, do not have a physical substance. Fixed assets are generally held as long-term assets and are not quickly convertible into cash. A business can purchase or acquire fixed assets, or the business can develop the fixed assets internally. Note that inventory is never a fixed asset.

Similarly, to inventory the verification of fixed assets poses additional risks for remote auditors. Using cameras to verify fixed assets is one way to mitigate this risk, but the auditor is still reliant on the client's employees for verifying fixed assets. Some auditors have used drones to help mitigate this risk.

Also, auditors should review to determine if the client has adjusted the useful life of any assets because of COVID-19 slowdowns or shutdowns. They should also verify if impairment testing, and adjustments if needed, were completed. Other things to consider when auditing fixed assets include, but are not limited to, the following:

- Existence
- Historical cost
- Depreciation
- Ownership
- Leased assets
- Impairments
- Dispositions
- Security of assets
- Internal controls
- Capital assets budget
- Insurance on assets
- Property taxes accrued and paid
- Maintenance and repairs
- Internally generated assets

Financial Statement Fraud

Financial statement fraud is usually done in conjunction with other frauds in order to conceal the fraud and hide the illegal activities. Financial statement fraud can also occur on its own and is the costliest of the occupational frauds. Readers are probably already aware of some of the famous financial statement frauds, such as Enron, WorldCom, Waste Management, and others. These financial statement frauds occurred when management wanted to give the appearance of increased profitability in order to drive up stock prices. Managers can add fictitious revenues or hide or capitalize expenses in order to make a company look more profitable. The executives at Enron used off-balance-sheet financing to move liabilities off the company's balance sheet and into special purpose and variable interest entities.

Note, however, that the vast majority of financial statement frauds are not designed to make a company look more profitable. Indeed, the business owners skim revenue out of the business and pay personal expenses from business funds for the sole purpose of making the company look *less* profitable. This is done to reduce the sales and income taxes the business owner would otherwise have to pay. There are far more small businesses in the country than there are large businesses, which is why this is a more common fraud. Don't be dismayed, however, because when it comes time to sell the business, these criminals are more than willing to cook the books to make the company appear more profitable for the buyer.

The easiest way to commit financial statement fraud is to record fictitious transactions on the books. This includes recording fake sales in order to increase revenue or recording fake expenses in order to reduce taxable income. Many times, fraudulent entries are input into the accounting system using top-sided or other journal entries. Businesses using the accrual method can also prematurely recognize revenue in order to manipulate the financial statements.

¶611

It is also possible to manipulate the financial statements by overstating the value of assets such as inventory, although intangible asset values are easy to manipulate. Failing to record or miss recording depreciation and amortization is another way to manipulate asset values. Companies have also been known to record consignment goods as part of the company's inventory. Understating liabilities or failing to disclose liabilities in the financial statements is another example of financial statement fraud.

Manipulating reserve accounts such as the allowance for doubtful accounts, warranty and repair allowances, environmental cleanup funds, and returns and allowances is another way to commit fraud. It is often common to see unrecorded liabilities, especially in small businesses where the owners are funding the business with personal loans or their personal credit cards. Failure to disclose contingent liabilities can also be an issue. Improperly recording transactions in the wrong period, either holding transactions for a future period before recording them or backdating transactions into past periods, is also an example of financial statement fraud.

While financial statement frauds are often undertaken to alter the balance sheet, income statement, or the statement of cash flows, failure to provide proper financial statement disclosures or filing misleading financial statement disclosures represent another type of financial statement fraud.

Additional fraud risks for financial statement frauds in remote audits occur because auditors can't directly interview the client's employees. As much as we would like to assume there is no difference between an in-person interview and a video interview, it is much harder to gauge body language when conducting a video interview.

¶ 612 DATA RISKS

When collecting and analyzing PII or PHI, care must be taken to ensure the information is not compromised or otherwise disclosed. With the General Data Protection Regulation (GDPR) and various federal and state laws on data security, organizations are required by law to take precautions when collecting, transmitting, using, storing, or destroying personal data that is considered to be confidential. Any organization, including auditors, collecting, or analyzing PII or PHI needs to have written internal controls for the data processes which are reviewed or audited on a regular basis.

When conducting remote audits, additional precautions should be taken when transferring or sharing information over the Internet. The use of an encrypted file transfer portal and virtual private network to create an encrypted connection over the Internet is highly recommended as a good cybersecurity internal control.

Relevance and Reliability of Data

When collecting data and audit evidence, an auditor must consider both the relevance and reliability of the data. GAAP indicates that when designing and performing audit procedures, the auditor should consider both the relevance and reliability of the information to be used as audit evidence. Characteristics that could affect relevance and reliability include the nature of the evidence, sources of the evidence, format of the evidence, timing of the evidence, extent of the evidence, verifiability of the evidence, and the level of aggregation of the data collected.

AU-C Section 330 specifically addresses the relevance of audit data. It indicates that a given set of audit procedures may provide audit evidence that is relevant to certain assertions but not others. Designing tests of controls to obtain relevant audit evidence includes identifying conditions (characteristics or attributes) that indicate performance of a control and identifying deviation conditions that indicate departures from adequate performance. Designing substantive procedures includes identifying conditions relevant to the purpose of the test that constitute a misstatement in the relevant assertion.

Auditors must also consider the reliability of the audit evidence they collect. Factors that can affect the reliability include, but are not limited to, the following:

- Reliability is increased when evidence is obtained from independent sources outside the entity.

- Reliability generated internally is increased when the related controls, including those over its preparation and maintenance, imposed by the entity are effective.

- Audit evidence obtained directly is more reliable than audit evidence obtained indirectly or by inference.

- Audit evidence in documentary form is more reliable than evidence obtained orally.

- Audit evidence provided by original documents is more reliable than audit evidence provided by photocopies, facsimiles, or documents that have been filmed, digitized, or otherwise transformed into electronic form.

With any audit in these uncertain times, it is necessary to use good professional judgement when considering going concern issues for a company. COVID-19 shutdowns, inflation, higher interest rates, the economic slowdown, worker shortages, higher rents, higher wages, and supply chain issues all add to risks of the client continuing as a going concern.

STUDY QUESTIONS

4. Which of the following creates an encrypted connection over the Internet?

- **a.** Virtual private network
- **b.** Hardware firewall
- **c.** PCI data security
- **d.** Biometrics

5. Taking cash before it is recorded in the accounting system is known as which of the following?

- **a.** Cash larceny
- **b.** Kiting
- **c.** Skimming
- **d.** Cash drawer loans

6. Which of the following is a type of inventory fraud?

- **a.** Bill and hold
- **b.** Lapping
- **c.** Cooking the books
- **d.** Short shipping

MODULE 2: TOP AUDITING ISSUES— CHAPTER 7: Environmental, Social, and Governance: A New Landscape

¶701 WELCOME

This chapter gives an overview of environmental, social, and governance (ESG) reporting requirements and standards and ESG's impact on generally accepted auditing standards (GAAS) and attestation.

On March 21, 2022, the U.S. Securities and Exchange Commission (SEC) proposed rules that would require public companies with periodic reporting obligations and companies filing registration statements to provide granular disclosures regarding greenhouse gas (GHG) emissions, climate-related risks and impacts, oversight of climate-related risks, climate-related goals, and climate-related financial statement metrics. It is one of the most significant developments in U.S. securities law in recent decades. Certain aspects of this information would also be subject to attestation or independent audit requirements. The proposed rules are intended to satisfy significant investor demand for climate-related disclosures that are consistent, comparable, and reliable.

¶702 LEARNING OBJECTIVES

Upon completion of this chapter, you will be able to:

- Describe the basics of ESG for management and auditors in ESG engagements, including ESG requirements and standards
- Identify issues for present and future situations and engagements with ESG positions
- Recognize the impacts ESG has on generally accepted auditing standards (GAAS) and attestation
- Identify what an auditor needs to know about management's policies and procedures that are unique to climate-related matters
- Differentiate relevant AU-C sections and how they apply
- Describe examples of climate-related matters that could raise substantial doubt about an entity's ability to continue as a going concern
- Describe the requirements proposed by the Securities and Exchange Commission (SEC) for public companies

¶703 BACKGROUND

Environmental, social, and governance (ESG) reporting enables companies to tell investors about their key ESG risks and opportunities, and their management of ESG; communicate progress on the company's commitments to the environment and society; show how the company's ESG strategy helps all owners; and increase confidence in leadership's ability to prioritize and push ESG commitments.

The terms *ESG*, *sustainability*, and *corporate social responsibility* are often used interchangeably, and different investors and stakeholders may describe ESG aspects differently. For the purpose of this chapter, the following is an explanation of each component of the ESG acronym.

The *environmental* component addresses how an entity is exposed to and manages risks and opportunities related to the environment, for example:

- Climate-related matters
- Natural resource scarcity
- Pollution
- Waste
- An entity's impact on the environment

The *social* component encompasses information about an entity's values and business relationships and addresses topics such as the following:

- Fair labor practices
- The use of ethically sourced material in the production of products
- Product quality and safety
- Human capital, such as employee health and safety, and diversity
- Inclusion policies and efforts

The *governance* component of ESG encompasses information about the system of rules, practices, and processes by which an entity is directed and controlled, and addresses topics such as the following:

- The structure and diversity of the board of directors
- Executive compensation
- Critical event responsiveness
- Entity resiliency
- Policies and practices related to lobbying, political contributions, bribery, and corruption
- Compliance with rules, regulations, and correct processes

GHG emissions disclosures are an issue for SEC filings. The proposed rules would mandate disclosures concerning a company's direct GHG emissions (Scope 1) and indirect GHG emissions from purchased electricity and other forms of energy (Scope 2). In addition, registrants would also be required to disclose indirect GHG emissions from the company's value chain, known as Scope 3 emissions, if material or if the company has set Scope 3 emissions targets or goals.

The proposed rules, if adopted, would go well beyond the statutory or regulatory requirements of any other federal agency, including the U.S. Environmental Protection Agency (EPA), in requiring the quantification and mandatory reporting of Scope 1, Scope 2, and, under certain circumstances, Scope 3 GHG emissions. Many of the proposed emissions disclosure requirements would create new challenges for public companies that have not made these disclosures in the past, including the new attestation requirements applicable to disclosures of Scope 1 and Scope 2 emissions by large, accelerated filers and accelerated filers. The proposed rules would require the attestation report to be included in a new separately captioned climate-related disclosure section in the relevant filing and include detailed disclosures about the experience, expertise, and independence of the GHG emissions attestation provider.

¶ 704 ENVIRONMENTAL ISSUES

Climate-Related Matters

Climate change is a topic that is increasingly important to stakeholders and has the potential to affect an increasing number of entities of all types and sizes. The effect of climate-related matters on financial reporting and the external audit may vary depending on a variety of factors. For certain entities, such as entities that insure, finance, or invest in entities that are more extensively affected by climate change, climate-related matters are more likely to have a pervasive effect.

For other entities, the effects of climate-related matters may be limited to an aspect of the entity's operations, such as its supply chain, input costs, customers, financing, insurance, or compliance with applicable laws and regulations.

Climate-related risks are often categorized as either physical risks arising from climate change, for example, flood, drought, and wildfire; or transition risks arising from the transition from an economy that relies on fossil fuels that produce GHG emissions to one that relies on alternative sources.

The independent auditor should be apprised of management's policies and procedures related to the following:

- Capturing information about climate-related matters that may affect the entity's financial statements

- Assessing the risks of material misstatement of the financial statements resulting from such matters

- Appropriately evaluating such matters to determine whether they may need to be reflected in the entity's financial statements

- How to consider and evaluate management's response to climate-related matters in an audit of financial statements conducted in accordance with generally accepted auditing standards (GAAS)

Management Responsibilities

Management is responsible for preparing the entity's financial statements in accordance with the applicable financial reporting framework. When applying current accounting standards, entities may consider climate-related changes in their business and operating environment when those changes have a material effect on the financial statements.

Risks associated with climate-related changes are considered in the context of the overall environment in which the entity operates, including industry, regulatory, and entity-specific factors.

Industry factors. Examples of industry factors include the degree of competitiveness within the industry, customer preferences, supplier relationships, and technological developments. Entities in certain industries or geographic locations may need to implement changes to enable their business activities to continue in the event of extreme climate-related events, such as wildfires or flooding. These measures may require significant expenditures (including long-term technological improvements) and may increase operating costs. Alternatively, entities in industries that do not take such actions may be subject to business disruption and property loss.

Regulatory factors. The regulatory environment encompasses, among other matters, the legal and political environment in which entities operate. The regulatory environment related to ESG matters continues to evolve, with a current emphasis on climate change.

Some entities face uncertainty about future climate regulations. For example, some regulations may create economic disincentives for entities to continue to emit carbon by imposing levies or taxes on high-emission sources, while other regulations may seek to incentivize entities to adopt specific operating practices, such as changing to lower emission or more sustainable land-use practices.

Changes in climate regulation or policy may affect a wide range of business inputs and outputs, such as energy pricing, carbon taxes, mandatory emission and energy standards, and industry targets. For example, the rapid emergence of climate-related legislation in different jurisdictions means that entities need to be aware of existing or proposed climate-related laws and regulations and the extent to which those laws and regulations may affect the entity's operating, investing, and financing activities.

Entity-specific factors. Management may need to consider entity-specific factors such as investor activism or the effects on the entity of shifting consumer preferences for environmentally friendly alternatives. For example, changes in consumer preferences may decrease the demand for certain products and create the need for the entity to obtain new technology and equipment to make innovations in its product, an accomplishment that may be dependent on another entity-specific factor, the entity's ability to obtain financing.

Entities may find it helpful to consider climate-related risks within the context of the entity's overall enterprise risk management (ERM) program; doing so may assist management in developing effective responses to, and provide increased transparency about, those risks and their potential effects on the entity.

Governance Responsibilities

Those charged with governance are responsible for overseeing the entity's strategic direction and the obligations related to the entity's accountability. This includes overseeing the financial reporting process and the external audit.

Therefore, those charged with governance have a role to play with respect to the consideration of climate-related risks in the context of overseeing the entity's financial reporting process. Examples of responsibilities of those charged with governance as they relate to climate-related matters may include obtaining information about management's risk assessment activities and its plans for mitigating those risks and exploring with management how climate-related risks may affect the entity's significant accounting policies, accounting estimates, and financial statement disclosures.

Entities may be at different stages in their consideration of climate-related matters as it relates to financial reporting, and those charged with governance must understand the entity's current status with respect to such considerations and whether the entity has begun to consider future risks and opportunities that may arise as a result of climate-related matters. In addition, how this is done may vary depending on the environment in which the entity operates and changes thereto.

Those charged with governance may also want to discuss these matters with the auditor, for example, to understand how climate-related risks may be considered in the audit and to share related insights. An effective audit of the financial statements requires a two-way dialogue between those charged with governance and the auditor so that the auditor can understand how risks are being identified and managed at the governance level.

¶ 705 AUDIT IMPACTS

Auditor Responsibilities

The auditor is responsible for planning and performing the audit to obtain reasonable assurance about whether the financial statements as a whole are free from material misstatement to enable the auditor to report on whether the financial statements are prepared, in all material respects, in accordance with the applicable financial reporting framework.

Climate-related risks may affect the auditor's determination of materiality in accordance with AU-C section 320, *Materiality in Planning and Performing an Audit.*

AU-C section 315A, *Understanding the Entity and Its Environment and Assessing the Risks of Material Misstatement,* requires the auditor to obtain an understanding of the entity and its environment, including the entity's internal control as it relates to the audit. In particular, understanding how management assesses and responds to risks (including climate-related risks) may help the auditor to:

- Identify risks such as natural disasters like hurricanes, floods, or tornadoes, or man-made situations like strip mining, tunneling, or construction defects
- Determine whether the effect of such risks could give rise to the risk of material misstatement of the entity's financial statements
- Develop appropriate audit responses to address these assessed risks

For example, in obtaining an understanding of the entity, its environment, and its risk assessment process, auditors may find it helpful to obtain information about the following matters:

- Whether and how the entity has considered climate-related risks and opportunities
- The extent of management's knowledge and awareness of the effects of climate-related matters on the entity, the industry, and geographic locations in which the entity operates
- Whether the entity has considered the effects of macroeconomic conditions such as inflation, which may occur when climate-related events result in, for example:
  — A shortage of an essential component of a product,
  — Reducing the availability of the product,
  — Causing the price of the product to rise, and
  — In some cases, causing consumers to move on to a replacement product
- The process management has used to identify aspects of its operations, suppliers, or markets that may be affected by:
  — Shifts in consumer preferences toward environmentally friendly alternatives
  — The transition to low-carbon economies, and
  — The transition by the entity itself to low-carbon alternatives
- The time horizon management has used in considering climate-related risks
- How the financial impacts of identified risks have been assessed and incorporated into financial budgeting, projections, and the financial reporting process
- What management has done to ensure that it complies with emerging climate-related regulations and meets requirements regarding climate-related disclosures in the entity's financial statements, including determining whether it has a

reasonable basis for information presented or disclosed in the entity's financial statements

- Management's decarbonization plan, if applicable

In accordance with paragraph .06 of AU-C section 315A, risk assessment procedures should include inquiries of management and other appropriate individuals within the entity, including individuals within the internal audit function (if the function exists).

To obtain an understanding of these matters, the auditor also may make inquiries of individuals in operations, legal, or product development. In addition, reviewing one or more internal or external sources (e.g., climate-related information disclosed in other information, separately produced sustainability reports, or management communications through press releases and website content) may give the auditor an understanding of climate-related matters that may affect the entity and its environment.

The knowledge obtained from risk assessment procedures forms the basis for identifying risks, including climate-related risks that could affect the entity and its financial statements, and for evaluating whether such risks give rise to a risk of material misstatement.

Auditing standards require auditors to design and implement overall responses to address the assessed risks of material misstatement at the financial statement level and to design and perform further audit procedures whose nature, timing, and extent are based on—and responsive to—the assessed risks of material misstatement at the relevant assertion level. These risks would include natural disasters and/or man-made disasters discussed earlier.

Risk Assessment and Responses

AU-C Section 315A, *Understanding the Entity and Its Environment and Assessing the Risks of Material Misstatement*, requires the auditor to do the following:

- Identify and assess the risks of material misstatement in the financial statements through understanding the entity and its environment, including the entity's internal control
- Perform risk assessment procedures to provide a basis for identifying and assessing risks of material misstatement at the financial statement and relevant assertion levels

If the auditor determines that risks of material misstatement represent a significant risk as described in paragraphs 28–29 of AU-C 315A, the auditor is required by AU-C 260.11 to communicate that to those charged with governance, as well as take other steps as outlined in AU-C 315A.

The following are some of the matters that AU-C Section 315A requires the auditor to obtain an understanding of, and examples of how they might relate to climate-related events or conditions:

- Relevant industry, regulatory, and other external factors, including the applicable financial reporting framework
  - For an automobile manufacturer, an industry trend toward manufacturing electric vehicles and phasing out the production of vehicles that use fossil fuels
  - For a mining entity, the enactment of new climate-related laws and regulations, the violation of which could result in penalties or the suspension of business
  - For a hotel located on a coast, a rise in the sea level and erosion of beaches that makes the hotel a less attractive destination

- The nature of the entity including its operations

  — The entity produces a product that requires a part that has become either unavailable or overpriced due to climate-related matters in the part of the world where the part is produced

  — A commercial real estate company owns properties located in areas subject to climate-related events and is required to pay above market for financing

  — An agricultural producer is affected by the occurrence of drought that reduces yields or volume

- The entity's objectives, strategies, and related business risks that may result in risks of material misstatement

  — The entity has begun to develop electric vehicles using a labor force that is relatively new to this technology, increasing the risk that the vehicles will be defective

  — The entity has no track record in manufacturing and selling electric vehicles, which increases estimation uncertainty when determining the provision for warranty claims

  — A manufacturer is implementing its net zero commitment to decrease its GHG emissions by a specified date, which affects almost every aspect of its manufacturing process

  — An online retailer is replacing the Styrofoam packaging it uses to ship its products with biodegradable packaging. The retailer hired a consultant to advise the company regarding the most suitable packaging materials and is phasing out the Styrofoam packaging in favor of the biodegradable packaging, which is made of plant matter. The biodegradable packaging is more costly and requires a change in packaging machinery and process

Materiality in Planning

AU-C Section 320, *Materiality in Planning and Performing an Audit*, addresses the auditor's responsibility to apply the concept of materiality in planning and performing an audit of financial statements. Misstatements, including omissions, are considered material if there is a substantial likelihood that, individually or in the aggregate, they would influence the judgment made by a reasonable user based on the financial statements.

The auditor's determination of materiality is a matter of professional judgment and is affected by the auditor's perception of the financial information needs of users of the financial statements. Auditors of entities that are affected by climate-related risks may take that into account when determining materiality.

Audit Procedures Responding to Assessed Risks

AU-C Section 330, *Performing Audit Procedures in Response to Assessed Risks and Evaluating the Audit Evidence Obtained*, addresses the auditor's responsibility to design and implement responses to the risks of material misstatement identified and assessed by the auditor in accordance with AU-C Section 315A–16 and to evaluate the audit evidence obtained in an audit of financial statements.

The nature, timing, and extent of the audit procedures performed to respond to risks of material misstatement associated with climate-related matters is a matter of professional judgment and depends on the nature of the assessed risk. The following are examples of further audit procedures an auditor might perform to respond to an assessed risk of material misstatement affected by climate-related matters:

- Obtaining third-party forecasts of future demand for refined petroleum products to evaluate the potential impairment of assets for an oil and gas refinery
- Holding discussions with the entity's attorneys regarding climate-related matters and conducting a search for climate litigation and claims brought against the entity to respond to the risk that provisions could be understated or that contingent liability disclosures may be omitted
- Determining if management has adjusted the residual valuation of equipment and related depreciation expense to reflect a decreased demand for the entity's product and the shortened useful life of equipment used to produce it

Laws and Regulations

AU-C Section 250, *Consideration of Laws and Regulations in an Audit of Financial Statements*, discusses the auditor's responsibility to consider laws and regulations in an audit of financial statements. It identifies two different kinds of laws and regulations and the auditor's responsibility when considering them. It requires the auditor to do the following:

- Obtain sufficient appropriate evidence regarding material amounts and disclosures in the financial statements that are determined by the provisions of those laws and regulations generally recognized to have a direct effect on their determination
- Perform specified audit procedures that may identify instances of noncompliance with other laws and regulations that do not have a direct effect on the determination of the amounts and disclosures in the financial statements, for which compliance may be fundamental to the operating aspects of the business and the entity's ability to continue as a going concern

> **NOTE:** Climate-related matters may affect the legal and regulatory environment in which the entity operates. An example is a law or regulation that prohibits the manufacturing of vehicles whose emissions exceed a specified amount. A breach of such law or regulation may have a material effect on the financial statements. For example, a breach may result in a contingent liability for potential litigation and fines or penalties.

Misstatements Evaluation

AU-C Section 450, *Evaluation of Misstatements Identified During the Audit*, discusses the auditor's responsibility to evaluate the effect of identified misstatements on the audit and the effect of uncorrected misstatements on the financial statements.

AU-C Section 450 indicates that circumstances related to some misstatements may cause the auditor to evaluate them as material, individually or when considered together with other misstatements, even if they are lower than materiality for the financial statements as a whole. An example of a circumstance related to climate-related matters that may affect the evaluation of misstatements is the extent to which the misstatement is an omission of qualitative disclosures about environmental matters that present certain risks and uncertainties that could significantly affect the amounts reported in the financial statements as required under the financial reporting framework.

Audit Evidence

AU-C Section 540A, *Auditing Accounting Estimates, Including Fair Value Accounting Estimates, and Related Disclosures*, addresses the auditor's responsibilities relating to accounting estimates, including fair value accounting estimates and related disclosures, in an audit of financial statements. The following are examples of estimates included in the financial statements that may be affected by climate-related matters:

- The valuation of property, plant, and equipment after a climate-related event has occurred or when there is a high probability of a recurrence of such an event
- The repair to a seawall after a hurricane
- Provisions for the cost of reforestation of abandoned strip mines
- The valuation of intangible assets, such as an entity's brand, after the entity has been publicly identified as being responsible for plastic pollution contributing to carbon emissions
- The net realizable value of inventory when the entity is affected by regulatory changes that could reduce the demand for a product and thereby make the inventory obsolete, or a significant weather event that causes physical damage to inventory

AU-C Section 540 requires the auditor to obtain an understanding of how management makes the accounting estimates and the data on which they are based. This includes understanding the entity's process for capturing information about climate-related matters and their possible effects on the financial statements, and the nature and source of the information and the circumstances under which it is obtained.

Matters that the auditor may consider in auditing accounting estimates include the following:

- Whether management has assessed the continued use of previous methods, assumptions, and data used in making estimates, and if not, whether the methods, assumptions, and data used remain appropriate. For example, insurance entities may need to increase their loss reserves, including incurred but not reported loss adjustment expense due to greater property damage from hurricanes with increased severity as a result of changes in weather patterns.
- The degree to which an accounting estimate is subject to estimation uncertainty. For example, climate-related matters may make it more difficult to make precise, reliable predictions about the incidence and effect of future events or conditions such as the frequency of extreme droughts.
- The degree to which the accounting estimate is subject to complexity, which may require the use of specialized skill or knowledge to determine the effects of the changing climate-related event or condition.

AU-C Section 540 also requires the auditor to obtain sufficient appropriate audit evidence about whether the disclosures in the financial statements related to accounting estimates are in accordance with the requirements of the applicable financial reporting framework and, for accounting estimates that give rise to significant risks, to evaluate the adequacy of the disclosure of estimation uncertainty in the financial statements in the context of that framework. Many of the estimates affected by climate-related matters may have a high degree of estimation uncertainty.

Examples of matters that the auditor may consider in auditing accounting estimates include the following:

- Whether management has assessed the continued use of previous methods, assumptions, and data used in making estimates, and if not, whether the methods, assumptions, and data used remain appropriate. For example, insurance entities may need to increase their loss reserves, including incurred but not reported loss adjustment expense due to greater property damage from hurricanes with increased severity as a result of changes in weather patterns.
- The degree to which an accounting estimate is subject to estimation uncertainty. For example, climate-related matters such as the frequency of extreme droughts

affecting harvests may make it more difficult to make precise and reliable predictions about the incidence and effect of future events or conditions.

- The degree to which the accounting estimate is subject to complexity, which may require the use of specialized skill or knowledge to determine the effects of the changing climate-related event or condition.

AU-C Section 540 also requires the auditor to obtain sufficient appropriate audit evidence about whether the disclosures in the financial statements related to accounting estimates are in accordance with the requirements of the applicable financial reporting framework and, for accounting estimates that give rise to significant risks, to evaluate the adequacy of the disclosure of estimation uncertainty in the financial statements in the context of that framework.

Many of the estimates affected by climate-related matters may have a high degree of estimation uncertainty.

AU-C Section 620A, *Using the Work of an Auditor's Specialist*, outlines the auditor's responsibilities relating to the work of an individual or organization that has expertise in a field other than accounting or auditing when that work is used to help the auditor obtain sufficient appropriate audit evidence.

When auditing areas affected by climate-related matters, a specialist with expertise or specialized skill in a field other than accounting and auditing may be needed.

The following are examples of how the work of a specialist may be used in an audit of an entity affected by climate-related matters:

- To test the reasonableness of management's calculation of the provision recognized for decommissioning offshore oil and gas operations or rehabilitating environmental damage, when required by law or regulation

- To assist in understanding how management has considered future demand for refined petroleum products

AU-C Section 570, *The Auditor's Consideration of an Entity's Ability to Continue as a Going Concern*, examines the auditor's responsibilities in the audit of financial statements relating to the entity's ability to continue as a going concern and the implications for the auditor's report.

This section applies to all audits of a complete set of financial statements, regardless of whether the financial statements are prepared in accordance with a general-purpose or a special-purpose framework. It includes guidance if events or conditions have been identified that may cast substantial doubt on the entity's ability to continue as a going concern.

AU-C Section 570 requires the auditor to conclude, based on the audit evidence obtained, whether substantial doubt exists about an entity's ability to continue as a going concern for a reasonable period of time and to evaluate the possible financial statement effects, including the adequacy of disclosure regarding the entity's ability to continue as a going concern for a reasonable period of time. If the auditor concludes that substantial doubt exists, the auditor must consider management's plans to alleviate that doubt and evaluate disclosures regarding these matters.

The following are examples of climate-related matters that could raise substantial doubt about an entity's ability to continue as a going concern, and factors that may or may not alleviate that doubt:

- The disruption of business and the uncertainty created by operating in a geographic location that has a history of being highly susceptible to extreme weather events mitigated by evidence that the entity has leased a plant in, and will relocate to, an area that is less vulnerable to such events

- Increased compliance costs related to enacted emissions regulations mitigated by a plan developed by a specialist that will enable the entity to comply with those regulations

- Significant litigation claims by a city vulnerable to sea level rise and flooding against an energy company responsible for carbon emissions and the views of attorneys regarding the likelihood that the litigation will succeed

Communication with Governance

One of the matters that AU-C Section 260, *The Auditor's Communication with Those Charged with Governance,* requires the auditor to communicate to those charged with governance is the auditor's views on the qualitative aspects of the entity's significant accounting practices, including accounting policies, accounting estimates, and financial statement disclosures.

An example of a matter that the auditor may communicate to those charged with governance is the effect of climate-related matters on significant assumptions used in accounting estimates, such as the impairment of nonfinancial and financial assets, and the degree of subjectivity involved in the development of the assumptions.

Opinion and Reporting

AU-C Section 700, *Forming an Opinion and Reporting on Financial Statements*, discusses the auditor's responsibility to form an opinion on the financial statements. It also addresses the form and content of the auditor's report issued as a result of an audit of financial statements.

To determine whether the financial statements are prepared, in all material respects, in accordance with the requirements of the applicable financial reporting framework, AU-C Section 700 requires the auditor to evaluate the matters in paragraph 15 of AU-C Section 700. One of those matters is whether the financial statements provide adequate disclosures to enable the intended users to understand the effect of material transactions and events on the information conveyed in the financial statements.

An example is disclosure about an entity's strategy to transition from manufacturing vehicles that use fossil fuels to manufacturing electric vehicles, a strategy that would have pervasive effects on the entity and its financial statements. The following are additional disclosures that may be needed in this circumstance:

- Risks related to the uncertainty of the demand for electric vehicles because of the market's perceptions about the quality, safety, performance (the range over which electric vehicles may be driven on a single battery charge), existing infrastructure (access to charging facilities), and cost of these vehicles

- Risks related to competition from other types of alternative fuel vehicles, plug-in hybrid electric vehicles, and high fuel-economy internal combustion engine vehicles

- The entity's dependence on the continued supply of lithium-ion battery cells for its vehicles and the limited number of such suppliers at the date of the financial statements

Key Audit Matters

An auditor's responsibility to communicate key audit matters (KAMs) in the auditor's report, when the auditor is engaged to do so, is prescribed by AU-C Section 701, *Communicating Key Audit Matters (KAMs) in the Independent Auditor's Report.*

It is intended to address both the auditor's judgment about what to communicate in the auditor's report and the form and content of the communication. However, it does not require the communication of KAMs.

The purpose of communicating KAMs is to provide report users with greater transparency about the audit that was performed. The communication of KAMs in the auditor's report may also give intended users of the financial statements a basis to further engage with management and those charged with governance about certain matters relating to the entity, the audited financial statements, or the audit that was performed.

When communicating KAMs, the auditor is required to identify matters that, in the auditor's professional judgment, were of most significance in the audit of the financial statements of the current period. KAMs are selected from matters communicated with those charged with governance.

Auditing account balances and disclosures affected by climate-related matters may involve especially challenging, subjective, or complex auditor judgment. These matters may be communicated to those charged with governance. If they are, and the auditor is engaged to communicate KAMs, those matters would be among the matters considered by the auditor as potential KAMs.

Other Information in Annual Reports

AU-C Section 720, *The Auditor's Responsibilities Relating to Other Information Included in Annual Reports*, addresses the auditor's responsibility relating to other information, whether financial or nonfinancial (other than financial statements and the auditor's report thereon), including in an entity's annual report.

When the auditor has obtained all the other information at the date of the auditor's report, the auditor *is required* to include a separate section in the auditor's report with the heading "Other Information" or other appropriate heading.

AU-C Section 720 requires the auditor to read the other information and consider whether a material inconsistency exists between the other information and the financial statements, and to remain alert for indications that a material misstatement of fact exists. It also requires the auditor to remain alert for indications that a material inconsistency exists between the other information and the auditor's knowledge obtained in the audit or the other information is otherwise misleading.

> **NOTE:** The credibility of the audited financial statements may be undermined by material inconsistencies between the other information and the audited financial statements or the auditor's knowledge obtained in the audit.

The following are examples of other information about climate-related matters that might be included in a document containing the audited financial statements and the auditor's report, which the auditor would be required to read and consider in accordance with AU-C Section 720:

- A discussion of the entity's short-term and long-term strategies for managing and responding to climate-related risks
- Disclosure of climate-related performance measures, such as carbon emissions attributable to activities for which the entity is responsible
- Potential future effects of climate change on the entity's operations

If the auditor identifies that a material inconsistency appears to exist (or becomes aware that the other information appears to be materially misstated) between the other information and the audited financial statements, AU-C Section 720 states the auditor should discuss the matter with management and, if necessary, perform other procedures to conclude whether a material misstatement of the other information exists, whether a material misstatement of the financial statements exists, and whether the auditor's understanding of the entity and its environment needs to be updated.

STUDY QUESTIONS

1. The governance component of ESG encompasses information about each of the following, *except?*

a. The structure and diversity of the board of directors

b. Inclusion policies and efforts

c. Executive compensation

d. Critical event responsiveness

2. Which of the following is an example of a regulatory factor?

a. The degree of competitiveness within the industry

b. Customer preferences

c. The legal and political environment in which entities operate

d. Supplier relationships

3. Climate-related risks may affect the auditor's determination of materiality in accordance with which of the following AU-C Sections?

a. AU-C Section 315

b. AU-C Section 320

c. AU-C Section 450

d. AU-C Section 530

¶ 706 ATTESTATION IMPACTS

As mentioned earlier, sustainability information is information about sustainability matters related to ESG. Preparers of sustainability information often seek to increase the credibility of their reported sustainability information to users. Accordingly, they may engage practitioners to perform an attestation engagement or others to perform some form of assurance engagement.

One type of sustainability information is greenhouse gas (GHG) emissions information. Sometimes practitioners are engaged to perform attestation engagements on GHG. Entities often prepare separate reports on GHG information, and later in this chapter is specific guidance on the application of American Institute of Certified Public Accountants (AICPA) attestation standards to such presentations.

Such guidance is intended to supplement the general guidance throughout this chapter and, though specific to performing an attestation engagement on a separate presentation of GHG emissions information, can also be considered when performing an attestation engagement on a sustainability report that includes GHG emissions information.

Examples of ways the reporting entity might hold out the subject matter as sustainability information include the following:

- Labeling the report containing the subject matter as a sustainability report; corporate social responsibility report; or environmental, social, and governance report, or a similar title

- Labeling the presentation of information as a GHG emissions schedule or statement
- Submitting the presentation in response to a third-party requirement for the submission of sustainability information (e.g., to sustainability rating bodies)
- Labeling sections of a broader report, such as a report submitted to a securities regulator (e.g., in the "Management Discussion and Analysis" section of an SEC Form 10-K), as sustainability; corporate social responsibility; or environmental, social, and governance information

Planning

AT-C Sections 205, *Examination Engagements*, and 210, *Review Engagements*, state that the practitioner should do the following in an examination or review engagement:

- In an *examination*, identify the characteristics of the engagement that define its scope and ascertain the reporting objectives of the engagement in order to plan the timing of the engagement and the nature of the communications required, and consider the factors that, in the practitioner's judgment, are significant in directing the engagement team's efforts.
- In a *review*, obtain a sufficient understanding of the subject matter and other engagement circumstances to provide a basis for designing and performing procedures to achieve the engagement objectives. That understanding should include the practices used to measure, recognize, and record the subject matter.

Understanding

Understanding the subject matter and other engagement circumstances in a sustainability *examination or review* engagement includes developing an understanding of the following:

- The nature and characteristics of the subject matter
- The organization's structure and nature of the entity's business
- The entity's organizational and operational boundaries and its approach to setting reporting boundaries, including the reporting boundary used by the entity to prepare the sustainability information
- The criteria used, the responsible party's interpretation of the criteria, and the availability of the criteria to measure particular components of and to present the sustainability information
- Definitions of key terms used, and assumptions made with respect to material components of the sustainability information
- The characteristics of the collection and reporting process of material components of the sustainability information
- Whether the criteria, measurement method reporting boundary, or measurement units employed are consistent with the prior period's
- Whether comparative information is presented and whether it is to be covered by the current examination or review engagement, or whether it was previously subjected to an examination or review engagement
- Whether the entity's internal audit function is relevant to the engagement
- Whether high measurement uncertainty exists in any of the quantitative sustainability information
- Whether the practitioner expects to use the work of another practitioner
- Whether the practitioner expects to use the work of a practitioner's specialist

Nature of Planning

The nature of planning will vary according to the nature and characteristics of the subject matter and the scope of the engagement.

EXAMPLES: Sustainability information related to biodiversity is likely to require more extensive procedures on measurement uncertainty and the methodologies for capturing and reporting such information than sustainability information related to health and safety or employment practices.

Materiality considerations will vary depending on whether the engagement is to include the entire sustainability report, a presentation of GHG emissions information, an identifiable section of a sustainability report, or only specified indicators.

The characteristics of the sustainability information affect the availability of sufficient evidence and the nature of the procedures to be performed. Sustainability information may have one or more of the following characteristics.

Quantified information:

- Numerical information including statistics, which may be produced internally or obtained externally (e.g., from other organizations outside its organizational boundary but within its operational boundary).

- These quantified indicators may be subject to high degrees of accuracy and precision (low measurement uncertainty), or the tool or methodology used to arrive at such quantifications may be subject to lower degrees of accuracy or precision (and may result in high measurement uncertainty).

- Some quantified indicators—such as those related to future-oriented matters—cannot be measured but may be supported by other types of evidence, such as board meeting minutes and policy statements.

Factual narrative:

- Nonnumerical information that is supported by events that have occurred and is objectively determinable; it may be evidenced in various ways, including through reporting systems and the entity's internally produced reports from such systems or in information externally reported by other organizations.

- This includes directional indications of an effect or anticipated outcome (e.g., increase or decrease, favorable or unfavorable).

Soft narrative:

- Nonnumerical information that is subjective. It may contain views or judgments of management and those charged with governance, but the substance of the narrative may be supported in the entity's operating practices and by various reports, internal communications, and the entity's internal or external websites.

Diagrams or graphs:

- These may be used as pictorial representations in conjunction with or instead of a narrative, schedule, or table. They can be representations of quantified measurements and factual information or of soft narrative information.

Nature of Business and Organizational Structure

An understanding of the entity's structure and the nature of the business is needed to be able to examine or review sustainability information. Therefore, it is important to understand characteristics about the entity, including the legal entities comprising the entity, its organizational boundary, and its governance; whether the entity has operations in multiple locations, and the types of products and services it offers; the underlying business processes; and significant changes thereto since the prior period. Sources of information to obtain the understanding include, but are not limited to, the following:

- Inquiries of management
- The entity's website and the sustainability site, which can provide information about the entity's structure, vision, products, and services, as well as key stakeholders and how sustainability relates to its strategy
- Internal documents that discuss strategy
- Minutes of the board and committee meetings
- Other entity documents

New Activity for the Entity

If collecting and reporting sustainability information is a relatively new activity for the entity, the information systems, processes, and controls over the sustainability information may not be fully developed and may consist of both automated and manual processes. Some information may be initially gathered electronically and then used in a manual process, particularly if that data is obtained from different systems.

Relevant considerations may include whether any of the following situations are present and the effects that any of these situations might have on planning and performing the examination or review engagement:

- Systems and processes that have been designed for purposes other than reporting information about sustainability; in such cases, they may not capture all the required information.

- Systems and processes that produce the sustainability information are not traditional accounting systems and processes and therefore have not been previously subject to assessment (e.g., by internal audit or in conjunction with external audit or attest services); in such cases, they may not produce or contain the necessary documentation.

- Systems and processes capturing measurements are complex and involve highly technical information involving engineering and other science skills; in such cases, specialized skills may be necessary.

- Systems for capturing sustainability information are not subject to the same backup requirements or information technology general controls as traditional accounting systems, and therefore data and subsequent system reports may be incomplete or inaccurate.

Materiality in Attestation

As required by AT-C Section 205, the practitioner should consider materiality for the subject matter when establishing the overall engagement strategy, including the determination of the nature, timing, and extent of procedures; and when evaluating whether uncorrected misstatements are material—individually or in the aggregate.

According to AT-C Section 210, the practitioner should consider materiality when planning and performing the *review* engagement, including the determination of the nature, timing, and extent of procedures; and when evaluating whether the practitioner is aware of any material modifications that should be made to the subject matter for it to be fairly presented in accordance with the criteria or the assertion in order for it to be fairly stated.

¶706

Materiality as a concept relates to both which information is material to users and thus should be included in the sustainability report; and whether an identified misstatement, including an omitted disclosure, would be material to users.

Assessing the significance of a misstatement of some items of the sustainability information may depend more on qualitative than on quantitative considerations. Qualitative aspects of materiality relate to the relevance and reliability of the information presented (e.g., qualitative aspects of materiality in assessing whether the underlying information, determinations, estimates, and assumptions of the entity provide a reasonable basis for the disclosures in the sustainability report).

Quantitative information is often more meaningful when accompanied by qualitative disclosures. For example, quantitative information about a measurement of GHG emissions may be more meaningful when accompanied by a narrative about the source and extent of measurement uncertainty of such measurement.

When high measurement uncertainty exists, materiality considered in planning and performing the engagement may be smaller than the range of values reasonably attributed to such sustainability information. Information with complex measurement methods that incorporate multiple assumptions may result in high measurement uncertainty, and therefore a point value in that range may not be as accurate or precise for such sustainability information as information that can be easily counted or measured.

When measurement uncertainty is material to the engagement, the practitioner should design procedures that focus on obtaining evidence regarding the quality of the measurement process, whether there are any known errors, and whether the disclosures related to the reported information are sufficient.

When the engagement is for an entire sustainability report, relevant materiality considerations may include:

- Obtaining an understanding of the process the entity's management used to identify what is material to the entity for sustainability reporting purposes

- Identifying the sustainability information that is most significant to the users of the report (material information); and

- Determining a threshold of materiality of misstatements for that information

It is likely that the sustainability information considered most significant to users of the report will cover several different topics or indicators, in which case a materiality of misstatement threshold would be assessed for each such topic or indicator. Relevant factors to consider in identifying the sustainability information most significant to users of the report may include management's view on the materiality of the information; the materiality determination process the entity undertakes to determine what information to include in the report; and the practitioner's understanding of the intended users.

Types of misstatements that could occur in sustainability information include the following:

- Misstatement of quantified information (e.g., understatement or overstatement of GHG emissions; omissions of activity for a period of time or a location; omission of the unit of measurement; or if the measurement uncertainty is high, the quantified extent of the measurement uncertainty)

- Misstatement of narrative (e.g., not balanced, or incomplete information, or inaccurate statement)

- Omitted disclosure (e.g., lack of disclosure called for by the criteria or lack of a disclosure about a material event affecting the sustainability information)

- Insufficient description of the criteria (e.g., for measurement of a particular indicator, the methodologies applied, measurement methods, assumptions, estimates, and factors used in making the measurement or evaluation might not be disclosed)

Performing Procedures

Under AT-C Section 205, *Examination Engagements*, the practitioner is required to identify and assess risks of material misstatement as the basis for designing and performing further procedures whose nature, timing, and extent (1) are responsive to assessed risks of material misstatement and (2) allow the practitioner to obtain reasonable assurance about whether the sustainability information is presented in accordance with the criteria, in all material respects.

In the case of specified indicators, the risk of material misstatement is assessed in relation to each indicator. For an identifiable section of a sustainability report, materiality and the risk of material misstatement are assessed in relation to that section. In an examination of an entire sustainability report, materiality and the risk of material misstatement are assessed in relation to the entire sustainability.

Review procedures. AT-C Section 210, *Review Engagements*, requires the practitioner to place increased focus on areas where he or she believes there are increased risks that the subject matter may be materially misstated. In the case of specified indicators, the increased focus in areas of increased risk relates to each indicator. For an identifiable section of a sustainability report, the increased focus in areas of increased risk relates to that section. In a review of an entire sustainability report, the increased focus in areas of increased risk relates to the entire sustainability report.

Examinations. Procedures performed in assessing risks of material misstatement can, among other procedures, include inquiries about the relationships of narrative statements to the sustainability metrics used and the source of the reported information.

Inquiries about relationships of narrative statements to metrics used can identify inconsistencies or possible sources of evidence to support the disclosure or corroborate the results of other inquiries. The specific procedures to be performed are a function of the characteristics of the sustainability information and may take into consideration the following:

- The industry in which the organization operates
- The reporting boundary for purposes of the examination engagement and whether information to be reported is based on data received by the entity from organizations in the supply chain.

In deciding whether to perform analytical procedures, the practitioner should consider whether the information to which the analytical procedures would be applied is appropriate for analytical procedures. Some sustainability information, although quantifiable in nature, may not be suitable for analytical procedures.

> **EXAMPLE:** The practitioner may be unable to obtain sufficient evidence for metrics, such as a health and safety statistic of fatalities per year, given the lack of a quantifiable relationship between the variables relating to such metric.

Review. Areas in which to place increased focus may be determined through inquiries about the reporting boundary, the relationships of narrative statements to the sustainability metrics used, and the source of the reported information.

Inquiries about relationships of narrative statements to metrics used can identify inconsistencies or possible sources of evidence to support the disclosure or corroborate the results of other inquiries. The specific inquiries to be made are a function of the characteristics of the sustainability information, and the practitioner's knowledge of the industry in which the entity operates may be taken into consideration.

The nature of procedures in a review engagement concerning sustainability information will vary according to whether analytical procedures can be performed. Some sustainability information, although quantifiable in nature, may not be suitable for analytical procedures (e.g., safety metrics).

Analytical procedures may not be possible when the subject matter is qualitative rather than quantitative. AT-C Section 210 states that in these situations, the practitioner should perform other procedures, in addition to inquiries, that provide equivalent levels of review evidence (such as inspection and observation).

Even when there is the ability to perform analytical procedures, conditions may exist that might not produce a reliable basis on which to perform the procedures or performing analytical procedures will be less effective and efficient than performing tests of details to obtain sufficient review evidence. For example, in obtaining review evidence related to an entity's community investment, it might be more effective to review documentary evidence of payments made or observe donated property in use.

Examination measurement uncertainty. The degree of measurement uncertainty associated with the reported information affects the identification and assessment of the risks of material misstatement in an examination of sustainability information and, accordingly, the practitioner should tailor further procedures to respond to the identified risks.

When high measurement uncertainty is identified in sustainability information, the practitioner should evaluate whether, in his or her professional judgment, the aspects of the measurement process (e.g., measurement techniques, assumptions, and conversion factors) give rise to an increased risk of material misstatement.

Review measurement uncertainty. When high measurement uncertainty is identified in sustainability information, the practitioner should place increased focus in those areas of measurement uncertainty arising from the various aspects of the measurement process (e.g., measurement techniques, assumptions, and conversion factors) in which the practitioner believes there are increased risks that the sustainability information may be materially misstated.

Factors that may be considered when assessing whether the process resulting in high measurement uncertainty in sustainability information gives rise to an increased risk of material misstatement include the following:

- How reported values were measured (i.e., the process used to arrive at the range of reasonable values)
- The source and extent of measurement uncertainty for reported point values included in the sustainability information
- How those reported point values were selected from the range of reasonable values
- Whether other methods may be more or less accurate and precise, and why management intends to use the selected method
- Whether and what management intends to include as disclosures related to such reported point values, including disclosures about the source(s) of measurement uncertainty and a quantified expression of the measurement uncertainty, such as the range of values that could be reasonably attributed to the reported point values

The following are examples of measurements that might be identified as having high measurement uncertainty:

- Measurements requiring high levels of judgment, such as when significant assumptions could fall within a range of reasonable values that could significantly affect the measurement
- Measurements with a less accurate or less precise process for measuring the information
- Measurements that require the summation of multiple values, each with its own significant measurement uncertainty

¶ 707 REPORTING ON ATTESTATION AGREEMENTS

In forming an opinion or conclusion, AT-C Sections 205, *Examination Engagements*, and 210, *Review Engagements*, require the practitioner to evaluate his or her conclusion regarding the sufficiency and appropriateness of engagement evidence obtained, and whether uncorrected misstatements are material, individually or in the aggregate.

AT-C sections 205 and 210 also require the practitioner to evaluate, based on the evidence obtained, whether the presentation of the subject matter or assertion is misleading within the context of the engagement. Aspects of sustainability information that should be considered by the practitioner in forming an opinion or conclusion on the sustainability information include the following:

- The overall presentation, structure, and content of the sustainability information
- Consistency of criteria and measurement method(s) used from the prior period
- The completeness of the sustainability information for the intended purpose
- Whether the disclosures are informative of matters that affect the use, understanding, and interpretation of the sustainability information in the context of its intended purpose

Other considerations in forming the opinion or conclusion include matters such as the following:

- Whether a change in the entity's organizational boundary has occurred and whether the entity is using a consistent approach to determine its reporting boundary for preparing the sustainability information. For example, if the organizational or reporting boundary has changed from the prior year, such as a change from reporting on the organization's domestic entities to reporting on the consolidated organization, regardless of whether comparative information is presented, whether such change is appropriately disclosed, and the sustainability information is appropriately labeled with the organizational boundary in the practitioner's identification of the entity.
- The adequacy of disclosures (e.g., for material matters, the measurement criteria used in the current period and whether they are comparable to those used in the prior period if prior period sustainability information is presented; the source and extent of inherent uncertainties related to such information).
- Whether sustainability information is being reported publicly for the first time with comparative information and, if so, whether the process employed in the prior year in measuring and accumulating such comparative information was consistent or sufficiently rigorous to enable reporting of comparative information.
- If diagrams, graphs, or other visual representations of data are presented, whether such presentation is reflective of the actual quantitative information or possibly may be misleading.
- The consistency of narrative disclosures to tables or graphics.

- Whether errors were identified and corrected in the current period that may indicate errors in prior period information that is included for comparative purposes.

Measurement Uncertainty

The criteria for sustainability information may not include explicit criteria for the disclosure of measurement uncertainty. In evaluating whether the sustainability information is misleading within the context of the engagement, the practitioner should consider whether it is necessary for the sustainability information to include disclosure about measurement uncertainty, even when the criteria do not require such disclosure.

The practitioner may conclude that sustainability information is misleading when it is not informative of material matters that may affect the use, understanding, and interpretation of the information, such as the extent of measurement uncertainty.

When measurement uncertainty is high for sustainability information covered by the engagement, considerations may include whether and how it is communicated to report users. For example, one way of identifying and communicating such uncertainty is by disclosing the range of reasonable outcomes associated with the reported point value within which the actual value may fall.

Although the disclosures with respect to the sustainability information may be in accordance with the criteria, the criteria may not have been designed to address all reporting situations that might be encountered. In forming the opinion or conclusion, AT-C Sections 205 and 2105 require the practitioner to evaluate, based on the engagement evidence obtained, whether the presentation of the subject matter or assertion is misleading within the context of the engagement. For sustainability information that is subject to high measurement uncertainty, the practitioner may conclude that a lack of disclosure of measurement uncertainty is misleading in light of the circumstances and facts involved.

To make the information reported understandable, useful, complete, and not misleading, it may be necessary for management to provide disclosures beyond those specifically required by the reporting criteria.

The practitioner's evaluation of the adequacy of disclosure of measurement uncertainty increases in importance the greater the range of reasonable outcomes of the measurement is in relation to materiality. In some cases, the practitioner may also consider it appropriate to encourage the responsible party to describe in the presentation of the sustainability information the circumstances giving rise to the high measurement uncertainty, such as by including a description of the key assumptions.

Report Preparation

In accordance with AT-C Sections 205 and 210, the practitioner's report should be in writing and identify the sustainability information or assertion being reported on, including the point in time or period to which the sustainability information relates.

> **NOTE:** Practitioners should not use terms such as *validation* or *verification* in their attest reports, regardless of whether the requirements of other organizations for assurance engagements use such terms, because AT-C Section 105, *Concepts Common to All Attestation Engagements*, requires the terms *examination* or *review* to be used to describe such engagements.

If the practitioner has been engaged to perform an examination of some specified indicators and a review of others, the practitioner should make clear in the practitioner's report which specified indicators are covered by the examination report and which are covered by the review report. Identifying the sustainability information being reported on under the examination or review engagement:

- Clarifies the level of assurance obtained by the practitioner on such information, and
- If information that was not the subject of the practitioner's engagement is included with the subject matter, helps clarify which information is not the subject matter of either the examination or review engagement

Report Content: Examination

Consistent with AT-C Section 205, the practitioner's report on an examination of sustainability information should include the following, unless the practitioner is disclaiming an opinion:

- A title that includes the word *independent*
- An appropriate addressee as required by the engagement circumstances
- An identification or description of the sustainability information or assertion being reported on, including the point in time or period to which the measurement or evaluation of the sustainability information or assertion relates
- An identification of the criteria against which the subject matter was measured or evaluated
- A statement that identifies the responsible party and its responsibility for the sustainability information in accordance with the criteria or for its assertion; and the practitioner's responsibility to express an opinion on the sustainability information or assertion, based on the practitioner's examination
- A statement that
  — The practitioner's examination was conducted in accordance with attestation standards established by the AICPA.
  — Those standards require that the practitioner plan and perform the examination to obtain reasonable assurance about whether the sustainability information is in accordance with the criteria, in all material respects (or equivalent language regarding the subject matter and criteria); or the responsible party's assertion is fairly stated, in all material respects.
  — The practitioner believes the evidence he or she obtained is sufficient and appropriate to provide a reasonable basis for the practitioner's opinion.
- A description of the nature of an examination engagement
- A statement that describes significant inherent limitations, if any, associated with the measurement or evaluation of the sustainability information against the criteria
- The practitioner's opinion about whether the sustainability information is in accordance with the criteria, in all material respects; or the responsible party's assertion is fairly stated, in all material respects
- The manual or printed signature of the practitioner's firm
- The city and state where the practitioner practices
- The date of the report. The report should be dated no earlier than the date the practitioner has obtained sufficient appropriate evidence on which to base the practitioner's opinion, including evidence that

— The attestation documentation has been reviewed,

— If applicable, the written presentation of the sustainability information has been prepared, and

— The responsible party has provided a written assertion or, in the circumstances described in paragraph.A66 of AT-C Section 205, an oral assertion.

The wording of the statement of the description of planning and performing the examination may depend on the nature of the sustainability information, such as described in the following examples:

- If the sustainability information is an entire sustainability report or specified indicators, the practitioner might state that those standards require that he or she plan and perform the examination to obtain reasonable assurance about whether the sustainability information is presented in accordance with the criteria in all material respects.

- If the sustainability information is a management assertion about specified indicators being presented in accordance with the criteria, the practitioner might state that those standards require that he or she plan and perform the examination to obtain reasonable assurance about whether management's assertion is fairly stated, in all material respects.

- When the program or registry contains specific materiality requirements that are more stringent than those of AT-C Sections 205 and 210, the practitioner may include a reference to those requirements in the attest report (e.g., materiality requirements under a GHG trading program or registry).

The wording of the statement of the description of planning and performing the examination may depend on the nature of the sustainability information, such as described in the following examples:

- If the sustainability information is an entire sustainability report or specified indicators, the practitioner might state that those standards require that the practitioner plan and perform the examination to obtain reasonable assurance about whether the sustainability information is presented in accordance with the criteria in all material respects.

- If the sustainability information is a management assertion about specified indicators being presented in accordance with the criteria, the practitioner might state that those standards require that the practitioner plan and perform the examination to obtain reasonable assurance about whether management's assertion is fairly stated, in all material respects.

- When the program or registry contains specific materiality requirements that are more stringent than those of AT-C sections 205 and 210, the practitioner may include a reference to those requirements in the attest report (for example, materiality requirements under a GHG trading program or registry).

Report Content: Review

Consistent with AT-C section 210, the practitioner's report on a review of sustainability information should include the following:

- A title that includes the word *independent*

- An appropriate addressee as required by the circumstances of the engagement

- An identification or description of the sustainability information or assertion being reported on, including the point in time or period of time to which the measurement or evaluation of the sustainability information or assertion relates

- An identification of the criteria against which the sustainability information was measured or evaluated. (See paragraph 4.14.)

- A statement that identifies the responsible party and its responsibility for the sustainability information in accordance with the criteria or for its assertion, and the practitioner's responsibility to express a conclusion on the sustainability information or assertion, based on the practitioner's review
- A statement that
  - The practitioner's review was conducted in accordance with attestation standards established by the American Institute of Certified Public Accountants.
  - Those standards require that the practitioner plan and perform the review to obtain limited assurance about whether any material modifications should be made to the sustainability information in order for it to be in accordance with the criteria (or equivalent language regarding the subject matter and criteria; or the responsible party's assertion in order for it to be fairly stated).
  - A review is substantially less in scope than an examination, the objective of which is to obtain reasonable assurance about whether the sustainability information is in accordance with the criteria, in all material respects, or the responsible party's assertion is fairly stated, in all material respects, in order to express an opinion. Accordingly, the practitioner does not express such an opinion.
  - The practitioner believes the review provides a reasonable basis for the practitioner's conclusion.
- A statement that describes significant inherent limitations, if any, associated with the measurement or evaluation of the sustainability information against the criteria.
- The practitioner's conclusion about whether, based on the review, the practitioner is aware of any material modifications that should be made to
  - The sustainability information in order for it to be in accordance with the criteria (or equivalent language regarding the subject matter and criteria) or
  - The responsible party's assertion in order for it to be fairly stated.
- The manual or printed signature of the practitioner's firm
- The city and state where the practitioner practices
- The date of the report. The report should be dated no earlier than the date on which the practitioner has obtained sufficient appropriate review evidence on which to base the practitioner's conclusion, including evidence that
  - The attestation documentation has been reviewed,
  - If applicable, the written presentation of the sustainability information has been prepared, and
  - The responsible party has provided a written assertion.

The wording of the statement of the description of planning and performing the review may depend on the nature of the sustainability information, such as described in the following examples:

- If the sustainability information is an entire sustainability report or specified indicators, the practitioner might state that those standards require that the practitioner plan and perform the review to obtain limited assurance about whether any material modifications should be made to the sustainability information in order for it to be presented in accordance with the criteria.
- If the sustainability information is a management assertion about specified indicators being in accordance with the criteria, the practitioner might state that

those standards require that the practitioner plan and perform the review to obtain limited assurance about whether any material modifications should be made to management's assertion in order for it to be fairly stated.

- When the program or registry contains specific materiality requirements that are more stringent than those of AT-C sections 205 and 210, the practitioner may include a reference to those requirements in the attest report (e.g., materiality requirements under a GHG trading program or registry).

The manner in which the practitioner states the practitioner's conclusion may depend on the nature of the sustainability information, such as described in the following examples:

- If the sustainability information is an entire sustainability report or specified indicators, the practitioner might state whether the practitioner is aware of any material modifications that should be made to the sustainability information in order for it to be presented in accordance with the criteria.

- If the sustainability information is a management assertion about specified indicators being in accordance with the criteria, the practitioner's conclusion might state whether the practitioner is aware of any material modifications that should be made to management's assertion in order for it to be fairly stated.

¶ 708 EXAMINATION REPORT EXAMPLES

Example 1: Practitioner's Examination Report on an Entire Sustainability Report; Reporting on Subject Matter; Unmodified Opinion

Independent Accountant's Report

[Appropriate Addressee]

We have examined [identify the subject matter, for example, XYZ Company's sustainability report for the year ended December 31, 20XX]. XYZ Company's management is responsible for preparing and presenting [identify the subject matter, for example, XYZ Company's sustainability report] in accordance with [identify the criteria, for example, the criteria specified on page XX of the accompanying sustainability report]. Our responsibility is to express an opinion on [identify the subject matter, for example, XYZ Company's sustainability report] based on our examination.

Our examination was conducted in accordance with attestation standards established by the American Institute of Certified Public Accountants. Those standards require that we plan and perform the examination to obtain reasonable assurance about whether [identify the subject matter, for example, the sustainability report]is presented in accordance with the criteria, in all material respects. An examination involves performing procedures to obtain evidence about [identify the subject matter, for example, the sustainability report]. The nature, timing, and extent of the procedures selected depend on our judgment, including an assessment of the risks of material misstatement of [identify the subject matter, for example, the sustainability report], whether due to fraud or error. We believe that the evidence we obtained is sufficient and appropriate to provide a reasonable basis for our opinion.

[Include a description of significant inherent limitations, if any, associated with the measurement or evaluation of the subject matter against the criteria, such as measurement uncertainty.]

[Additional paragraph(s) may be added to emphasize certain matters relating to the examination engagement or the subject matter.]

In our opinion, [identify the subject matter, for example, XYZ Company's sustainability report] is presented in accordance with [identify the criteria, for example, the criteria specified within the report] in all material respects.

[Practitioner's signature]

[Practitioner's city and state]

[Date of practitioner's report]

Example 2: Practitioner's Review Report on an Entire Sustainability Report; Reporting on the Subject Matter; Unmodified Conclusion

Independent Accountant's Review Report

[Appropriate Addressee]

We have reviewed [identify the subject matter, for example, the sustainability report of XYZ Company for the year ended December 31, 20XX]. XYZ Company's management is responsible for preparing and presenting [identify the subject matter, for example, the sustainability report] in accordance with [identify the criteria, for example, ABC criteria as further described [on pages X-X of the sustainability report]/[in the accompanying notes]]. Our responsibility is to express a conclusion on [identify the subject matter, for example, the sustainability report] based on our review.

Our review was conducted in accordance with attestation standards established by the American Institute of Certified Public Accountants. Those standards require that we plan and perform the review to obtain limited assurance about whether any material modifications should be made to [identify the subject matter, for example, the sustainability report] in order for it to be presented in accordance with the criteria. A review is substantially less in scope than an examination, the objective of which is to obtain reasonable assurance about whether [identify the subject matter, for example, the sustainability report] is [presented]in accordance with the criteria, in all material respects, in order to express an opinion. Accordingly, we do not express such an opinion. We believe that our review provides a reasonable basis for our conclusion.

[Include a description of significant inherent limitations, if any, associated with the measurement or evaluation of the subject matter against the criteria, such as measurement uncertainty.]

[Additional paragraph(s) may be added to emphasize certain matters relating to the review engagement or the subject matter.]

Based on our review, we are not aware of any material modifications that should be made to [identify the subject matter, for example, the accompanying sustainability report of XYZ Company for the year ended December 31, 20XX], in order for it to be presented in accordance with [identify the criteria, for example, ABC criteria as further described [on pages X to X of the sustainability report]/[in the accompanying notes]].

[Practitioner's signature]

[Practitioner's city and state]

[Date of practitioner's report]

STUDY QUESTIONS

4. Which of the following statements is correct with respect to attestation impacts?

   a. Preparers of sustainability information have always sought to increase the credibility of their reported sustainability information to users.

   b. Entities have always prepared separate reports on GHG information.

   c. The nature of planning will vary according to the nature and characteristics of the subject matter and the scope of the engagement.

   d. The characteristics of sustainability information will not affect the availability of sufficient evidence.

5. Which of the following statements is correct with respect to materiality in an attestation engagement?

    a. The practitioner should consider materiality for the subject matter when establishing the overall engagement strategy.

    b. As required by AT-C Section 210, the practitioner should consider materiality when planning and performing an agreed-upon procedures engagement.

    c. Materiality as a concept relates to only what information is material to users and thus should be included in the sustainability report.

    d. Assessing the significance of a misstatement of some items of the sustainability information will always be more dependent on quantitative considerations.

6. Which of the following statements is *incorrect* regarding attestation reporting on sustainability information?

    a. In forming an opinion or conclusion, the practitioner should evaluate his or her conclusion regarding the sufficiency and appropriateness of engagement evidence obtained.

    b. The criteria for sustainability information may include explicit criteria for the disclosure of measurement uncertainty.

    c. The overall presentation, structure, and content of the sustainability information should be considered when forming an opinion.

    d. The completeness of the sustainability information for the intended purpose should be considered when forming an opinion.

CPE NOTE: When you have completed your study and review of chapters 4-7, which comprise Module 2, you may wish to take the Final Exam for this Module. Go to **cchcpelink.com/printcpe** to take this Final Exam online.

MODULE 3: SEC REPORTING—CHAPTER 8: Management's Discussion and Analysis (MD&A)

¶ 801 WELCOME

This chapter provides an overview of the rules and regulations with respect to the management's discussion and analysis (MD&A) section of an entity's consolidated financial statements filed with the U.S. Securities and Exchange Commission (SEC). MD&A has been, and continues to be, a primary focus area of the SEC when reviewing public company filings. In fact, it has consistently ranked in the top 10 of the most frequent comment letters issued by the SEC.

¶ 802 LEARNING OBJECTIVES

Upon completion of this chapter, you will be able to:

- Identify the SEC Regulation applicable to MD&A
- Recognize the primary objective and focus areas related to MD&A
- Identify key information that should be included within a company's MD&A
- Recognize the types of transactions that should be discussed in MD&A
- Identify methods to enhance the presentation of MD&A

¶ 803 INTRODUCTION

If you've perused some Form 10-Qs and 10-Ks recently, you likely know that one of the largest sections included within these filings is the section titled "Management's Discussion and Analysis of Financial Condition and Results of Operations," or simply MD&A for short. Consequently, this is also the area of a company's consolidated financial statements which often receives a significant amount of the attention by the SEC. In fact, in several of the Big 4 accounting firms recent (and historical) SEC Comment Letter trend publications, the topic of MD&A has consistently ranked in the Top 10 areas for SEC comments. For example, in PwC's "SEC Comment Letter Trends" publication published on March 28, 2022, the firm notes that MD&A was #2 on the list of the Top 10 most frequent comment letters. Similarly, in EY's publication "SEC Reporting Update—Highlights of Trends in 2021 SEC Comment Letters," the firm also notes that MD&A was #2 on the Top 10 list. While this ranking has moved up or down in the past, the MD&A topic has consistently been included in the Top 10.

Given the importance of this area within a company's consolidated financial statements, it's important to have a clear understanding of the rules and regulations with respect to this area. To that end, this chapter provides a detailed overview of the SEC requirements along with other interpretations and best practices offered up by the SEC. This chapter also includes comment letter examples included within several of the Big 4 accounting firm's comment letter analysis publications.

¶ 804 WHERE DO I GO FOR GUIDANCE?

Knowing where to look for guidance on MD&A requirements is the first step in the process of better understanding this important area of a company's consolidated financial statements. If you navigate to the actual Form 10-Q and Form 10-K instructions, you'll note that both forms will direct you to Item 303 of Regulation S-K. More specifically, Part I, Item 2 of the 10-Q and Part II, Item 7, of the 10-K will direct you to Item 303.

Item 303 is filled with several pages of guidance which lays out the information that should be included within the MD&A section. Additionally, the guidance also provides information on some of the objectives with respect to these areas and what disclosure is seeking to accomplish. In addition to the guidance included in Item 303, there is also significant interpretive guidance provided by the SEC. You can also find additional best practices outlined within several of the Big 4 accounting firms' publications.

¶ 805 OBJECTIVE OF MD&A

Before we get too deep into the actual guidance outlined in Item 303, it's important to first understand the overall objective of MD&A, and what the primary purpose is for including it in a company's 10-Q and 10-K. As noted in the objective section of Item 303, the objective of MD&A is to do the following:

- Provide material information relevant to an assessment of the financial condition and results of operations of an entity including:
  — An evaluation of the amounts; and
  — Certainty of cash flows from operations and from outside sources.

The SEC further notes in Item 303 that MD&A should focus specifically on **"material events and uncertainties** known to management that are **reasonably likely** to cause reported financial information not to be necessarily indicative of future operating results or of future financial condition." In other words, the expectation here is to provide additional context that cannot already be inferred by an investor looking at the consolidated financial statements of a company. In doing this, entities should include descriptions and amounts of matters that have had a material impact on reported operations, as well as matters that are reasonably likely based on management's assessment to have a material impact on future operations.

Overall, the SEC notes that MD&A must be "of the financial statements and other statistical data that the registrant believes will **enhance a reader's understanding** of the registrant's financial condition, cash flows and other changes in financial condition and results of operations." In other words, MD&A should be viewed as an additional supplement to provide key information to inventors which, again, they cannot readily ascertain from the other parts of the consolidated financial statements. Said another way, the SEC notes that by including MD&A, it is expected to allow investors to "view the entity from management's perspective."

In the SEC's interpretation "Commission Guidance Regarding Management's Discussion and Analysis of Financial Condition and Results of Operations" (https://www.sec.gov/rules/interp/33-8350.htm), the SEC provides additional context with respect to the primary objectives of MD&A. In it, the SEC notes that "the purpose of MD&A is not complicated. It is to provide readers information necessary to an understanding of a company's financial condition, changes in financial condition and results of operations." In its interpretation, the SEC outlines the following three principal objectives:

- Provide a narrative explanation of a company's financial statements that enables investors to see the company through the eyes of management
- Enhance the overall financial disclosure and provide the context within which financial information should be analyzed

- Provide information about the quality of, and potential variability of, a company's earnings and cash flow, so that investors can ascertain the likelihood that past performance is indicative of future performance

Refer to the following Exhibit, which provides some additional comments from the SEC with respect to the purpose of and presentation of MD&A.

Exhibit 1: Commission Guidance Regarding Management's Discussion and Analysis of Financial Condition and Results of Operations

(III) Overall Approach to MD&A

A. The Presentation of MD&A

Since the introduction of our MD&A requirements, many companies have become larger, more global, and more complex. At the same time, the combination of our rules and investors' demands have led to an increase in the number of subjects and matters addressed in MD&A. For these and other reasons, many companies' MD&A have become necessarily lengthy and complex. Unfortunately, the presentation of the MD&A of too many companies also may have become unnecessarily lengthy, difficult to understand and confusing.

MD&A, like other disclosure, should be presented in clear and understandable language. We understand that complex companies and situations require disclosure of complex matters, and we are not in any way seeking over-simplification or "dumbing down" of MD&A. However, we believe that companies can improve the clarity and understandability of their MD&A by using language that is clearer and less convoluted. We believe that efforts by companies to provide clearer and better organized presentations of MD&A can result in more understandable disclosure that does not sacrifice the appropriate level of complexity or nuance. In order to engender better understanding, companies should prepare MD&A with a strong focus on the most important information, provided in a manner intended to address the objectives of MD&A.

Within its above referenced publication, the SEC further notes that they expect a "good introduction or overview to provide a balanced, executive-level discussion that identifies the most important themes or other significant matters with which management is concerned primarily in evaluating the company's financial condition and operating results." Furthermore, the SEC notes that this "good introduction" would include the following information:

- Economic or industry-wide factors relevant to the company
- Informs readers about how the company earns revenues and income and generates cash
- Discusses a company's lines of business, location or locations of operations, and principal products and services
  - The SEC cautions here that it should not merely duplicate disclosure in the "Description of Business" section
- Provides insight into material opportunities, challenges, and risks, such as those presented by known material trends and uncertainties, on which the company's executives are most focused for both the short and long term, as well as the actions they are taking to address these opportunities, challenges, and risks

In its interpretation, the SEC further notes the following:

Because these matters do not generally remain static from period to period, we would expect the introduction to change over time to remain current. As is true with all sections of MD&A, boilerplate disclaimers and other generic language generally are not helpful in providing useful information or achieving balance and would detract from the purpose of the introduction or overview.

¶805

Refer to the following Exhibit, which provides some additional insight from the SEC with respect to the overall purpose and preparation of MD&A.

Exhibit 2: Commission Guidance Regarding Management's Discussion and Analysis of Financial Condition and Results of Operations

(III) Overall Approach to MD&A

A. The Presentation of MD&A

An introduction or overview, by its very nature, cannot disclose everything and should not be considered by itself in determining whether a company has made full disclosure. Further, the failure to include disclosure of every material item in an introduction or overview should not automatically trigger the application of the "buried facts" doctrine, in which a court would consider disclosure to be false and misleading if its overall significance is obscured because material is "buried," such as in a footnote or an appendix.

Throughout MD&A, including in an introduction or overview, discussion and analysis of financial condition and operating performance includes both past and prospective matters. In addressing prospective financial condition and operating performance, there are circumstances, particularly regarding known material trends and uncertainties, where forward-looking information is required to be disclosed. We also encourage companies to discuss prospective matters and include forward-looking information in circumstances where that information may not be required but will provide useful material information for investors that promotes understanding.

¶ 806 ITEM 303—FULL FISCAL YEAR REQUIREMENTS

Now that you know the overall objective of MD&A, as well as some of the main principles outlined by the SEC, let's next address more specifically some of the information that is required to be disclosed. There are several subsections included within Item 303. Additionally, you should note that there is guidance that is applicable to full fiscal years (i.e., to be included in a company's Form 10-K) as well as guidance that is applicable only to interim periods (i.e., to be included in a company's Form 10-Q).

In this first section of the chapter addressing the Item 303 requirements, we'll start with the full fiscal year requirements. In a later section of the chapter, we'll go over those requirements that are applicable only to interim periods. In an attempt to help illustrate application of the guidance (but not necessarily best practices per se), we'll include illustrative examples from SEC filers along the way.

¶ 807 ITEM 303—LIQUIDITY AND CAPITAL RESOURCES

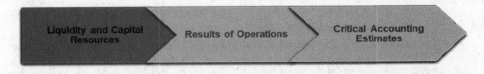

We'll use the above roadmap to help illustrate the three key areas within Item 303 for full fiscal year filings. In this section addressing liquidity and capital resources, as well as the subsequent ones addressing results of operations and critical accounting estimates, we'll present the actual text from the SEC guidance and then discuss that guidance in additional detail.

Refer to the following Exhibit, which includes the SEC guidance related to liquidity and capital resources.

Exhibit 3: § 229.303 (Item 303)(b)(1)—Liquidity and Capital Resources

(1) Liquidity and capital resources. Analyze the registrant's ability to generate and obtain adequate amounts of cash to meet its requirements and its plans for cash in the short-term (i.e., the next 12 months from the most recent fiscal period end required to be presented) and separately in the long-term (i.e., beyond the next 12 months). The discussion should analyze material cash requirements from known contractual and other obligations. Such disclosures must specify the type of obligation and the relevant time period for the related cash requirements. As part of this analysis, provide the information in paragraphs (b)(1)(i) and (ii) of this section.

   (i) Liquidity. Identify any known trends or any known demands, commitments, events, or uncertainties that will result in or that are reasonably likely to result in the registrant's liquidity increasing or decreasing in any material way. If a material deficiency is identified, indicate the course of action that the registrant has taken or proposes to take to remedy the deficiency. Also identify and separately describe internal and external sources of liquidity, and briefly discuss any material unused sources of liquid assets.

   (ii) Capital resources.

      (A) Describe the registrant's material cash requirements, including commitments for capital expenditures, as of the end of the latest fiscal period, the anticipated source of funds needed to satisfy such cash requirements and the general purpose of such requirements.

      (B) Describe any known material trends, favorable or unfavorable, in the registrant's capital resources. Indicate any reasonably likely material changes in the mix and relative cost of such resources. The discussion must consider changes among equity, debt, and any off-balance sheet financing arrangements.

As you'll note from the guidance above, the primary goal of the liquidity and capital resources section is to provide additional information and context related to a company's ability to meet its short-term obligations as well as a company's plans for using cash (both in the short and long-term). Specifically, the guidance requires that companies discuss known contractual obligations in this section.

Liquidity

In its most basic form, liquidity refers to a company's ability to convert an asset or a security into cash. In other words, how quickly can an asset be bought or sold and turned into cash by the owner of that asset. At the risk of stating the obvious, having liquidity is generally preferred as opposed to having more value tied up in those types of assets that aren't as readily convertible into cash.

Cash Requirements

The topic of cash, and more specifically, cash requirements, is an area that is further explored within the previous SEC interpretive guidance. In it, the SEC notes that in order to identify known material cash requirements, companies should consider whether the following information would have a **material impact** on liquidity:

- Funds necessary to:
  - Maintain current operations
  - Complete projects underway
  - Achieve stated objectives or plans

- Commitments for capital or other expenditures

- The reasonably likely exposure to future cash requirements associated with known trends or uncertainties

  — Including an indication of the time periods of likely resolution

In its interpretive guidance, the SEC notes that ". . . one starting point for a company's discussion and analysis of cash requirements is the tabular disclosure of contractual obligations, supplemented with additional information that is material to an understanding of the company's cash requirements." Refer to the following Exhibit, which further expands on this point.

Exhibit 4: Commission Guidance Regarding Management's Discussion and Analysis of Financial Condition and Results of Operations

(IV) Liquidity and Capital Resources

A. Cash Requirements

For example, if a company has incurred debt in material amounts, it should explain the reasons for incurring that debt and the use of the proceeds and analyze how the incurrence of that debt fits into the overall business plan, in each case to the extent material. Where debt has been incurred for general working capital purposes, the anticipated amount and timing of working capital needs should be discussed, to the extent material.

Companies should address, where material, the difficulties involved in assessing the effect of the amount and timing of uncertain events, such as loss contingencies, on cash requirements and liquidity. Any such discussion should be specific to the circumstances and informative, and companies should avoid generic or boilerplate disclosure. In addition, because of these difficulties and uncertainties, companies should consider whether they need to make or change disclosure in connection with quarterly as well as annual reports.

As you'll note from the preceding Exhibit, the SEC notes that a company should explain the reasons for incurring debt and the use of the proceeds. As an example of how this disclosure objective is achieved, the SEC notes that debt may have been issued to fund the construction of a new plant, which will allow the company to expand its operations into a specific geographic area. Furthermore, the SEC notes that understanding this relationship as well as the expected commencement date of plant operations puts the cash requirement for the debt into an appropriate context to understand liquidity.

Sources and Uses of Cash

Another key focus area with respect to liquidity relates to the sources and uses of cash. However, this section of the MD&A should not simply give a description of the various inflows and outflows of cash (which would instead simply be found within the statement of cash flows). Recall the purposes of MD&A in general. It should reflect information that is not already evident based on an investors review of a company's consolidated financial statements. That said, an investor can generally understand how cash has been earned and used by looking at a company's statement of cash flows. Because of this, the SEC notes that MD&A should focus on the "primary drivers of and other material factors necessary to an understanding of the company's cash flows and the indicative value of historical cash flows." The SEC further notes that "in addition to explaining how the cash requirements identified in MD&A fit into a company's overall business plan, the company should focus on the resources available to satisfy those cash requirements." Refer to the following Exhibit, which offers some additional interpretive guidance from the SEC on this topic.

¶807

> **Exhibit 5: Commission Guidance Regarding Management's Discussion and Analysis of Financial Condition and Results of Operations**
>
> (IV) Liquidity and Capital Resources
>
> B. Sources and Uses of Cash
>
> Where there has been material variability in historical cash flows, MD&A should focus on the underlying reasons for the changes, as well as on their reasonably likely impact on future cash flows and cash management decisions. Even where reported amounts of cash provided and used by operations, investing activities or financing have been consistent, if the underlying sources of those cash flows have materially varied, analysis of that variability should be provided. The discussion and analysis of liquidity should focus on material changes in operating, investing, and financing cash flows, as depicted in the statement of cash flows, and the reasons underlying those changes.

As you know, cash flows on a company's statement of cash flows are categorized as cash flows from operating activities, cash flows from financing activities, or cash flows from investing activities. The accounting requirements with respect to the statement of cash flows are prescribed within ASC Topic No. 230. Like other ASC Topics, this topic includes a discussion of the objectives of the guidance, certain scope exceptions, a glossary, as well as presentation and disclosure matters.

Of particular interest in the MD&A guidance provided by the SEC is cash flows from operating activities. As a refresher, ASC Topic 230 provides specific examples of both inflows and outflows as it relates to operating activities. Examples of cash inflows (from the ASC Topic) as it relates to operating activities include the following:

- Cash receipts from returns on loans, other debt instruments of other entities, and equity securities—interest and dividends;
- Cash receipts from sales of goods or services, including receipts from collection or sale of accounts and both short- and long-term notes receivable from customers arising from those sales;
- All other cash receipts that do not stem from transactions defined as investing or financing activities, such as amounts received to settle lawsuits or certain proceeds of insurance settlements

On the other hand, the following transactions are examples of cash outflows as it relates to operating activities:

- Cash payments to acquire materials for manufacture or goods for resale, including principal payments on accounts and both short- and long-term notes payable to suppliers for those materials or goods;
- Cash payments to governments for taxes, duties, fines, and other fees or penalties;
  - This would include the cash that would have been paid for income taxes if increases in the value of equity instruments issued under share-based payment arrangements that are not included in the cost of goods or services recognizable for financial reporting purposes also had not been deductible in determining taxable income;
- Cash payments to other suppliers and employees for other goods or services;
- Cash payment made to settle an asset retirement obligation;
- Cash payments to lenders and other creditors for interest; and
- All other cash payments that do not stem from transactions defined as investing or financing activities, such as payments to settle lawsuits, cash contributions to charities, and cash refunds to customers.

¶807

Now that you have a good refresher on what are cash flows from operating activities, let's explore the guidance further on this topic. Take a look at the following Exhibit, which provides some of the interpretive guidance provided by the SEC on this topic.

Exhibit 6: Commission Guidance Regarding Management's Discussion and Analysis of Financial Condition and Results of Operations

(IV) Liquidity and Capital Resources

B. Sources and Uses of Cash—I. Operations

The discussion and analysis of operating cash flows should not be limited by the manner of presentation in the statement of cash flows. Alternate accounting methods of deriving and presenting cash flows exist, and while they generally yield the same numeric result in the major captions, they involve the disclosure of different types of information. When preparing the discussion and analysis of operating cash flows, companies should address material changes in the underlying drivers (e.g., cash receipts from the sale of goods and services and cash payments to acquire materials for manufacture or goods for resale), rather than merely describe items identified on the face of the statement of cash flows, such as the reconciling items used in the indirect method of presenting cash flows.

For example, consider a company that reports an overall increase in the components of its working capital other than cash with the effect of having a material decrease in net cash provided by operations in the current period. If the increase in working capital was driven principally by an increase in accounts receivable that is attributable not to an increase in sales, but rather to a revised credit policy resulting in an extended payment period for customers, these facts would need to be addressed in MD&A to the extent material, along with the resulting decrease in cash provided by operations, if not otherwise apparent. In addition, if there is a material trend or uncertainty, the impact of the new credit policy on cash flows from operations should be disclosed. While a cash flow statement prepared using the indirect method would report that various individual components of working capital increased or decreased during the period by a specified amount, it would not provide a sufficient basis for a reader to analyze the change. If the company reports negative cash flows from operations, the disclosure provided in MD&A should clearly identify this condition, discuss the operational reasons for the condition if material, and explain how the company intends to meet its cash requirements and maintain operations. If the company relies on external financing in these situations, disclosure of that fact and the company's assessment of whether this financing will continue to be available, and on what terms, should be considered and may be required.

As you'll note from the Exhibit above, the key takeaway is that companies shouldn't limit their discussion in MD&A based on the presentation format within the statement of cash flows. Instead, companies should strive to address material changes in the underlying drivers instead of simply describing items identified included within the statement of cash flows.

Financing Considerations

Another important area the SEC expects appropriate information be included in MD&A relates to financing. More specifically, this relates to areas such as debt instruments, guarantees, as well as related covenants. In situations when these financing considerations are material, companies are required to provide information about their historical financing arrangements and their importance to cash flows. Examples cited by the SEC for which they would expect disclosure include the following (if applicable):

- The company's external debt financing
- The company's use of off-balance sheet financing arrangements
- The company's issuance or purchase of derivative instruments linked to its stock
- The company's use of stock as a form of liquidity

The SEC also requires that companies provide appropriate disclosure about their plans to raise capital, either through debt or equity. The SEC notes the following as an example of a situation where they would likely expect to see appropriate disclosure:

> Where a company has decided to raise or seeks to raise material external equity or debt financing, or if it is reasonably likely to do so in the future, discussion and analysis of the amounts or ranges involved, the nature and the terms of the financing, other features of the financing and plans, and the impact on the company's cash position and liquidity (as well as results of operations in the case of matters such as interest payments) should be considered and may be required.

Recall from the preceding paragraph that covenants are an area where the SEC would look to companies to provide certain disclosures in MD&A. As you likely know, a debt covenant (sometimes also called a *loan covenant*) is simply a condition (or conditions) in a loan agreement that requires the borrower to meet certain conditions or to not take certain action. Simply put, it's restrictions on what a borrower can and can't do while they are subject to a loan agreement. The SEC notes that there are "at least **two scenarios** in which companies should consider whether discussion and analysis of material covenants related to their outstanding debt may be required." These two scenarios are presented in the following Exhibit.

Exhibit 7: Commission Guidance Regarding Management's Discussion and Analysis of Financial Condition and Results of Operations

(IV) Liquidity and Capital Resources

C. Debt Instruments, Guarantees and Related Covenants

First, companies that are, or are reasonably likely to be, in breach of such covenants must disclose material information about that breach and analyze the impact on the company if material. That analysis should include, as applicable and to the extent material:

• The steps that the company is taking to avoid the breach;
• The steps that the company intends to take to cure, obtain a waiver of or otherwise address the breach;
• The impact or reasonably likely impact of the breach (including the effects of any cross-default or cross-acceleration or similar provisions) on financial condition or operating performance; and
• Alternate sources of funding to pay off resulting obligations or replace funding.

Second, companies should consider the impact of debt covenants on their ability to undertake additional debt or equity financing. Examples of these covenants include, but are not limited to, debt incurrence restrictions, limitations on interest payments, restrictions on dividend payments and various debt ratio limits. If these covenants limit, or are reasonably likely to limit, a company's ability to undertake financing to a material extent, the company is required to discuss the covenants in question and the consequences of the limitation to the company's financial condition and operating performance. Disclosure of alternate sources of funding and, to the extent material, the consequences (including but not limited to the cost) of accessing them should also be considered and may be required.

¶ 808 ITEM 303—LIQUIDITY AND CAPITAL RESOURCES: ILLUSTRATIVE EXAMPLES

Now that you've familiarized yourself with some of the requirements with respect to what should and should not be disclosed within this section of the MD&A, let's take a look at some real-world examples of public companies. A quick word of caution: The following examples are just that, examples. They are not being presented here to suggest that they reflect a best practice and/or that their disclosures presented satisfy all of the preceding guidance. You'll also note that as you look through the respective

SEC filings, while MD&A shows up at Item 7 in all the 10-Ks, the names of the sections as well as the expansiveness of the information provided can vary considerably. That said, some of the examples presented will only be excerpts from the referenced filing. If you want to review the entirety of the filing, you can pull it up on the SEC.gov website.

EXAMPLE: HP, Inc. Form 10-K for the fiscal year ended October 31, 2021

Item 7. Management's Discussion and Analysis of Financial Condition and Results of Operations

Liquidity and Capital Resources (*partial excerpt*)

We use cash generated by operations as our primary source of liquidity. While the impacts from the COVID-19 pandemic were originally expected to be temporary, however, with the emergence of new variants, there remains uncertainty around the extent and duration of the pandemic and how our liquidity and working capital needs may be impacted in the future periods as a result. We believe that current cash, cash flow from operating activities, new borrowings, available commercial paper authorization and the credit facilities will be sufficient to meet HP's operating cash requirements, planned capital expenditures, interest and principal payments on all borrowings, pension and post-retirement funding requirements, authorized share repurchases and annual dividend payments for the foreseeable future. Additionally, if suitable acquisition opportunities arise, the Company may obtain all or a portion of the required financing through additional borrowings. While our access to capital markets may be constrained and our cost of borrowing may increase under certain business, market and economic conditions, our access to a variety of funding sources to meet our liquidity needs is designed to facilitate continued access to capital resources under all such conditions. Our liquidity is subject to various risks including the risks identified in the section entitled "Risk Factors" in Item 1A and market risks identified in the section entitled "Quantitative and Qualitative Disclosures about Market Risk" in Item 7A, which are incorporated herein by reference.

During the fiscal year 2021, HP completed four acquisitions with a combined purchase price of $854 million, net of cash acquired, of which $400 million was recorded as goodwill and $385 million as intangible assets related to these acquisitions. For more information, see Note 18, "Acquisitions", to the Consolidated Financial Statements in Item 8 of Part II of this report, which is incorporated herein by reference.

Our cash and cash equivalents balances are held in numerous locations throughout the world. We utilize a variety of planning and financing strategies in an effort to ensure that our worldwide cash is available when and where it is needed. Amounts held outside of the United States are generally utilized to support non-U.S. liquidity needs and may from time to time be distributed to the United States. The Tax Cuts and Jobs Act ("TCJA") made significant changes to the U.S. tax law, including a one-time transition tax on accumulated foreign earnings. The payments associated with this one-time transition tax will be paid over eight years and began in fiscal year 2019. We expect a significant portion of the cash and cash equivalents held by our foreign subsidiaries will no longer be subject to U.S. income tax upon a subsequent repatriation to the United States as a result of the transition tax on accumulated foreign earnings. However, a portion of this cash may still be subject to foreign income tax or withholding tax upon repatriation. As we evaluate the future cash needs of our operations, we may revise the amount of foreign earnings considered to be permanently reinvested in our foreign subsidiaries and how to utilize such funds, including reducing our gross debt level, or other uses.

EXAMPLE: Apple Inc. Form 10-K for the fiscal year ended September 25, 2021

Item 7. Management's Discussion and Analysis of Financial Condition and Results of Operations

Liquidity and Capital Resources

The Company believes its balances of cash, cash equivalents and unrestricted marketable securities, which totaled $172.6 billion as of September 25, 2021, along with cash generated by ongoing operations and continued access to debt markets, will be sufficient to satisfy its cash requirements and capital return program over the next 12 months and beyond.

The Company's material cash requirements include the following contractual and other obligations.

Debt

As of September 25, 2021, the Company had outstanding floating-and fixed-rate notes with varying maturities for an aggregate principal amount of $118.1 billion (collectively the "Notes"), with $9.6 billion payable within 12 months. Future interest payments associated with the Notes total $39.5 billion, with $2.9 billion payable within 12 months.

The Company also issues unsecured short-term promissory notes ("Commercial Paper") pursuant to a commercial paper program. As of September 25, 2021, the Company had $6.0 billion of Commercial Paper outstanding, all of which was payable within 12 months.

Leases

The Company has lease arrangements for certain equipment and facilities, including retail, corporate, manufacturing and data center space. As of September 25, 2021, the Company had fixed lease payment obligations of $14.6 billion, with $1.8 billion payable within 12 months.

Manufacturing Purchase Obligations

The Company utilizes several outsourcing partners to manufacture subassemblies for the Company's products and to perform final assembly and testing of finished products. The Company also obtains individual components for its products from a wide variety of individual suppliers. Outsourcing partners acquire components and build product based on demand information supplied by the Company, which typically covers periods up to 150 days. As of September 25, 2021, the Company had manufacturing purchase obligations of $54.8 billion, with $54.7 billion payable within 12 months. The Company's manufacturing purchase obligations are primarily noncancelable.

Other Purchase Obligations

The Company's other purchase obligations primarily consist of noncancelable obligations to acquire capital assets, including product tooling and manufacturing process equipment, and noncancelable obligations related to advertising, content creation and Internet and telecommunications services. As of September 25, 2021, the Company had other purchase obligations of $8.3 billion, with $4.8 billion payable within 12 months.

¶808

Deemed Repatriation Tax Payable

As of September 25, 2021, the balance of the deemed repatriation tax payable imposed by the U.S. Tax Cuts and Jobs Act of 2017 (the "Act") was $24.6 billion, none of which is payable within 12 months.

In addition to its cash requirements, the Company has a capital return program authorized by the Board of Directors. The Program does not obligate the Company to acquire any specific number of shares. As of September 25, 2021, the Company's quarterly cash dividend was $0.22 per share. The Company intends to increase its dividend on an annual basis, subject to declaration by the Board of Directors.

STUDY QUESTIONS

1. In its interpretive guidance, the SEC notes that a "good introduction" in the MD&A should include each of the following, *except?*

   a. The accounting principle methods used by the company

   b. Economic or industry-wide factors relevant to the company

   c. Discussion about how the company earns revenues and income and generates cash

   d. Insight into material opportunities, challenges, and risks

2. A discussion of the sources and uses of cash should be included in which section of MD&A?

   a. Results of operations

   b. Critical accounting estimates

   c. Liquidity and capital resources

   d. Risks and uncertainties

¶ 809 ITEM 303—RESULTS OF OPERATIONS

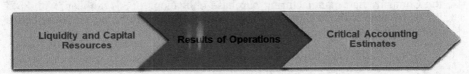

With the discussion of liquidity and capital resources behind us, let's now focus on the next primary area related to the results of operations. Continuing with our approach from the last area, let's first take a look at the detailed guidance provided by the SEC related to this area in the following Exhibit.

¶809

Exhibit 8: § 229.303 (Item 303)(b)(2) – Results of Operations

(i) Describe any unusual or infrequent events or transactions or any significant economic changes that materially affected the amount of reported income from continuing operations and, in each case, indicate the extent to which income was so affected. In addition, describe any other significant components of revenues or expenses that, in the registrant's judgment, would be material to an understanding of the registrant's results of operations.

(ii) Describe any known trends or uncertainties that have had or that are reasonably likely to have a material favorable or unfavorable impact on net sales or revenues or income from continuing operations. If the registrant knows of events that are reasonably likely to cause a material change in the relationship between costs and revenues (such as known or reasonably likely future increases in costs of labor or materials or price increases or inventory adjustments), the change in the relationship must be disclosed.

(iii) If the statement of comprehensive income presents material changes from period to period in net sales or revenue, if applicable, describe the extent to which such changes are attributable to changes in prices or to changes in the volume or amount of goods or services being sold or to the introduction of new products or services.

Clearly you know that the results of operations can often be reviewed by studying a company's income statement and its statement of cash flows. However, remember that the MD&A section is not meant to serve as simply a "rinse and repeat" type description of information that can already be gleaned from several of the financial statements. Instead, you'll note the theme in the previous exhibit, most prominently in the first two bullet points. The results of operations area of MD&A should present those transactions/events that are **unusual or infrequent**, and it should present **significant economic changes** that materially affected the amount of income reported. In addition to these points, it should be reserved for discussions about **known trends or uncertainties** that may have had a positive or negative impact on income from continuing operations.

Let's take a look at some more specifics with respect to this area. If you refer to the SEC's Division of Corporate Finance—Financial Reporting Manual, specifically Topic 9 ("Management's Discussion and Analysis of Financial Position and Results of Operations (MD&A)"), Section 9220 ("Results of Operations") notes that the following disclosures are required by Item 303:

- Any unusual or infrequent event or transaction or any significant economic change that materially affected the amount of reported income from continuing operations

- Significant components of revenues and expenses that are necessary in order to understand the results of operations (e.g., segmental information)

- Any known trends or uncertainties that have had or that the registrant reasonably expects will have a material favorable or unfavorable impact on net sales or revenues or income from continuing operations

- If events that are likely to cause a material change in the relationship between costs and revenues (increases in labor costs or raw materials for example), the change in the relationship should be disclosed

- To the extent there is a material increase in net sales, discuss the price versus volume mix (whether the overall increase is attributable to increases in prices or increases in the volume of goods and services being sold)

Additionally, refer to the following Exhibit, which provides additional guidance included within the Financial Reporting Manual related to the area of results of operations.

¶809

Exhibit 9: SEC Division of Corporate Finance—Financial Reporting Manual

Topic 9220.3 through 5

In order to comply with the requirement to discuss significant components of revenue and expenses, registrants will often provide a discussion along segmental lines (as determined under SFAS 131 [ASC 280]). Segment analysis is usually necessary to enable a reader to understand the consolidated amounts, but it should not result in repetitive disclosure that lengthens MD&A unnecessarily, or obscures salient information. The discussion and analysis of segments may be integrated with the discussion of the consolidated amounts to avoid unnecessary duplication. The discussion and analysis should be comprehensive. All components of the registrant's results of operations, including those that may not be allocated to the segments in determining the segmental profit or loss (such as certain corporate overhead items or income taxes for example) should be discussed.

Registrants should consider discussing and analyzing the tax implications related to material transactions, trends and other important items impacting their business as disclosed elsewhere in MD&A. A discussion of the nature and impact of significant tax rate reconciling items should also be considered. For example, discuss the tax rate reconciling item resulting from a change in assumptions related to an unrecognized tax benefit or a different final resolution related to the unrecognized benefit. Similarly, when uncertain tax positions are a critical accounting policy, MD&A should address why the assumptions were changed or why the actual resolution differed from management's assumption.

Registrants should address the underlying reasons for changes in the price versus volume mix. For example, if sales declined because the volume of goods sold decreased by 20%, but this was offset by a 10% increase in price, the discussion in MD&A should not stop once it identifies the price and volume components. In this example, the underlying factors that contributed to the decline in volume as well as the increase in selling prices should also be discussed. In addition, discussions about changes in the price vs. volume mix should consider changes in foreign currency fluctuations.

The SEC's Financial Reporting Manual notes that the results of operations may not always be prepared on a consistent basis. In other words, events such as a material acquisition or disposition could make the results of operations not perfectly comparable as if one of these significant events did not occur. When this occurs, the SEC notes companies may need to consider whether they need to supplement the discussion based upon pro forma financial information. Furthermore, the SEC notes that "this supplemental discussion may be meaningful in the case of a material acquisition, but generally would not be appropriate in the case of freshstart accounting." An example provided within the SEC's Reporting Manual is included below (9220.8):

> Assume a material acquisition occurs on August 31, 2007, and the registrant is a calendar year-end company. In accordance with the Form 8-K requirements, pro forma financial information prepared in accordance with S-X Article 11 is prepared for the year ended December 31, 2006, and the interim period ended June 30, 2007, and filed on the Form 8-K. When preparing its MD&A for the Form 10-K for the year ended December 31, 2007, the registrant could elect to supplement the discussion of its historical results with a discussion based on S-X Article 11 pro forma information for the year ended December 31, 2007, that gives effect to the August 31, 2007, acquisition. The pro forma December 31, 2007, information would then be compared to the pro forma information for the year ended December 31, 2006, previously filed via a Form 8-K. This discussion would be in addition to a comparison of the audited financial statements, which would reflect the acquisition occurring in mid-2007. A supplemental discussion based on pro forma financial information in more detail than revenues and costs of revenues for the year ended December 31, 2005, would not be appropriate. The comparison of results of operations and financial condition for the year ended December 31, 2005, to December 31, 2006, would be on an as

reported (and audited) basis and would not reflect any impact of the acquisition. In its Form 10-K for the year ended December 31, 2008, the registrant may carry forward the discussion of the pro forma results for the year ended December 31, 2006, and 2007 as a supplement to the discussion of the audited financial statements. No adjustments would be appropriate or necessary to the year ended December 31, 2008, as the acquisition would be reflected in the audited financial statements for the entire year.

To summarize, the discussion in MD&A related to the results of operations should not simply present results. Instead, recall that one of the fundamental objectives of MD&A is to see through the eyes of management. In order to meet this objective, companies should strive to explain the results such that it is informative to the investor and provides them important information that cannot be readily determined from a cursory review of the actual financial statements.

¶ 810 ITEM 303—RESULTS OF OPERATIONS: ILLUSTRATIVE EXAMPLE

Continuing on with our previous approach, we'll now take a look at an example of how the results of operations are presented from a public company. Again, it is not being presented here to suggest that it reflects a best practice and/or that the company's disclosures presented satisfy all of the preceding guidance presented. Instead, it serves to provide a bit of a real-world example of how some companies elect to meet these disclosure requirements.

EXAMPLE: Walmart Inc. Form 10-K for the fiscal year ended January 31, 2022

Item 7. Management's Discussion and Analysis of Financial Condition and Results of Operations

Results of Operations (*partial excerpt*)

Our total revenues, which includes net sales and membership and other income, increased $13.6 billion or 2.4% and $35.2 billion or 6.7% for fiscal 2022 and 2021, respectively, when compared to the previous fiscal year. These increases in revenues were primarily due to increases in net sales, which increased $12.5 billion or 2.3% and $35.3 billion or 6.8% for fiscal 2022 and 2021, respectively, when compared to the previous fiscal year. For fiscal 2022, the increase was primarily due to strong positive comparable sales for the Walmart U.S. and Sam's Club segments which benefited from strong U.S. consumer spending and some inflation, along with positive comparable sales in most of our remaining international markets. The increase was partially offset by a $32.6 billion net sales decrease primarily related to the divestiture of our operations in the U.K. and Japan, which closed in the first quarter of fiscal 2022. Net sales also benefited from a $4.5 billion positive impact of fluctuations in currency exchange rates during fiscal 2022. For fiscal 2021, the increase was primarily due to strong positive comparable sales for the Walmart U.S. and Sam's Club segments as well as positive comparable sales in the majority of our international markets resulting from increased demand stemming from the COVID-19 pandemic. Overall net sales growth was strong despite certain operating limitations in several international markets in the second quarter of fiscal 2021 due to government regulations and precautionary measures taken as a result of the COVID-19 pandemic. The net sales increase was partially offset by a negative impact from fluctuations in currency exchange rates of $5.0 billion.

Our gross profit rate increased 14 and 20 basis points for fiscal 2022 and 2021, respectively, when compared to the previous fiscal year. For fiscal 2022, the increase was primarily due to price management in the Walmart U.S. segment driven by cost inflation as well as merchandise mix, partially offset by increased supply chain costs. For fiscal 2021, the increase was primarily due to strategic sourcing initiatives, strong sales in higher margin categories, and fewer markdowns. This was partially offset in the Walmart U.S. segment by carryover of prior year price investment as well as the temporary closure of our Auto Care Centers and Vision Centers in response to the COVID-19 pandemic.

For fiscal 2022, operating expenses as a percentage of net sales decreased 19 basis points when compared to the previous fiscal year. Operating expenses as a percentage of net sales benefited from growth in comparable sales and lower incremental COVID-19 related costs of $2.5 billion as compared to the previous year, partially offset by increased wage investments primarily in the Walmart U.S. segment. For fiscal 2021, operating expenses as a percentage of net sales was flat when compared to the previous fiscal year. Operating expenses as a percentage of net sales benefited from strong growth in comparable sales, offset by $4.0 billion of incremental costs related to the COVID-19 pandemic.

STUDY QUESTIONS

3. Which of the following MD&A areas should present those transactions/events that are unusual or infrequent, as well as significant economic changes that materially affected the amount of income reported?

   a. Critical accounting estimates

   b. Liquidity and capital resources

   c. Sources and uses of cash

   d. Results of operations

4. Each of the following statements is correct with respect to the results of operations section as noted in the SEC's Division of Corporate Finance—Financial Reporting Manual, *except?*

   a. Companies do not need to consider underlying reasons for changes in the price versus volume mix.

   b. Segment analysis is usually necessary to enable a reader to understand the consolidated amounts.

   c. Discussion and analysis of segments may be integrated with the discussion of the consolidated amounts to avoid unnecessary duplication.

   d. Companies should consider discussing and analyzing the tax implications related to material transactions.

¶ 811 ITEM 303—CRITICAL ACCOUNTING ESTIMATES

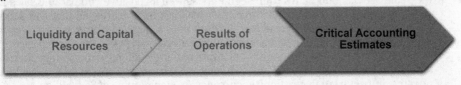

Our third and final section, as noted in the illustration above, relates to critical accounting estimates. Continuing with our approach from the last two areas, let's first take a look at the detailed guidance provided by the SEC related to this area in the following Exhibit.

Exhibit 10: § 229.303 (Item 303)(b)(3)—Critical Accounting Estimates

Critical accounting estimates are those estimates made in accordance with generally accepted accounting principles that involve a significant level of estimation uncertainty and have had or are reasonably likely to have a material impact on the financial condition or results of operations of the registrant. Provide qualitative and quantitative information necessary to understand the estimation uncertainty and the impact the critical accounting estimate has had or is reasonably likely to have on financial condition or results of operations to the extent the information is material and reasonably available. This information should include why each critical accounting estimate is subject to uncertainty and, to the extent the information is material and reasonably available, how much each estimate and/or assumption has changed over a relevant period, and the sensitivity of the reported amount to the methods, assumptions and estimates underlying its calculation.

As the name suggests, partially at least, critical accounting estimates reflect those types of estimates which involve either a significant level of uncertainty and/or a potential material impact on a company's income statement or balance sheet. As the name also suggests, this guidance doesn't simply require companies to disclose all of their accounting estimates. Far from it. Instead, it requires only those estimates that are in fact critical.

In its interpretations publication, the SEC notes that companies should consider whether they have made accounting estimates or assumptions where both of the following are applicable:

- The nature of the estimates or assumptions are material due to the levels of subjectivity and judgment necessary to account for highly uncertain matters or the susceptibility of such matters to change

- The impact of the estimates and assumptions on financial condition or operating performance is material

When both of the conditions are met, companies should make appropriate disclosures of their critical accounting estimates. If the contrary holds true, it is likely that disclosure is unnecessary.

Accounting Policy Disclosures versus Critical Accounting Estimates

One question that often arises in this area is the difference in the critical accounting estimates section in MD&A versus that of the accounting policies disclosures in a company's notes to its financial statements. Simply put, the SEC notes that "the discussion in MD&A should present a company's analysis of the **uncertainties involved** in applying a principle at a given time or the variability that is reasonably likely to result from its application over time." This is in contrast to the disclosure of a company's accounting principles which center more so around the **methods involved** and may or may not involve this enhanced discussion of the uncertainties involved in applying those principles. Additionally, the discussion of critical accounting estimates in the MD&A section should "supplement, not duplicate, the description of accounting policies that are already disclosed in the notes to the financial statements" and "provide greater insight into the quality and variability of information regarding financial condition and operating performance." Refer to the following Exhibit, which provides additional information from the SEC with respect to this area.

¶811

Exhibit 11: Commission Guidance Regarding Management's Discussion and Analysis of Financial Condition and Results of Operations

(V) Critical Accounting Estimates

A company should address specifically why its accounting estimates or assumptions bear the risk of change. The reason may be that there is an uncertainty attached to the estimate or assumption, or it just may be difficult to measure or value. Equally important, companies should address the questions that arise once the critical accounting estimate or assumption has been identified, by analyzing, to the extent material, such factors as how they arrived at the estimate, how accurate the estimate/assumption has been in the past, how much the estimate/assumption has changed in the past, and whether the estimate/assumption is reasonably likely to change in the future. Since critical accounting estimates and assumptions are based on matters that are highly uncertain, a company should analyze their specific sensitivity to change, based on other outcomes that are reasonably likely to occur and would have a material effect. Companies should provide quantitative as well as qualitative disclosure when quantitative information is reasonably available and will provide material information for investors.

For example, if reasonably likely changes in the long-term rate of return used in accounting for a company's pension plan would have a material effect on the financial condition or operating performance of the company, the impact that could result given the range of reasonably likely outcomes should be disclosed and, because of the nature of estimates of long-term rates of return, quantified.

¶ 812 ITEM 303—CRITICAL ACCOUNTING ESTIMATES: ILLUSTRATIVE EXAMPLES

Continuing on with our previous approach, we'll now take a look at an example of how critical accounting estimates are presented. This example is from Best Buy and only includes a couple of the critical accounting estimates that the company disclosed in their referenced 10-K. You'll note for each one, the company provides a description of the accounting estimate, describes why there are judgments/uncertainties inherent in the process, and also discusses the effects if those estimates were to materially differ from actual results.

EXAMPLE: Best Buy Co. Inc. Form 10-K for the fiscal year ended January 29, 2022

Item 7. Management's Discussion and Analysis of Financial Condition and Results of Operations

Critical Accounting Estimates (*partial excerpt*)

The preparation of our financial statements requires us to make assumptions and estimates about future events and apply judgments that affect the reported amounts of assets, liabilities, revenue, expenses, and the related disclosures. We base our assumptions, estimates and judgments on historical experience, current trends and other factors believed to be relevant at the time our consolidated financial statements are prepared. Because future events and their effects cannot be determined with certainty, actual results could differ from our assumptions and estimates, and such differences could be material.

Vendor Allowances

Description

We receive funds from our merchandise vendors through a variety of programs and arrangements, primarily in the form of purchases-based or sales-based volumes and for product advertising and placement. We recognize allowances based on purchases and sales as a reduction of cost of sales when the associated inventory is sold. Allowances for advertising and placement are recognized as a reduction of cost of sales ratably over the corresponding performance period. Funds that are determined to be a reimbursement of specific, incremental, and identifiable costs incurred to sell a vendor's products are recorded as an offset to the related expense within SG&A when incurred.

Judgments and uncertainties involved in the estimate

Due to the quantity and diverse nature of our vendor agreements, estimates are made to determine the amount of funding to be recognized in earnings or deferred as an offset to inventory. These estimates require a detailed analysis of complex factors, including (1) proper classification of the type of funding received; and (2) the methodology to estimate the portion of purchases-based funding that should be recognized in cost of sales in each period, which considers factors such as inventory turn by product category and actual sell-through of inventory.

Effect if actual results differ from assumptions

A 10% change in our vendor funding deferral as of January 29, 2022, would have affected net earnings by approximately $35 million in fiscal 2022. The overall level of vendor funding deferral has remained relatively stable over the last three fiscal years.

Inventory Markdown

Description

Our merchandise inventories were $6.0 billion as of January 29, 2022. We value our inventory at the lower of cost or net realizable value through the establishment of inventory markdown adjustments. Markdown adjustments reflect the excess of cost over the net recovery we expect to realize from the ultimate sale or other disposal of inventory and establish a new cost basis. No adjustment is recorded for inventory that we are able to return to our vendors for full credit.

Judgments and uncertainties involved in the estimate

Markdown adjustments involve uncertainty because the calculations require management to make assumptions and to apply judgment about the expected revenue and incremental costs we will generate for current inventory. Such estimates include the evaluation of historical recovery rates, as well as factors such as product type and condition, forecasted consumer demand, product lifecycles, promotional environment, vendor return rights and the expected sales channel of ultimate disposition. We also apply judgment in the assumptions about other components of net realizable value, such as vendor allowances and selling costs.

Effect if actual results differ from assumptions

A 10% change in our markdown adjustment as of January 29, 2022, would have affected net earnings by approximately $12 million in fiscal 2022. The level of markdown adjustments has remained relatively stable over the last three fiscal years.

¶ 813 ITEM 303—INTERIM REPORTING REQUIREMENTS

Up until this point in the chapter, we have addressed the three main disclosure categories with respect to Item 303—liquidity and capital resources, results of operations, and critical accounting estimates. As you'll also recall, these are areas that are required to be disclosed with respect to full fiscal years (i.e., 10-Ks). In this section of the chapter, we shift gears and focus on those requirements related to interim periods (i.e., 10-Qs).

The overall guidance for interim periods is pretty straightforward. In short, MD&A discussion in the interim period should focus on **material changes** in those items disclosed in the annual filing. In other words, MD&A would focus on material changes in liquidity and capital resources, material changes in results of operations, and material changes in critical accounting estimates from the most recent 10-K. To continue on with our approach in the earlier sections, let's take a look at the specific SEC guidance in Item 303 related to this area.

Exhibit 12: § 229.303 (Item 303)(c)—Interim Periods

(1) **Material changes in financial condition.** Discuss any material changes in financial condition from the end of the preceding fiscal year to the date of the most recent interim balance sheet provided. If the interim financial statements include an interim balance sheet as of the corresponding interim date of the preceding fiscal year, any material changes in financial condition from that date to the date of the most recent interim balance sheet provided also must be discussed. If discussions of changes from both the end and the corresponding interim date of the preceding fiscal year are required, the discussions may be combined at the discretion of the registrant.

(2) **Material changes in results of operations**

(i) Discuss any material changes in the registrant's results of operations with respect to the most recent fiscal year-to-date period for which a statement of comprehensive income is provided and the corresponding year-to-date period of the preceding fiscal year.

(ii) Discuss any material changes in the registrant's results of operations with respect to either the most recent quarter for which a statement of comprehensive income is provided and the corresponding quarter for the preceding fiscal year or, in the alternative, the most recent quarter for which a statement of comprehensive income is provided and the immediately preceding sequential quarter. If the latter immediately preceding sequential quarter is discussed, then provide in summary form the financial information for that immediately preceding sequential quarter that is subject of the discussion or identify the registrant's prior filings on EDGAR that present such information. If there is a change in the form of presentation from period to period that forms the basis of comparison from previous periods provided pursuant to this paragraph, the registrant must discuss the reasons for changing the basis of comparison and provide both comparisons in the first filing in which the change is made.

As you'll note from the guidance above, it's fairly simple to understand the key takeaway here. If there have been material changes to those areas previously disclosed in the most recent 10-K, then those need to be properly addressed within the respective interim period. If there have not been material changes, then no disclosures are likely necessary.

¶ 814 ITEM 303—INTERIM REPORTING REQUIREMENTS: ILLUSTRATIVE EXAMPLE

Continuing on with our previous approach, we'll take a look at an example of how this interim information is presented within the MD&A section. Again, this example is not being presented to reflect a best practice and/or that their disclosures presented satisfy all of the preceding guidance presented.

EXAMPLE: IBM Corporation Form 10-Q For the quarterly period ended September 30, 2021

Item 2. Management's Discussion and Analysis of Financial Condition and Results of Operations

Liquidity and Capital Resources

In our 2020 Annual Report, on pages 56 to 58, there is a discussion of our liquidity including two tables that present three years of data. The table presented on page 56 includes net cash from operating activities, cash and cash equivalents, restricted cash and short-term marketable securities, and the size of our global credit facilities for each of the past three years. For the nine months ended, or at, as applicable, September 30, 2021, those amounts are $10.3 billion of net cash from operating activities, $8.4 billion of cash and cash equivalents, restricted cash, and short-term marketable securities and $10.0 billion in global credit facilities, respectively. While we have no current plans to draw on these credit facilities, they are available as back-up liquidity.

On July 9, 2019, we closed the acquisition of Red Hat for cash consideration of $34.8 billion. The transaction was funded through a combination of cash on hand and proceeds from debt issuances. In order to reduce this debt and return to target leverage ratios within a couple of years, we suspended our share repurchase program at the time of the Red Hat acquisition closing.

In October 2021, Moody's downgraded our long-term debt rating from A2 to A3 and our commercial paper rating from Prime-1 to Prime-2. IBM has ample financial flexibility, supported by our strong liquidity position and cash flows, to operate at a single A credit rating. Debt levels have decreased $7.0 billion from December 31, 2020, and $18.5 billion from our peak levels on June 30, 2019 (immediately preceding the Red Hat acquisition) and we will continue to deleverage throughout 2021 utilizing our debt maturities schedule.

¶ 815 SEC VIEWS—HOW TO IMPROVE MD&A

Up to this point in the chapter, we've focused on the core requirements of MD&A and presented lots of real-world examples of disclosures made by well-known public companies. In this section of the chapter, we turn our attention to some of the points made by the SEC as it relates to these requirements, and how companies can better achieve the objectives.

In its previously referenced interpretations document, the SEC notes the following:

In addition to enhancing MD&A through the use of clearer language and presentation, many companies could improve their MD&A by focusing on the most important information disclosed in MD&A. Disclosure should emphasize material information that is required or promotes understanding and de-emphasize (or, if appropriate, delete) immaterial information that is not required and does not promote understanding.

In order to accomplish the objective of enhancing MD&A, the SEC provides the following four suggestions. We'll discuss each of these in the following few sections of this chapter:

- Focus on key indicators of financial condition and operating performance
- Focus on materiality
- Focus on material trends and uncertainties
- Focus on analysis

Focus on Key Indicators of Financial Condition and Operating Performance

As you recall from some of the earlier discussions, one of the key objectives of MD&A is to provide investors with a view of the company similar to that with which management is provided (i.e., through the eyes of management). The SEC notes that "financial measures generally are the starting point in ascertaining these key variables and other factors." They go on to note that "however, financial measures often tell only part of how a company manages its business" and companies should consider whether "disclosure of all key variables and other factors that management uses to manage the business would be material to investors, and therefore required." Refer to the following Exhibit, which provides additional guidance provided by the SEC.

Exhibit 13: Commission Guidance Regarding Management's Discussion and Analysis of Financial Condition and Results of Operations

B. The Content and Focus of MD&A

Many companies currently disclose non-financial business and operational data. Academics, authors, and consultants also have researched the types of information, outside of financial statement measures, that would be helpful to investors and other users. Such information may relate to external or macro-economic matters as well as those specific to a company or industry. For example, interest rates or economic growth rates and their anticipated trends can be important variables for many companies. Industry-specific measures can also be important for analysis, although common standards for the measures also are important. Some industries commonly use non-financial data, such as industry metrics and value drivers. Where a company discloses such information, and there is no commonly accepted method of calculating a particular non-financial metric, it should provide an explanation of its calculation to promote comparability across companies within the industry. Finally, companies may use non-financial performance measures that are company-specific.

In addition, if companies disclose material information (historical or forward-looking) other than in their filed documents (such as in earnings releases or publicly accessible analysts' calls or companion website postings) they also should evaluate that material information to determine whether it is required to be included in MD&A, either because it falls within a specific disclosure requirement or because its omission would render misleading the filed document in which the MD&A appears. We are not seeking to sweep into MD&A all the information that a company communicates. Rather, companies should consider their communications and determine what information is material and is required in, or would promote understanding of, MD&A.

The key takeaway from the SEC is that "the focus on key performance indicators can be enhanced not only through the language and content of the discussion, but also through a format that will enhance the understanding of the discussion and analysis." For example, the SEC notes that the order of the information is not required to follow the order necessarily presented in the guidance prescribed by Item 303 (i.e., substances over form).

The SEC also notes that MD&A should provide a "frame of reference that allows readers to understand the effects of material changes and events and known material trends and uncertainties arising during the periods being discussed, as well as their relative importance." In order to do this, companies should strive to provide a "**balanced view** of the underlying dynamics of the business." For example, they shouldn't limit themselves to the company's successes.

Focus on Materiality

If you've sensed a theme so far throughout, it's that a company's MD&A must specifically focus on known **material** events and uncertainties that would cause reported financial information not to be necessarily indicative of future operating performance or of future financial condition. At the risk of stating the obvious though, materiality is different based on the company involved. For example, compare the materiality threshold for a company like Apple versus a small publicly traded company. Because of this, the SEC notes that companies must determine "based on their own particular facts and circumstances, whether disclosure of a particular matter is required in MD&A." The SEC does caution that "however, the effectiveness of MD&A decreases with the accumulation of unnecessary detail or duplicative or uninformative disclosure that obscures material information." Refer to the following Exhibit, which provides additional information on the materiality topic.

Exhibit 14: Commission Guidance Regarding Management's Discussion and Analysis of Financial Condition and Results of Operations

B. The Content and Focus of MD&A

As the complexity of business structures and financial transactions increase, and as the activities undertaken by companies become more diverse, it is increasingly important for companies to focus their MD&A on material information. In preparing MD&A, companies should evaluate issues presented in previous periods and consider reducing or omitting discussion of those that may no longer be material or helpful, or revise discussions where a revision would make the continuing relevance of an issue more apparent.

Companies also should focus on an analysis of the consolidated financial condition and operating performance, with segment data provided where material to an understanding of consolidated information. Segment discussion and analysis should be designed to avoid unnecessary duplication and immaterial detail that is not required and does not promote understanding of a company's overall financial condition and operating performance.

One subtle, yet important, point to note here relates to interim period. The SEC notes that companies also must assess the materiality of items in preparing disclosure in their quarterly reports. This is because there may be different "quantitative and qualitative factors to consider when deciding whether to include certain information in a specific quarterly or annual report."

Focus on Material Trends and Uncertainties

The SEC notes in order to understand a company's performance, and the extent to which reported financial information is indicative of future results, one must understand the trends, demands, commitments, events, and uncertainties. Without having this information, investors would not have a good sense for company performance. Because of this, the SEC notes that these disclosures should include the following:

- Consideration of financial, operational, and other information known to the company
- Identification, based on this information, of known trends and uncertainties
- Assessment of whether these trends and uncertainties will have, or are reasonably likely to have, a material impact on the company's liquidity, capital resources or results of operations

The SEC goes on to further note that "in identifying known material trends and uncertainties, companies should consider the substantial amount of financial and non-financial information available to them, and whether or not the available information itself is required to be disclosed." Said another way, over time this information may in fact reveal a trend or general pattern in activity.

Focus on Analysis

The last key area noted by the SEC is to focus on the analysis. In other words, while companies should be focused on the discussion, they shouldn't lose sight of also incorporating an appropriate analysis. Specifically, this relates to an analysis of those material trends, events, demands, commitments, and uncertainties discussed in the previous section. Refer to the following Exhibit for some additional information from the SEC on this topic.

Exhibit 15: Commission Guidance Regarding Management's Discussion and Analysis of Financial Condition and Results of Operations

B. The Content and Focus of MD&A

Identifying the intermediate effects of trends, events, demands, commitments, and uncertainties alone, without describing the reasons underlying these effects, may not provide sufficient insight for a reader to see the business through the eyes of management. A thorough analysis often will involve discussing both the intermediate effects of those matters and the reasons underlying those intermediate effects. For example, if a company's financial statements reflect materially lower revenues resulting from a decline in the volume of products sold when compared to a prior period, MD&A should not only identify the decline in sales volume, but also should analyze the reasons underlying the decline in sales when the reasons are also material and determinable. The analysis should reveal underlying material causes of the matters described, including for example, if applicable, difficulties in the manufacturing process, a decline in the quality of a product, loss in competitive position and market share, or a combination of conditions.

Similarly, where a company's financial statements reflect material restructuring or impairment charges, or a decline in the profitability of a plant or other business activity, MD&A should also, where material, analyze the reasons underlying these matters, such as an inability to realize previously projected economies of scale, a failure to renew or secure key customer contracts, or a failure to keep downtime at acceptable levels due to aging equipment. Whether favorable or unfavorable conditions constitute or give rise to the material trends, demands, commitments, events, or uncertainties being discussed, the analysis should consist of material substantive information and present a balanced view of the underlying dynamics of the business.

¶ 816 BIG 4 VIEWS—COMMENT LETTER ANALYSIS ON MD&A

As we noted in the introductory section to this chapter, the topic of MD&A has consistently ranked at the top in the overall frequency of SEC comment letters. In PwC's "SEC Comment Letter Trends" publication published on March 28, 2022, the firm notes that MD&A was #2 on the list of the Top 10 most frequent comment letter areas. In EY's publication "SEC Reporting Update—Highlights of Trends in 2021 SEC Comment Letters," the firm notes that MD&A was #2 on the Top 10 list. Additionally, in Deloitte's similar publication, the firm has MD&A ranked at the top of the list for most frequent comment letters. In this final section of the chapter, we'll explore some of the reasons for this "popularity" as well as offer up some insight from several of the Big 4 firms.

Results of Operations

As you recall, this area of MD&A requires companies to disclose any unusual/infrequent events or transactions or any significant economic changes that materially affected the amount of reported income from continuing operations. It also requires companies to disclose any known trends or uncertainties that have had or that are reasonably likely to have a material favorable or unfavorable impact on net sales or revenues or income from continuing operations.

In EY's publication "SEC Reporting Update: Highlights of Trends in 2021 SEC Comment Letters," the firm notes the following with respect to this area:

> The SEC staff often requests that registrants explain the results of their operations with greater specificity, including identifying underlying drivers for each material factor that affected their earnings or is reasonably likely to

have a material effect on future earnings. In addition to commenting on the analysis of changes in revenue, the SEC staff has been commenting on significant components of expenses and provisions. The SEC staff also focuses on performance metrics, including whether registrants have disclosed key metrics used by management that would be material to investors and how those metrics correlate to material changes in the results of operations.

When material effects on results of operations are attributed to a decrease in headcount or other restructuring activities, the SEC staff may ask registrants to discuss their expectations about these activities. When registrants discuss changes in economic conditions, laws, regulations or foreign exchange rates, the SEC staff may ask about the expected effects of these items on revenues, income, and liquidity in future periods.

In its publication, the firm also provides the following excerpt from an actual SEC comment letter:

We note your disclosures regarding the tariff on imports that could adversely affect your costs, supply, or have other material adverse impacts on your business. When considering the requirements of Item 303 (a)(3)(ii) of Regulation S-K, please tell us how you concluded you did not need to describe trends or uncertainties related to these tariffs that have had or that you reasonably expect will have a material favorable or unfavorable impact on net sales or revenues or income from continuing operations, or any material changes in the relationship between costs and revenues.

Deloitte has also provided interpretive guidance in their publication around the results of operations area of MD&A. The firm notes that "SEC staff frequently comments on how a registrant can improve its discussion and analysis of known trends, demands, commitments, events, and uncertainties and their impact on the results of operations." Deloitte further notes that the SEC has also encouraged companies to "use appropriate metrics to help them tell their story" and to "present changes in a tabular format." Take a look at the following Exhibit, which provides a few comment letter examples provided by Deloitte in their referenced publication.

Exhibit 16: Deloitte—SEC Comment Letter Considerations, Including Industry Insights (November 2021)

Examples of SEC Comments

Please revise your disclosures to comply with Item 303 of Regulation S-K. In doing so, please be sure to describe the reasons for significant changes in revenues, expenses, cash flows and financial position. It is not sufficient to merely recite the information that is available on the face of the financial statements without describing the events, transactions and economic changes that materially affected the reported amounts.

We note that direct operating expenses increased significantly and in a higher proportion as compared to the percentage increase in revenue for each of your segments and on a consolidated basis. Please revise your disclosures in future filings to separately discuss direct operating expenses and to quantify and discuss factors responsible for changes pursuant to Item 303 of Regulation S-K. As part of your revised disclosure for direct operating expenses and for your existing expense discussion, please quantify each material component when a change is attributed to more than one factor. For example, you state that certain increases were "primarily" attributed to one factor, or "partially offset" by another [factor], or you cite several other factors responsible for the change. In your response, please provide us with an example of the disclosure to be included in future filings. Refer to SEC Release No. 33-8350.

PwC also has similar views which echo that of EY and Deloitte. In their comment letter publication, the firm also highlights that the SEC has a particular focus on the "discussion and analysis of results of operations, including the description and quantification of each material factor, offsetting factors, unusual or infrequent events, and economic developments causing changes in results between periods." Consistent with the other firms, PwC also notes that the SEC is keenly interested in the discussion of "known trends or uncertainties that are reasonably expected to impact near and long-term results."

Critical Accounting Estimates

The MD&A area related to critical accounting estimates is another area that is frequently reviewed by the SEC, though (anecdotally at least) it's likely not as common to receive SEC comments on this area as compared to the results of operations. As you recall from the discussion earlier in this chapter, critical accounting estimates reflect those types of estimates which involve either a significant level of uncertainty and/or a potential material impact on a company's income statement or balance sheet.

In its comment letter publication, EY notes that the SEC staff has frequently found companies' disclosures about critical accounting estimates to be "too general" and that they should "provide a more robust analysis than what is in the significant accounting policies note to the financial statements." Recall from earlier that we indicated that while accounting policies in the notes to the financial statements describe the methods used, the MD&A should instead provide more information and analysis into uncertainties involved in applying the principles disclosed. In its publication, the firm offers the following as an example comment letter from the SEC to a company regarding its critical accounting estimates.

> We note that a sharp decline in your stock price resulted in a significant decline in your market capitalization; however, you concluded that goodwill was not impaired for any business unit but did not provide a discussion of the methodology used to estimate fair value. Tell us how you reconciled and evaluated your market capitalization to the fair value of your reporting units and describe the reasons for significant differences, if any. Please also provide the method(s) you used to estimate the fair value of your reporting units. If more than one method was used, please indicate how you weighted each method. In this regard, please provide qualitative and quantitative descriptions of the material assumptions and factors (e.g., stock prices) used to support each reporting unit's fair value determination and describe the degree of uncertainty associated with your key assumptions. Please refer to Item 303 (a) (3) (ii) of Regulation S-K and SEC Release No. 34-48960.

Liquidity and Capital Resources

The MD&A area related to liquidity and capital resources is again another area that is frequently reviewed and commented on by the SEC. In its publication, EY notes that the SEC frequently requests that companies disclose the following:

- Whether identified trends will continue, and if so, how long they will continue and steps the registrant is taking to address the trends, including plans to remedy any identified material uncertainties or unfavorable trends in short- or long-term liquidity

- An analysis of all internal and external sources of liquidity, beyond cash on hand, as of the balance sheet date

- Amounts outstanding and available at the balance sheet date under each source of liquidity, with a comparison to cash needs over the next 12 months, including any significant planned capital expenditures

- The sufficiency of the amounts available under existing credit arrangements, the anticipated circumstances requiring their use, any uncertainty about the registrant's ability to access these funds when needed and the implications of not being able to access the arrangements

Continuing on with our previous approach, included below is a referenced comment letter example provided by EY in its publication.

> We note that you recently entered into a series agreement with your lenders to extend a significant portion of your near-term debt maturities and to stabilize collateral requirements for your existing surety bond portfolio. Separately, you recently indicated on the earnings call that you may be at risk of breaching a key financial covenant. Please disclose whether you are in compliance with all financial covenants and address the actual or reasonably likely effects of compliance or noncompliance with the financial covenants on your financial condition and liquidity. Refer to section IV.C. of SEC Interpretive Release No. 33-8350.

Deloitte has also offered similar analysis on this MD&A topic. In its publication, the firm notes that SEC staff frequently requests "more meaningful analysis in a registrant's MD&A of material cash requirements, historical sources and uses of cash, and material trends and uncertainties so that investors can understand the registrant's ability to generate cash and meet cash requirements." To help illustrate this point, take a look at the comment letter example included in the following Exhibit.

Exhibit 17: Deloitte—SEC Comment Letter Considerations, Including Industry Insights (November 2021)

3.1.3 Liquidity and Capital Resources

Examples of SEC Comments

In future filings, including your quarterly reports, please revise to disclose whether you believe you have sufficient cash and other types of liquidity available to fund operations and meet your obligations on both a long-term and short-term basis. We would consider long-term to be greater than twelve months.

Your discussion of operating cash flows appears to be a recitation of changes disclosed on the consolidated statement of cash flows. Please revise and expand this discussion to include the primary drivers of, and other material factors necessary to understand, the company's cash flows from operating activities. Refer to section IV.B of SEC Release 33-8350.

[Please] revise the MD&A in your Form 10-Q to address your capital needs for the next twelve months, the material uncertainties surrounding your liquidity, and the impact that those uncertainties could have on your business. Refer to Item 303 of Regulation S-K.

¶ 817 CONCLUSION

As you can note from the discussions throughout this chapter, the topic of MD&A is on the SEC's radar and frequently ranks as one of the most common areas in which the SEC provides comment letters to companies. While it's important to have a good understanding of the requirements outlined within Item 303 with respect to the various areas requiring disclosures, it's equally as important to perform sufficient benchmarking of other similar companies to understand what they are and are not disclosing. Chances are if your industry peers are providing significantly more detail in the areas discussed throughout this chapter, it may be helpful to do a more thorough review of your disclosures to ensure you're meeting the objectives of the guidance.

STUDY QUESTIONS

5. Critical accounting estimates are those estimates made in accordance with GAAP that involve a significant level of _____ and have had or are reasonably likely to have a _____ impact on the financial condition or results of operations of a company.

    a. Judgment / likely

    b. Estimation uncertainty / likely

    c. Judgment / material

    d. Estimation uncertainty / material

6. MD&A discussion in the interim period should focus on _____ changes in those items disclosed in the most recent annual filing.

    a. Material

    b. Likely

    c. Measurable

    d. Remote

MODULE 3: SEC REPORTING—CHAPTER 9: Non-GAAP Financial Measures

¶ 901 WELCOME

This chapter provides an overview of non-GAAP financial measures with a particular emphasis on comments from the U.S. Securities and Exchange Commission (SEC) and the Financial Accounting Standards Board (FASB), as well as comment letter analysis from several of the Big 4 accounting firms. Non-GAAP financial measures continue to rank at the top of the most frequent comment letters issued by the SEC. As a result, it's important to understand the guidance with respect to these measures to ensure that an entity's financial statements remain GAAP compliant and are not misleading.

¶ 902 LEARNING OBJECTIVES

Upon completion of this chapter, you will be able to:

- Differentiate between a GAAP financial measure and a non-GAAP financial measure
- Recognize examples of different types of non-GAAP financial measures
- Identify which SEC guidance is applicable to different types of non-GAAP financial measures
- Recognize disclosures within the scope of Regulation G
- Identify key requirements included within both Regulation G and Regulation S-K related to these measures

¶ 903 INTRODUCTION

If you're a CPA reviewing this chapter, you're probably quite familiar with many areas of U.S. GAAP (generally accepted accounting principles) and how entities record transactions and present their consolidated financial statements in accordance with U.S. GAAP. However, would it surprise you to know that a vast majority of the entities out there actually provide significant non-GAAP financial measures in their financial filings? You probably have lots of questions to start (e.g., what is a non-GAAP financial measure, why do the regulators care, how do you prevent receiving an SEC comment letter for inappropriate use of one of these measures, etc.). Several of these questions will be explored throughout this chapter. Given the subject of this chapter, there will be many references throughout to relevant SEC guidance and FASB comments, as well as insights and analysis from several of the Big 4 public accounting firms. In the final part of this chapter, we'll review some real-world examples of SEC comment letters issued to entities challenging their use of certain non-GAAP financial measures. You're encouraged to explore many of these resources on your own to obtain a more comprehensive appreciation of the importance of the topic.

¶ 904 WHAT IS A NON-GAAP FINANCIAL MEASURE?

Let's start at the most obvious starting point and define what is a non-GAAP financial measure. Sure, it's a financial measure that is not based on U.S. GAAP, but there's more to it that's worth understanding. Based on the SEC's Financial Reporting Manual (Topic 8: Non-GAAP Measures of Financial Performance, Liquidity, and Net Worth, Section 8120.1), the SEC defines a non-GAAP financial measure as the following:

A non-GAAP financial measure is a numerical measure of a registrant's historical or future financial performance, financial position, or cash flow that:

- Excludes amounts, or is subject to adjustments that have the effect of excluding amounts, that are included in the most directly comparable measure calculated and presented in accordance with GAAP in the statement of comprehensive income, balance sheet or statement of cash flows of the issuer; or

- Includes amounts or is subject to adjustments that have the effect of including amounts, that are excluded from the most directly comparable GAAP measure so calculated and presented.

Furthermore, in the *CPA Journal* article "The Gap Between GAAP and Non-GAAP" (published February 2020), the authors (Theresa F. Henry, PhD, CPA; Rob R. Weitz, PhD; and David A. Rosenthal, PhD) note the following with respect to non-GAAP financial measures:

A non-GAAP financial measure adjusts the most directly comparable GAAP measure reported on the audited financial statements by excluding items the company believes are not good indicators of its performance. One such measure is non-GAAP earnings. The calculation of this measure is highly subjective and is not comparable across entities or industries. Non-GAAP earnings is not a required disclosure, nor is it audited. Initial SEC regulation surrounding this disclosure was issued in 2003, entitled "Conditions for Use of Non-GAAP Financial Measures." The original rule was updated in 2010 and 2016 with the SEC's "Non-GAAP Financial Measures Compliance and Disclosure Interpretations." This guidance has offered varying degrees of rigor with respect to the way non-GAAP earnings should be reported and presented.

Non-GAAP financial measures are not a new thing entities are doing—far from it. However, they have been increasing in use and, in turn, have been increasingly coming into the radar of the regulators over the last several years. As we'll explore later in this chapter, you'll soon note that the topic of non-GAAP financial measures is one of the most frequently received comment letter topics by entities. While other topics such as revenue recognition, segment reporting, MD&A, and others round out some of the other top areas, the topic of non-GAAP financial measures has consistently ranked at the top for several years.

¶ 905 EXAMPLES OF NON-GAAP FINANCIAL MEASURES

There is certainly not an exhaustive list of non-GAAP financial measures. And it goes without saying that as entities continue to stretch the limits on what information they represent as non-GAAP financial measures, the listing will never be complete. We'll take a look at several common examples in the following sections.

In the previously referenced SEC Reporting Manual, Section 8120.2 identifies the following as common examples of measures that meet the definition of non-GAAP financial measures:

- Funds from operations (FFO)
- EBIT / EBITDA / adjusted EBITDA
- Adjusted revenues
- Broadcast cash flow (BCF)

- Free cash flow (FCF)
- Core earnings
- Measures presented on a constant-currency basis (e.g., revenues, operating expenses, etc.)

While you may not be familiar with all of the non-GAAP financial measure examples listed above, you have likely seen several throughout various entities' notes to their financial statements. In fact, EBIT and EBITDA are likely financial metrics that you first came across in one of your first accounting courses in college. It may be puzzling to some to realize that the concept of earnings before interest and taxes (EBIT) is non-GAAP. Other ones, such as free cash flow and/or measures presented on a constant-currency basis, may also be equally as puzzling as they're frequently used by many companies.

As noted above, there are many different types of non-GAAP financial measures. Another common example of these is key performance indicators, or KPIs for short. You've likely heard this term as well. Key performance indicators, as defined by Investopedia, refer to a set of "quantifiable measurements used to gauge a company's overall long-term performance." The Investopedia article on KPIs further notes that they "specifically help determine a company's strategic, financial, and operational achievements, especially compared to those of other businesses within the same sector."

Examples of KPIs are numerous and vary from industry to industry. Still, KPIs can be either financial or nonfinancial in nature. In the FASB online publication "Why the FASB Cares About Non-GAAP Performance Measures," the FASB notes the following as examples of both financial KPIs and nonfinancial KPIs:

- Nonfinancial KPIs:
  - Number of stores
  - Number of employees
  - Number of subscribers
- Financial KPIs:
  - Same-store sales
  - Average revenue per customer
  - Sales per square foot

What Are *Not* Non-GAAP Financial Measures

You have a good awareness now of what is a non-GAAP financial measure. But it's also important to understand what a non-GAAP financial measure is not. Within Regulation G ("General Rules Regarding Disclosure of Non-GAAP Financial Measures") issued by the SEC, the SEC notes the following as *not* being non-GAAP financial measures:

- Operating and other financial measures and ratios or statistical measures calculated using exclusively one or both of:
  - Financial measures calculated in accordance with GAAP; and
  - Operating measures or other measures that are not non-GAAP financial measures
- Financial measures required to be disclosed by GAAP, Commission rules, or a system of regulation of a government or governmental authority or self-regulatory organization that is applicable to the registrant.

Should Stakeholders Trust Non-GAAP Financial Measures?

This is likely a common question that is being asked, especially for those stakeholders that see the term "non-GAAP" and instinctively think something is not on the up-and-up. As long as non-GAAP financial measures are properly presented, properly disclosed, and respective Regulations are followed, then yes, these measures can be perfectly acceptable and provide certain insights into an entity's performance.

In its publication titled "To GAAP or Non-GAAP? The SEC Is Watching," the public accounting firm PwC notes the following with respect to the trust factor of non-GAAP financial measures.

> The use of GAAP provides uniformity in how companies report their financial performance. But most S&P 500 companies choose to report non-GAAP metrics in addition to GAAP measures. If done appropriately, non-GAAP measures can provide insights into a company's business, past performance, and potential prospects.

However, with the proliferation of the use of non-GAAP measures—the majority of which show non-GAAP results exceeding GAAP results—critics have questioned whether, in some instances, the alternative metrics are painting too rosy a financial picture. In addition, non-GAAP measures are not audited, and the preparation of non-GAAP information is not typically covered by a company's internal control over financial reporting. These factors have led to an overall lack of trust in non-GAAP measures.

¶ 906 WHERE DO NON-GAAP FINANCIAL MEASURES SHOW UP?

Believe it or not, but you likely come across non-GAAP financial measures almost every day if you frequent financial news reports, earnings releases, investor publications, etc. The fact of the matter is that these non-GAAP financial measures are prevalent throughout. For example, you're likely to come across them in earnings calls, media interviews, investor and/or industry presentations, earnings guidance, and filings with the SEC (e.g., Form 10-K, Form 10-Q, registration statements, etc.). In this section of the chapter, we'll explore a few examples of these to help you better understand how these are presented as well as the explanatory language that entities often include to call attention to the fact that some of the information being presented is not based on U.S. GAAP.

Let's take a look at our first example from HP, Inc.'s Fiscal Year 2021 Second Quarter results press release. Note that the following Exhibit only provides an excerpt from the respective earnings release.

Exhibit 1: HP Earnings Release
HP Inc. Reports Fiscal 2021 Full Year and Fourth Quarter Results

PALO ALTO, Calif., Nov. 23, 2021 (GLOBE NEWSWIRE) – HP (NYSE: HPQ)

• Fiscal 2021 GAAP diluted net earnings per share ("EPS") of $5.33[1], above the previously provided outlook of $3.56 to $3.62 per share
• Fiscal 2021 **non-GAAP** diluted net EPS of $3.79, above the previously provided outlook of $3.69 to $3.75 per share
• Fiscal 2021 net revenue of $63.5 billion, up 12.1% from the prior-year period
• Fiscal 2021 net cash provided by operating activities of $6.4 billion[1], **free cash flow** of $4.2 billion

• Fiscal 2021 returned $7.2 billion to shareholders in the form of share repurchases and dividends
• Fourth quarter GAAP diluted net EPS of $2.71, above the previously provided outlook of $0.82 to $0.88 per share
• Fourth quarter **non-GAAP** diluted net EPS of $0.94, above the previously provided outlook of $0.84 to $0.90 per share
• Fourth quarter net revenue of $16.7 billion, up 9.3% from the prior-year period
• Fourth quarter net cash provided by operating activities of $2.8 billion, **free cash flow** of $0.9 billion

• Fourth quarter returned $2.0 billion to shareholders in the form of share repurchases and dividends

Use of non-GAAP financial information

To supplement HP's consolidated condensed financial statements presented on a generally accepted accounting principles ("GAAP") basis, HP provides net revenue on a constant currency basis, non-GAAP total operating expense, non-GAAP operating profit, non-GAAP operating margin, non-GAAP tax rate, non-GAAP net earnings, non-GAAP diluted net EPS, free cash flow, gross cash, and net cash (debt) financial measures. HP also provides forecasts of non-GAAP diluted net EPS and free cash flow. Reconciliations of these non-GAAP financial measures to the most directly comparable GAAP financial measures are included in the tables below or elsewhere in the materials accompanying this news release. In addition, an explanation of the ways in which HP's management uses these non-GAAP measures to evaluate its business, the substance behind HP's decision to use these non-GAAP measures, the material limitations associated with the use of these non-GAAP measures, the manner in which HP's management compensates for those limitations, and the substantive reasons why HP's management believes that these non-GAAP measures provide useful information to investors is included under "Use of non-GAAP financial measures" after the tables below. This additional non-GAAP financial information is not meant to be considered in isolation or as a substitute for net revenue, operating expense, operating profit, operating margin, tax rate, net earnings, diluted net EPS, cash (used in)/ provided by operating activities or cash and cash equivalents prepared in accordance with GAAP.

From the example press release above, you'll note the prevalent use of the term "non-GAAP" in the first few bullet points. Additionally, you may have also identified some other examples we mentioned earlier including the use of "free cash flow" as well as "constant currency." We'll discuss these in the next few sections of this chapter.

Free Cash Flow

Cash is king! Or is it free cash flow is king? The Corporate Financial Institute identifies the generic free cash flow formula as " . . . cash from operations minus capital expenditures." Said another way, the Corporate Financial Institute notes that "free cash flow is intended to represent the amount of cash generated by a business, after accounting for reinvestment in non-current capital assets by the company." Free cash flow can generally be easily derived by looking at an entity's statement of cash flows. If that's not available for some reason, it's also possible to derive it through a backdoor approach using net income and adjusting for non-cash expenses, working capital, and capital expenditures.

Free cash flow is an important non-GAAP financial measure used by many companies. Investopedia notes the following with respect to free cash flow:

> Free cash flow is an important measurement since it shows how efficient a company is at generating cash. Investors use free cash flow to measure whether a company might have enough cash for dividends or share buybacks. In addition, the more free cash flow a company has, the better it is placed to pay down debt and pursue opportunities that can enhance its business, making it an attractive choice for investors.

Let's take a look at an example of a 10-K filing that references the non-GAAP financial measure of free cash flow, as well as some others presented earlier. Refer to the following Exhibit.

Exhibit 2: Valvoline, Inc.—Form 10-K For the Fiscal Year Ended September 30, 2021
Use of Non-GAAP Measures

To aid in the understanding of Valvoline's ongoing business performance, certain items within this document are presented on an adjusted, non-GAAP basis. These non-GAAP measures, presented both on a consolidated and reportable segment basis, have limitations as analytical tools and should not be considered in isolation from, or as an alternative to, or more meaningful than, the financial statements presented in accordance with U.S. GAAP. The financial results presented in accordance with U.S. GAAP and reconciliations of non-GAAP measures included within this Annual Report on Form 10-K should be carefully evaluated. The following are the non-GAAP measures management has included and how management defines them:

- EBITDA – defined as net income/loss, plus income tax expense/benefit, net interest and other financing expenses, and depreciation and amortization;
- Adjusted EBITDA – defined as EBITDA adjusted for certain unusual, infrequent, or non-operational activity not directly attributable to the underlying business, which management believes impacts the comparability of operational results between periods ("key items," as further described below);
- Segment adjusted EBITDA – defined as segment operating income adjusted for depreciation and amortization, in addition to key items impacting comparability;
- Free cash flow – defined as cash flows from operating activities less capital expenditures and certain other adjustments as applicable; and
- Discretionary free cash flow – defined as cash flows from operating activities less maintenance capital expenditures and certain other adjustments as applicable.

Constant Currency

The use of constant currencies is another popular non-GAAP financial measure. This is certainly the case for large multinational entities with significant operations outside the United States (especially those with operations in countries with exchange rates that are highly volatile). At its core, constant currency is when certain exchange rates are used to eliminate the effect of these significant fluctuations when calculating financial performance numbers. Simply put, it is a method in which to provide investors an overview of how the entity performed without the material impacts of currency fluctuation (which is inherently outside the control of the entity).

Continuing on with the previous press release example from HP, Inc., refer to the following excerpt from that same press release where the concept of constant currency was highlighted by the entity.

Exhibit 3: HP Earnings Release
HP Inc. Reports Fiscal 2021 Full Year and Fourth Quarter Results

PALO ALTO, Calif., Nov. 23, 2021 (GLOBE NEWSWIRE) – HP (NYSE: HPQ)

Fiscal 2021 fourth quarter segment results

Personal Systems net revenue was $11.8 billion, up 13% year over year (up 10% in **constant** currency) with a 6.5% operating margin. Consumer PCs net revenue decreased 3% and Commercial PCs net revenue increased 25%. Total units were down 9% with Notebooks units down 12% and Desktops units up 2%.

Printing net revenue was $4.9 billion, up 1% year over year (flat in **constant** currency) with a 17.0% operating margin. Total hardware units were down 26% with Consumer units down 28% and Commercial units down 12%. Consumer net revenue was down 6% and Commercial net revenue was up 19%. Supplies net revenue was down 2% (down 3% in constant currency).

STUDY QUESTIONS

---

1. Which of the following identifies an example of a non-GAAP financial measure?

    a. Diluted EPS

    b. Cash flows from operating activities

    c. Net income

    d. Free cash flow

2. Which of the following is a type of nonfinancial key performance indicator?

    a. Number of subscribers

    b. Same-store sales

    c. Average revenue per customer

    d. Sales per square foot

¶ 907 WHAT DROVE THE INCREASE IN NON-GAAP FINANCIAL MEASURES?

You know what a non-GAAP financial measure is by definition and are aware of some of the different types commonly used. The next question you may be asking yourself is what drove the increased use of these measures. You're not alone in this regard. In fact, this is something the FASB has considered, and certainly continues to consider in its standard-setting activities. Refer to the following Exhibit, which provides some insight from the FASB on the increased use of these measures.

**Exhibit 4: From the Chairman's Desk: By Russell G. Golden, FASB Chairman
Why the FASB Cares About Non-GAAP Performance Measures**

One of the growing controversies in financial reporting in 2016 was over public companies' use of non-GAAP reporting to describe their business performance to investors. For example, 88 percent of S&P 500 companies disclose non-GAAP measures in earnings releases.

While the number of non-GAAP measures garnered significant attention, the nature of some of the non-GAAP measures were particularly troubling. Those measures lacked credibility because they ignored GAAP recognition and measurement principles altogether and inaccurately depicted the underlying transaction or event.

The challenge lies in the potential for investors to misunderstand performance if they selectively use highly customized or tailored non-GAAP-based figures. The Securities and Exchange Commission (SEC) has clearly signaled to companies it is concerned about this, and companies are on notice that the SEC is paying close attention to how non-GAAP measures are used in investor communications.

If you've read parts of the FASB Codification lately and specifically stumbled into some of the more complex areas of U.S. GAAP, you'll note that U.S. GAAP can be hard and sometimes difficult to interpret. Even for seasoned professionals with years of experience, knowing how to account for a transaction or present a certain transaction within a financial statement can be hard. Look at the vast number of technical accounting and/or accounting policy positions included within some entities' accounting/finance departments. If U.S. GAAP was easy to read, easy to apply, and easy to understand from an investor's standpoint, so much specialized knowledge from these experts would not be needed. If U.S. GAAP is hard for seasoned professionals, how easy is it to understand for an uninformed investor? Does an investor know what goodwill is? Does an investor know it's not amortized but tested for impairment? The questions can go on and on. How well informed is an everyday investor about how an entity accounts for a significant acquisition or a significant disposition? This begs the question, if U.S. GAAP is the gold standard, why are companies increasingly using more and more non-GAAP financial measures to present their financial and operating performance?

The trouble with GAAP-based financial statements is an area that was addressed by McKinsey & Company in its article "Building a Better Income Statement." In the article, the company notes the following:

> Strict adherence to the conceptual principles of accounting often leads to confusion and distortions in an income statement. When companies make an acquisition, for example, GAAP requires that they allocate part of the difference between the purchase price and current market value to intangible assets. It then requires companies to amortize the value of those assets over some period of time, reducing their future earnings—in the same way they would depreciate physical assets. The calculation is theoretically consistent but provides no insight into future required cash investments. The annual amortization of acquired intangibles is a noncash expense and, unlike physical assets, companies either don't replace them or, if they do invest in them, those investments show up as expenses, not on the balance sheet.

> A bigger problem with GAAP is its emphasis on producing a single number, net income, that is supposed to be useful to the company, as well as its investors and creditors. But sophisticated investors don't care about reported net income. They want to know its components—or, specifically, to be able to distinguish operating items (sales to customers less the costs of those sales) from nonoperating items (interest income or interest expense). They also want to know which items are likely to be recurring and which

are likely to be nonrecurring (that is, restructuring charges). Finally, they want to know which items are real and which, like the amortization of intangibles, are merely accounting concepts.

¶ 908 WHY DO REGULATORS CARE ABOUT NON-GAAP FINANCIAL MEASURES?

Simply put, the use of U.S. GAAP provides uniformity and comparability in how entities report their financial performance. When everyone is applying the same U.S. GAAP, in a perfect world it results in a near apples-to-apples comparison. However, what if a group of entities in a given sector are reporting performance using different metrics? In this case, investors are left struggling with how to compare two entities or compare an entity to its industry average. What if Entity A only provides cash from operating activities (a GAAP measure) but Entity B provides both cash from operations and free cash flow? Which term is more relevant, and how do you compare the two?

One of the overarching principles with respect to non-GAAP financial measures is that they cannot be misleading. In other words, they can't be used in a way that seemingly shows a company is doing better than its counterpart that is not using the same non-GAAP financial measures (if it's not the case). Simply put, the SEC is watching. To highlight this, refer to the following Exhibit for an overview of why the SEC continues to have a heightened interest in this area.

Exhibit 5: The CPA Journal

The Expanding Use of Non-GAAP Financial Measures—Understanding Their Utility and Regulatory Limitations

When they first began to be used, non-GAAP earnings were presented in accordance with GAAP but would highlight a material change in the operating structure or accounting method of the company. In the late 1990s, non-GAAP financial measures evolved into a way for companies to exclude certain nonrecurring revenues or expenses from the GAAP-based earnings number. The motive for this adjustment was to eliminate these revenues or expenses to provide investors with a greater degree of understanding of the company's ongoing core business; however, a lack of guidance gave companies the opportunity to report potentially misleading non-GAAP financial measures.

The SEC has become proactive in providing guidance for and monitoring of the use of non-GAAP financial measures after companies have presented potentially misleading non-GAAP measures. It is currently focusing on the comparability of non-GAAP financial measures across periods and the use of creative accounting principles. Financial reporting executives and CPAs are encouraged to continue to monitor the SEC and IASB for future guidance relating to non-GAAP financial measures.

We know the SEC cares about the topic of non-GAAP financial measures, but what about the FASB? As noted on the FASB's previously referenced online article, the FASB is actually using the increased use of non-GAAP financial measures to determine if improvements are needed in GAAP. In other words, while the FASB likes to regard U.S. GAAP as the gold standard, then why do entities choose to make such extensive use of non-GAAP financial measures? Refer to the following excerpt from that article, which delves into this discussion more:

> We recently discussed non-GAAP reporting with our Financial Accounting Standards Advisory Council (FASAC). FASAC members informed us that investors rely on non-GAAP measures primarily because they are derived from GAAP information and affirmed our thinking about the potential standard-setting implications of non-GAAP reporting. They encouraged us to continue to monitor the use of non-GAAP measures and observed that certain non-GAAP adjustments might help the FASB identify where improvements could be considered.

Another way to learn from non-GAAP measures is to identify cases in which changes to GAAP might reduce the need for non-GAAP reporting. Some non-GAAP reporting develops because investors request and help shape the information provided by companies. Changing GAAP in these situations can help develop a standardized approach that is more consistent with common reporting practices that investors find useful. In other words, it would improve the credibility of financial reporting.

To give one recent example, the FASB decided that debt-valuation adjustments for a company's own credit risk should be recorded through other comprehensive income rather than net income. This change eliminates the need for companies to make non-GAAP adjustments for such gains and losses, which many investors found to be counterintuitive.

¶ 909   WHERE DO I LOOK FOR GUIDANCE?

While this chapter is a good start for some of the general insights and some of the key observations from the Big 4 accounting firms and regulators, it's not comprehensive by any stretch of the imagination. Unfortunately, there is not a single authoritative publication by the SEC or the FASB that concisely summarizes all the rules and regulations with respect to non-GAAP financial measures. In its publication titled "To GAAP or Non-GAAP? The SEC Is Watching," the public accounting firm PwC notes the following with respect to the source of guidance with respect to non-GAAP financial measures.

> Unless you are steeped in the SEC rules covering non-GAAP information, they can be confusing. Part of this is caused by rules that are dependent on where or how the non-GAAP information is communicated. We summarize elements of the various rules but cannot address all aspects of the regulations and interpretive guidance. For more information, see the SEC's website at www.sec.gov.

> Which non-GAAP rules govern the presentation of non-GAAP measures depends on where the disclosure will appear. The disclosure requirements vary based on the applicable regulation. Regardless of the source, all of the governing regulations share an overarching principle that non-GAAP information cannot be misleading.

The above answer is probably not comforting for someone wanting to become more well-versed in the area of non-GAAP financial measures. SEC Regulations are difficult to read and span hundreds if not thousands of pages. Getting a handle on how the respective SEC Regulations are organized, not to mention how to interpret the actual guidance, is a job best left handled by those with several, if not many, years of experience in that niche area of accounting. However, you have to start somewhere.

As noted in the article excerpt above, the relevant rules are dependent on where/how the non-GAAP information is presented. Recall that there are many areas where non-GAAP information is presented. One of these is earnings releases issued by most entities on a quarterly basis. For this area, the respective guidance is within Form 8-K Item 2.02. If instead, you're looking for the relevant guidance with respect to an entity's Form 10-K, you'd look to Regulation S-K. Finally, if you're looking for guidance as it relates to earnings calls or investor presentations, you would look to Regulation G.

As you'll note, knowing where to go for the governing regulations is one of biggest challenges. Actually, going into the respective regulations and trying to find what you're looking for, presents an even bigger challenge. However, you should note that Regulations G and S-K are the areas that you should be most familiar with as it relates to non-GAAP financial measures. We'll explore the first Regulation in the next section of this chapter.

¶ 910 REGULATION G

While we've harped on the fact that you have to look to many different places for guidance, and that guidance depends on the information for which the non-GAAP financial measure is included, Regulation G is a great starting point to develop a baseline understanding of the principles/requirements related to non-GAAP financial measures.

How Did We Get Here?

Regulation G, and many other non-GAAP financial measures rules and regulations, came about as a direct result of the Sarbanes-Oxley Act of 2002. Regulation G, in fact, was just one of several new/revised regulations as the SEC took on the task of reigning in the rampant use of non-GAAP financial measures. Refer to the summary in the following Exhibit.

Exhibit 6: SEC Final Rule—Conditions for Use of Non-GAAP Financial Measures

As directed by the Sarbanes-Oxley Act of 2002, we are adopting new rules and amendments to address public companies' disclosure or release of certain financial information that is calculated and presented on the basis of methodologies other than in accordance with generally accepted accounting principles (GAAP). We are adopting a new disclosure regulation, Regulation G, which will require public companies that disclose or release such non-GAAP financial measures to include, in that disclosure or release, a presentation of the most directly comparable GAAP financial measure and a reconciliation of the disclosed non-GAAP financial measure to the most directly comparable GAAP financial measure. We also are adopting amendments to Item 10 of Regulation S-K and Item 10 of Regulation S-B to provide additional guidance to those registrants that include non-GAAP financial measures in Commission filings. Additionally, we are adopting amendments to Form 20-F to incorporate into that form the amendments to Item 10 of Regulation S-K. Finally, we are adopting amendments that require registrants to furnish to the Commission, on Form 8-K, earnings releases, or similar announcements.

Scope

Before diving too deep into Regulation G, it's important that you understand what entities are within the scope of the Regulation. As noted in the SEC's Final Rule ("Conditions for Use of Non-GAAP Financial Measures"), Regulation G applies to "any entity that is required to file reports pursuant to Sections 13(a) or 15(d) of the Exchange Act, other than a registered investment company." Perhaps more importantly, you should note that Regulation G "applies whenever such a registrant, or a person acting on its behalf, discloses publicly or releases publicly any material information that includes a non-GAAP financial measure."

In the SEC's Final Rule, the SEC also notes that non-GAAP financial measures do not include financial information that does not have the effect of providing numerical measures that are different from the comparable GAAP measure. The SEC further notes that examples of measures to which Regulation G *does not apply* include the following:

- Disclosure of amounts of expected indebtedness, including contracted and anticipated amounts;

- Disclosure of amounts of repayments that have been planned or decided upon but not yet made;

- Disclosure of estimated revenues or expenses of a new product line, so long as such amounts were estimated in the same manner as would be computed under GAAP; and

- Measures of profit or loss and total assets for each segment required to be disclosed in accordance with GAAP.

Refer to the following Exhibit, which provides additional context and explanation from the Final Rule related to Regulation G and what financial measures are in scope.

Exhibit 7: SEC Final Rule—Discussion of the Definition of Non-GAAP Financial Measures

An example of a non-GAAP financial measure would be a measure of operating income that excludes one or more expense or revenue items that are identified as "non-recurring." Another example would be EBITDA, which could be calculated using elements derived from GAAP financial presentations but, in any event, is not presented in accordance with GAAP. Examples of ratios and measures that would not be non-GAAP financial measures would include sales per square foot (assuming that the sales figure was calculated in accordance with GAAP) or same store sales (again assuming the sales figures for the stores were calculated in accordance with GAAP).

An example of a ratio that would not be a non-GAAP financial measure would be a measure of operating margin that is calculated by dividing revenues into operating income, where both revenue and operating income are calculated in accordance with GAAP. Conversely, an example of a ratio that would be a non-GAAP financial measure would be a measure of operating margin that is calculated by dividing revenues into operating income, where either revenue or operating income, or both, were not calculated in accordance with GAAP.

We received comment regarding the exclusion of financial measures used for regulatory purposes from the definition. In response to these comments, we have provided an exclusion from the definition of "non-GAAP financial measure" for financial measures required to be disclosed by GAAP, Commission rules, or a system of regulation of a government or governmental authority or self-regulatory organization that is applicable to the registrant. Examples of such financial measures would include measures of capital or reserves calculated for such a regulatory purpose.

General Requirements of Regulation G

The overarching principles outlined within Regulation G includes the following:

> A registrant, or a person acting on its behalf, shall not make public a non-GAAP financial measure that, taken together with the information accompanying that measure, contains an untrue statement of a material fact or omits to state a material fact necessary in order to make the presentation of the non-GAAP financial measure, in light of the circumstances under which it is presented, not misleading.

While this general disclosure requirement is fairly simple to understand (the principle, that is—preventing information from being misleading), let's explore further how this general requirement is more specifically prescribed within the guidance of Regulation G. Overall, Regulation G requires that whenever a registrant, or person acting on its behalf, publicly discloses material information that includes a non-GAAP financial measure, the registrant must accompany that non-GAAP financial measure with all of the following information:

- A presentation of the most directly comparable financial measure calculated and presented in accordance with GAAP

- A reconciliation (by schedule or other clearly understandable method), which is quantitative for historical non-GAAP measures presented, and quantitative, to the extent available without unreasonable efforts, for forward-looking information, of the differences between the non-GAAP financial measure disclosed or released with the most comparable financial measure, or measures calculated and presented in accordance with GAAP identified in above

As you'll note from above, the first requirement is that when an entity provides certain non-GAAP financial information, they are required to also include the most comparable measure calculated in accordance with U.S. GAAP. Take the following non-GAAP disclosure (related to constant currency), which was presented in an earlier exhibit from HP's annual earnings release:

> Personal Systems net revenue was $11.8 billion, up 13% year over year (up 10% in constant currency) with a 6.5% operating margin. Consumer PCs net revenue decreased 3% and Commercial PCs net revenue increased 25%. Total units were down 9% with Notebooks units down 12% and Desktops units up 2%.

> Printing net revenue was $4.9 billion, up 1% year over year (flat in constant currency) with a 17.0% operating margin. Total hardware units were down 26% with Consumer units down 28% and Commercial units down 12%. Consumer net revenue was down 6% and Commercial net revenue was up 19%. Supplies net revenue was down 2% (down 3% in constant currency).

In the two paragraphs above, you will note that while the entity chose to present the revenue increase in constant currency (i.e., a non-GAAP financial measure), the entity also provided the most comparable U.S. GAAP measure with change in revenue. In other words, had the entity instead made the following excerpted disclosures, this would have likely conflicted with the rules included within Regulation G:

- Personal Systems net revenue was $11.8 billion, up 10% in constant currency.

- Printing net revenue was $4.9 billion, flat in constant currency.

- Supplies net revenue was down 3% in constant currency.

In each of the above three "hypothetical" excerpts, the entity has provided a non-GAAP financial measure but has not included a comparable GAAP measure. To further emphasize, refer to the following Exhibit, which provides an excerpt from a hypothetical entity.

Exhibit 8: Example Company ABC

Inappropriate Disclosure Under Regulation G

- Fiscal 2021 free cash flow of $4.1 billion
- Fourth quarter non-GAAP diluted net EPS of $0.12, above the previously provided outlook of $0.09 to $0.10 per share

Acceptable Disclosure Under Regulation G

- Fiscal 2021 net cash flow provided by operating activities of $5.3 billion, free cash flow of $4.1 billion

Fourth quarter GAAP diluted EPS of $0.14, non-GAAP diluted net EPS of $0.12

Disclosure by Other Means

The example above with the hypothetical press release excerpts is simple to understand and relatively easy to apply (especially for an entity that has been a public company and has released public financial information for several years). However, there are obviously times when information is not released through a press release or a type of SEC filing (e.g., Form 10-Q, Form 10-K, etc.) but is instead issued by other means such as the following:

- Orally

- Telephonically

- Through a webcast

Even though the information is being disseminated through another "non-written" channel, the overall requirements of Regulation G hold true. In short, the Regulation requires that an entity post that information on their website and disclose the location and availability of the required accompanying information during its presentation.

STUDY QUESTIONS

3. Which of the following organizations noted that non-GAAP financial measures "lacked credibility because they ignored GAAP recognition and measurement principles altogether and inaccurately depicted the underlying transaction or event"?

    a. SEC

    b. PCAOB

    c. IASB

    d. FASB

4. Which SEC Regulation would you reference as it relates to earnings calls or investor presentations?

    a. Regulation G

    b. Regulation D

    c. Regulation S-X

    d. Regulation S-K

¶ 911   REGULATION S-K

You may have seen this Regulation from time to time. In short, Regulation S-K includes the SEC rules that prescribe the detailed disclosure requirements applicable to registration statements, periodic reports (e.g., Form 10-Qs and Form 10-Ks), proxy statements, and other filings under the Securities Act and the Exchange Act. When the SEC issued its "Final Rule: Conditions for Use of Non-GAAP Financial Measures" previously referenced, in doing so, the SEC provided certain amendments to Regulation S-K to address the topic of non-GAAP financial measures (this was in addition to releasing the new Regulation G we just discussed).

Recall from the earlier discussion that depending on what type of information includes the non-GAAP financial measure, that will generally dictate which Regulation is applicable. For earnings calls and certain press releases, Regulation G is the go-to. However, for filings with the SEC such as 10-Qs and 10-Ks, Regulation S-K (Item 10) is the go-to.

The amendments included in Regulation S-K require entities using non-GAAP financial measures in SEC filings to provide the following:

- A presentation, with equal or greater prominence, of the most directly comparable financial measure calculated and presented in accordance with GAAP;

- A reconciliation (by schedule or other clearly understandable method), which shall be quantitative for historical non-GAAP measures presented, and quantitative, to the extent available without unreasonable efforts, for forward-looking information, of the differences between the non-GAAP financial measure disclosed or released with the most directly comparable financial measure or measures calculated and presented in accordance with GAAP;

- A statement disclosing the reasons why the registrant's management believes that presentation of the non-GAAP financial measure provides useful information to investors regarding the registrant's financial condition and results of operations; and

- To the extent material, a statement disclosing the additional purposes, if any, for which the registrant's management uses the non-GAAP financial measure that are not otherwise disclosed.

As you'll note from the above requirements, they are similar in some respects to those presented earlier when we discussed Regulation G. For example, both Regulation G and Regulation S-K require a comparable GAAP presentation along with an appropriate reconciliation. However, Regulation S-K takes it a step further and requires that an entity also disclose reasons why the entity believes that presentation of the non-GAAP financial measure provides useful information to investors regarding the registrant's financial condition and results of operations.

In order to help illustrate how these requirements are applied, let's take a look at a real-world example from Walmart's Form 10-Q for the quarterly period ending October 31, 2021. As with all other SEC filings, you can directly access this SEC filing on the SEC.gov site. In its filing, Walmart identifies three separate non-GAAP financial measures, which include the following:

- Return on Assets
- Return on Investments
- Free Cash Flow

Refer to the following Exhibit, which provides the relevant excerpts from the filing. In it, you'll note that the entity identifies the non-GAAP measure, describes the comparable GAAP measure (Note: it's presented elsewhere and not included in the following exhibit), and also addresses how the entity believes presentation is useful information for investors regarding their results of operations.

Exhibit 9: Walmart Inc.—Form 10-Q for the Quarterly Period Ending October 31, 2021
Note: Certain sections omitted for presentation purposes.

Item 2. Management's Discussion and Analysis of Financial Condition and Results of Operations

Return on Assets and Return on Investment
We include Return on Assets ("ROA"), the most directly comparable measure based on our financial statements presented in accordance with generally accepted accounting principles in the U.S. ("GAAP") and Return on Investment ("ROI") as metrics to assess returns on assets. While ROI is considered a non-GAAP financial measure, management believes ROI is a meaningful metric to share with investors because it helps investors assess how effectively Walmart is deploying its assets. Trends in ROI can fluctuate over time as management balances long-term strategic initiatives with possible short-term impacts.

Our calculation of ROI is considered a non-GAAP financial measure because we calculate ROI using financial measures that exclude and include amounts that are included and excluded in the most directly comparable GAAP financial measure. For example, we exclude the impact of depreciation and amortization from our reported operating income in calculating the numerator of our calculation of ROI. As mentioned above, we consider ROA to be the financial measure computed in accordance with GAAP most directly comparable to our calculation of ROI. ROI differs from ROA (which is consolidated net income for the period divided by average total assets for the period) because ROI: adjusts operating income to exclude certain expense items and adds interest income; and adjusts total assets for the impact of accumulated depreciation and amortization, accounts payable and accrued liabilities to arrive at total invested capital. Because of the adjustments mentioned above, we believe ROI more accurately measures how we are deploying our key assets and is more meaningful to investors than ROA. Although ROI is a standard financial measure, numerous methods exist for calculating a company's ROI. As a result, the method used by management to calculate our ROI may differ from the methods used by other companies to calculate their ROI.

Free Cash Flow
Free cash flow is considered a non-GAAP financial measure. Management believes, however, that free cash flow, which measures our ability to generate cash from our business operations, is an important financial measure for use in evaluating the Company's financial performance. Free cash flow should be considered in addition to, rather than as a substitute for, consolidated net income as a measure of our performance and net cash provided by operating activities as a measure of our liquidity. See Liquidity and Capital Resources for discussions of GAAP metrics including net cash provided by operating activities, net cash used in investing activities and net cash used in financing activities.

We define free cash flow as net cash provided by operating activities in a period minus payments for property and equipment made in that period. Walmart's definition of free cash flow is limited in that it does not represent residual cash flows available for discretionary expenditures due to the fact that the measure does not deduct the payments required for debt service and other contractual obligations or payments made for business acquisitions. Therefore, we believe it is important to view free cash flow as a measure that provides supplemental information to our Condensed Consolidated Statements of Cash Flows. Although other companies report their free cash flow, numerous methods may exist for calculating a company's free cash flow. As a result, the method used by management to calculate our free cash flow may differ from the methods used by other companies to calculate their free cash flow.

You should note that in addition to the information provided as excerpted in the above Exhibit, Walmart also included relevant reconciliations (as required by Regulation S-K) for each of the above non-GAAP financial measures. Let's take a look at another example, from Lowes's Form 10-Q for the quarterly period ended October 29, 2021. In its form, the entity calls out the following as its non-GAAP financial measures:

- Adjusted Diluted Earnings Per Share

- Return on Invested Capital

Refer to the following Exhibit, which provides the relevant excerpts from the filing. In it, you'll note that the entity identifies the non-GAAP measure, describes the comparable GAAP measure, and also addresses how the entity believes presentation is useful information for investors regarding their results of operations.

> **Exhibit 10: Lowes Companies, Inc.—Form 10-Q for the quarterly period ending October 29, 2021**
>
> *Note: Certain sections omitted for presentation purposes.*
>
> **Item 2. Management's Discussion and Analysis of Financial Condition and Results of Operations**
>
> **Adjusted Diluted Earnings Per Share**
> Adjusted diluted earnings per share is considered a non-GAAP financial measure. The Company believes this non-GAAP financial measure provides useful insight for analysts and investors in evaluating what management considers the Company's core financial performance. Adjusted diluted earnings per share excludes the impact of discrete items, further described below, not contemplated in the Company's business outlook for the third quarter of fiscal 2020. Unless otherwise noted, the income tax effect of these adjustments is calculated using the marginal rate for the period.
>
> **Return on Invested Capital**
> Return on Invested Capital (ROIC) is calculated using a non-GAAP financial measure. Management believes ROIC is a meaningful metric for analysts and investors as a measure of how effectively the Company is using capital to generate profits. Although ROIC is a common financial metric, numerous methods exist for calculating ROIC. Accordingly, the method used by our management may differ from the methods used by other companies. We encourage you to understand the methods used by another company to calculate ROIC before comparing its ROIC to ours.

Prior to these examples, we touched on the amendments included in Regulation S-K that require entities using non-GAAP financial measures in SEC filings to also provide certain information. On the flip side of this is information that is prohibited by Regulation S-K. This includes the following:

- Excluding charges or liabilities that required, or will require, cash settlement, or would have required cash settlement absent an ability to settle in another manner, from non-GAAP liquidity measures, other than the measures EBIT and EBITDA;
- Adjusting a non-GAAP performance measure to eliminate or smooth items identified as non-recurring, infrequent or unusual, when
  — the nature of the charge or gain is such that it is reasonably likely to recur within two years, or
  — there was a similar charge or gain within the prior two years;
- Presenting non-GAAP financial measures on the face of the registrant's financial statements prepared in accordance with GAAP or in the accompanying notes;
- Presenting non-GAAP financial measures on the face of any pro forma financial information required to be disclosed by Article 11 of Regulation S-X;
- Using titles or descriptions of non-GAAP financial measures that are the same as, or confusingly similar to, titles or descriptions used for GAAP financial measures.

As you can note, the requirements for information that must be included and the prohibition on certain items as prescribed by Regulation S-K are more extensive than those rules outlined in Regulation G. As noted within the SEC's release of these amendments, the SEC noted the following with respect to this difference:

> The requirements and prohibitions for filed information are more extensive and detailed than those of Regulation G. The additional requirements and prohibitions are generally consistent with the staff's historical practice in situations where it has reviewed filings containing non-GAAP financial measures.

¶911

Unreasonable Effort Considerations

As we've already discussed, there is a reconciliation requirement prescribed by Regulation S-K (and Regulation G) as well. The intent of this reconciliation is to illustrate how a certain non-GAAP financial measure is being presented and how it compares to the closest related GAAP financial measure. For example, in the previous Exhibit, which provides an overview of Lowes' press release of its second quarter results, the entity included non-GAAP operating income as a measure. There, the entity also included a reconciliation which basically "walks back" to GAAP operating income by factoring in intangible asset amortization and certain restructuring charges. In other words, the entity bridges the gap between the non-GAAP financial measure and the closest related GAAP financial measure by including this reconciliation.

Oftentimes this reconciliation is fairly routine. However, for certain non-GAAP financial measures, this reconciliation may be overly difficult, especially if it relates to new information or the facts and circumstances surrounding the metric make it overly difficult to reconcile appropriately. As a result, you'll note in the reconciliation requirement as reflected below, there is an "unreasonable effort" exception noted.

- A reconciliation (by schedule or other clearly understandable method), which shall be quantitative for historical non-GAAP measures presented, and quantitative, to the extent available **without unreasonable efforts**, for forward-looking information, of the differences between the non-GAAP financial measure disclosed or released with the most directly comparable financial measure or measures calculated and presented in accordance with GAAP;

Refer to the following Exhibit, which provides additional context from the SEC's final rules with respect to reasonable effort exception.

Exhibit 11: SEC Final Rule—Discussion of the Definition of Non-GAAP Financial Measures

Unreasonable Effort "Exception"

We had proposed that the requirements for a reconciliation to the most directly comparable GAAP financial measure be slightly more stringent than those set forth under Regulation G. In particular, in filings with the Commission, it was proposed that there not be an "unreasonable effort" exception for forward-looking information to the requirement for a quantitative reconciliation between the non-GAAP financial measure and the comparable GAAP financial measure. Commenters expressed the view that the need for such an exception was present equally in disclosure that was filed with the Commission and disclosure that was not filed. In response to these comments, we have revised the requirement for filed documents to include the same exception as in Regulation G. Accordingly, with regard to the quantitative reconciliation of non-GAAP financial measures that are forward-looking, Item 10 of Regulation S-K and Item 10 of Regulation S-B require a schedule or other presentation detailing the differences between the forward-looking non-GAAP financial measure and the appropriate forward-looking GAAP financial measure. If the GAAP financial measure is not accessible on a forward-looking basis, the registrant must disclose that fact and provide reconciling information that is available without an unreasonable effort. Furthermore, the registrant must identify information that is unavailable and disclose its probable significance.

As you'll note from Exhibit 11 and the preceding guidance, entities cannot simply assert that it is too hard to provide the reconciliation. If they do take this position, significant additional disclosures, and the reasons thereof, are required to be made.

Boilerplate Concerns

Boilerplate is essentially any text, such as a financial statement disclosure, that is/can be reused more than once in a new context without any substantial changes to the original. Unfortunately, boilerplate disclosures are commonplace throughout the industry.

This boilerplate risk was a concern of the SEC when these Regulations were issued. That said, the SEC doesn't want entities to just simply "rinse and repeat" a disclosure. Instead, they want clear, pertinent, and current information about the non-GAAP financial measure. In its release of the final rules, the SEC noted the following with respect to the risk of boilerplate disclosures:

> The required statements of the purposes for which management uses the non-GAAP financial measure and the utility of the information to investors should not be boilerplate. We intend these statements to be clear and understandable. We also intend these statements to be specific to the non-GAAP financial measure used, the registrant, the nature of the registrant's business and industry, and the manner in which management assesses the non-GAAP financial measure and applies it to management decisions.

¶ 912 SEC COMPLIANCE AND DISCLOSURE INTERPRETATIONS

Up to this point in the chapter, we've addressed the main requirements outlined within Regulation G and Regulation S-K released by the SEC many years ago. While no super-recent updated guidance has been released, the SEC did provide many updated interpretations to these rules back in 2016 (with other clarifying amendments continuing to this day). The updated rules, referred to as the Compliance & Disclosure Interpretations, relate to the SEC's interpretations of the rules and regulations on the use of non-GAAP financial measures. Some of these rules/interpretations are very specific and outside the scope of this chapter; however, there are several interpretations that we'll review in this section of this chapter that have broader appeal. Many of these interpretations deal with the reconciliation and how it should be properly presented, but many of the other Q&As address several other important areas.

¶ 913 MISLEADING CONCERNS

Recall that the overall principle is that a non-GAAP financial measure cannot be misleading. While this is fairly simple to understand, sometimes the term *misleading* can be interpreted differently. As a result, the SEC has provided three interpretations that primarily address this concept. The following is an overview of these three interpretations sourced from the SEC's Compliance & Disclosure Interpretations.

Question 100.01

Can certain adjustments, although not explicitly prohibited, result in a non-GAAP measure that is misleading?

Answer: Yes. Certain adjustments may violate Rule 100(b) of Regulation G because they cause the presentation of the non-GAAP measure to be misleading. For example, presenting a performance measure that excludes normal, recurring, cash operating expenses necessary to operate a registrant's business could be misleading.

Question 100.02

Can a non-GAAP measure be misleading if it is presented inconsistently between periods?

Answer: Yes. For example, a non-GAAP measure that adjusts a particular charge or gain in the current period and for which other, similar charges or gains were not also adjusted in prior periods could violate Rule 100(b) of

Regulation G unless the change between periods is disclosed and the reasons for it explained. In addition, depending on the significance of the change, it may be necessary to recast prior measures to conform to the current presentation and place the disclosure in the appropriate context.

Question 100.03

Can a non-GAAP measure be misleading if the measure excludes charges, but does not exclude any gains?

Answer: Yes. For example, a non-GAAP measure that is adjusted only for non-recurring charges when there were non-recurring gains that occurred during the same period could violate Rule 100(b) of Regulation G.

¶ 914 EARNINGS MANAGEMENT

It may be interpreted by some that non-GAAP financial measures are intended to be used to help "smooth" over earnings. For example, take the situation where an entity receives a very significant legal settlement in the last month of a quarter and recognizes it in income (based on U.S. GAAP requirements). In this situation, the receipt and recognition of this settlement may significantly skew the earnings per share (EPS) metric (a GAAP measure). As a result, an entity would likely exclude this significant settlement in order to show a more apples-to-apples comparison quarter over quarter. If not, an investor may see the significant spike in EPS from the prior period and draw inappropriate conclusions about the entity's performance.

However, there may be times when entities abuse the use of non-GAAP financial measures in order to smooth items identified as non-recurring, infrequent, or unusual. While this is generally inappropriate at times, at other times it is not. Refer to the following interpretation on this topic released by the SEC.

Question 102.03

Item 10(e) of Regulation S-K prohibits adjusting a non-GAAP financial performance measure to eliminate or smooth items identified as non-recurring, infrequent or unusual when the nature of the charge or gain is such that it is reasonably likely to recur within two years or there was a similar charge or gain within the prior two years. Is this prohibition based on the description of the charge or gain, or is it based on the nature of the charge or gain?

Answer: The prohibition is based on the description of the charge or gain that is being adjusted. It would not be appropriate to state that a charge or gain is non-recurring, infrequent or unusual unless it meets the specified criteria. The fact that a registrant cannot describe a charge or gain as non-recurring, infrequent or unusual, however, does not mean that the registrant cannot adjust for that charge or gain. Registrants can make adjustments they believe are appropriate, subject to Regulation G and the other requirements of Item 10(e) of Regulation S-K.

¶ 915 PROMINENT PRESENTATION

As you recall, when a non-GAAP financial measure is presented, the most comparable GAAP financial measure must also be presented. More specifically, Item 10(e)(1)(i)(A) of Regulation S-K provides that "an issuer, when including a non-GAAP financial measure in a filing with the Commission, must include a presentation, with **equal or greater prominence**, of the most directly comparable financial measure or measures calculated and presented in accordance with GAAP."

Again, the concept of equal or greater prominence is something that can be interpreted differently by different entities. As a result, this is an area where the SEC provided additional interpretations. Specifically, in Question 102.10 of the SEC's Compliance & Disclosure Interpretations, the SEC notes the following as examples where a non-GAAP financial disclosure is more prominent (i.e., "don't do this"):

- Presenting a full income statement of non-GAAP measures or presenting a full non-GAAP income statement when reconciling non-GAAP measures to the most directly comparable GAAP measures;

- Omitting comparable GAAP measures from an earnings release headline or caption that includes non-GAAP measures;

- Presenting a non-GAAP measure using a style of presentation (e.g., bold, larger font) that emphasizes the non-GAAP measure over the comparable GAAP measure;

- A non-GAAP measure that precedes the most directly comparable GAAP measure (including in an earnings release headline or caption);

- Describing a non-GAAP measure as, for example, "record performance" or "exceptional" without at least an equally prominent descriptive characterization of the comparable GAAP measure;

- Providing tabular disclosure of non-GAAP financial measures without preceding it with an equally prominent tabular disclosure of the comparable GAAP measures or including the comparable GAAP measures in the same table;

- Excluding a quantitative reconciliation with respect to a forward-looking non-GAAP measure in reliance on the "unreasonable efforts" exception in Item 10(e)(1)(i)(B) without disclosing that fact and identifying the information that is unavailable and its probable significance in a location of equal or greater prominence; and

- Providing discussion and analysis of a non-GAAP measure without a similar discussion and analysis of the comparable GAAP measure in a location with equal or greater prominence.

While the SEC provides examples in its interpretive guidance, the SEC does understand and recognize that "whether a non-GAAP measure is more prominent than the comparable GAAP measure generally depends on the facts and circumstances in which the disclosure is made."

¶ 916 TAX IMPACTS

The consideration of how tax impacts are presented is another area that is addressed by the SEC. Refer to the following question, which addresses the situation of whether or not tax impacts on the adjustments should or should not be presented.

Question 102.11

How should income tax effects related to adjustments to arrive at a non-GAAP measure be calculated and presented?

Answer: A registrant should provide income tax effects on its non-GAAP measures depending on the nature of the measures. If a measure is a liquidity measure that includes income taxes, it might be acceptable to adjust GAAP taxes to show taxes paid in cash. If a measure is a performance measure, the registrant should include current and deferred income tax expense commensurate with the non-GAAP measure of profitability. In addition, adjustments to arrive at a non-GAAP measure should not be presented "net of tax." Rather, income taxes should be shown as a separate adjustment and clearly explained.

¶ 917 EBIT AND EBITDA

These are metrics that you come across in nearly every earnings release from a publicly traded entity. Given their importance, this is an area that is further addressed by the SEC within its Compliance & Disclosure Interpretations. In it, the SEC provides guidance on two specific issues as noted below.

Question 103.01

Exchange Act Release No. 47226 describes EBIT as "earnings before interest and taxes" and EBITDA as "earnings before interest, taxes, depreciation and amortization." What GAAP measure is intended by the term "earnings"? May measures other than those described in the release be characterized as "EBIT" or "EBITDA"? Does the exception for EBIT and EBITDA from the prohibition in Item 10(e)(1)(ii)(A) of Regulation S-K apply to these other measures?

Answer: "Earnings" means net income as presented in the statement of operations under GAAP. Measures that are calculated differently than those described as EBIT and EBITDA in Exchange Act Release No. 47226 should not be characterized as "EBIT" or "EBITDA" and their titles should be distinguished from "EBIT" or "EBITDA," such as "Adjusted EBITDA." These measures are not exempt from the prohibition in Item 10(e)(1)(ii)(A) of Regulation S-K, with the exception of measures addressed in Question 102.09. [Jan. 11, 2010]

Question 103.02

If EBIT or EBITDA is presented as a performance measure, to which GAAP financial measure should it be reconciled?

Answer: If a company presents EBIT or EBITDA as a performance measure, such measures should be reconciled to net income as presented in the statement of operations under GAAP. Operating income would not be considered the most directly comparable GAAP financial measure because EBIT and EBITDA make adjustments for items that are not included in operating income. In addition, these measures must not be presented on a per share basis.

¶ 918 FREE CASH FLOW

Recall that free cash flow is intended to represent the amount of cash generated by a business, after accounting for reinvestment in non-current capital assets by the company. Given its importance and frequent use by entities, it is also an area for which the SEC provides certain interpretations. Refer to the following question/answer below for an overview of the SEC's interpretation.

Question 102.07

Some companies present a measure of "free cash flow," which is typically calculated as cash flows from operating activities as presented in the statement of cash flows under GAAP, less capital expenditures. Does Item 10(e)(1)(ii) of Regulation S-K prohibit this measure in documents filed with the Commission?

Answer: No. The deduction of capital expenditures from the GAAP financial measure of cash flows from operating activities would not violate the prohibitions in Item 10(e)(1)(ii). However, companies should be aware that this measure does not have a uniform definition and its title does not describe how it is calculated. Accordingly, a clear description of how this measure is calculated, as well as the necessary reconciliation, should accompany the measure where it is used. Companies should also avoid inappropriate or potentially misleading inferences about its usefulness. For example, "free cash flow" should not be used in a manner that inappropriately implies that the measure represents the residual cash flow available for discretionary expenditures, since many companies have mandatory debt service requirements or other non-discretionary expenditures that are not deducted from the measure. Also, free cash flow is a liquidity measure that must not be presented on a per share basis.

¶ 919 SEGMENT INFORMATION

There are several interpretations provided by the SEC regarding segment reporting as well as non-GAAP considerations for segments. The accounting, reporting, and disclosure requirements with respect to segment reporting are prescribed by ASC Topic 280. The information included within ASC Topic 280 provides guidance to public entities on how to report certain information about operating segments in both complete sets of financial statements as well as condensed financial statements of interim periods. In general, ASC Topic 280 requires that public entities report certain information about their products and services, the geographic areas in which they operate, and their major customers. These objectives are achieved by using what is referred to as the management approach to segment reporting.

ASC Topic 280 notes that an operating segment is a component of an entity that has all of the following characteristics:

- It engages in business activities from which it may recognize revenues and incur expenses (including revenues and expenses relating to transactions with other components of the same public entity).

- Its operating results are regularly reviewed by the public entity's chief operating decision maker to make decisions about resources to be allocated to the segment and assess its performance.

- Its discrete financial information is available.

Within ASC Topic 280, the required disclosures are broken out into several categories to include the following:
- General Information
- Information about Profit or Loss and Assets
- Measurement
- Reconciliations
- Interim Period Information
- Restatement of Previously Reported Information

While there are significant disclosure requirements related to disclosures, one of the primary categories of disclosure relates to profit and loss. Overall, ACS Topic 280 notes that an entity should report a measure of profit or loss and total assets for each reportable segment.

Now that you have a baseline understanding of segments and some of the disclosure requirements, let's take a look at several of the SEC interpretations on the topic.

Note that the last interpretation presented also addresses the topic along with considerations for constant currency.

Question 104.01

Is segment information that is presented in conformity with Accounting Standards Codification 280, pursuant to which a company may determine segment profitability on a basis that differs from the amounts in the consolidated financial statements determined in accordance with GAAP, considered to be a non-GAAP financial measure under Regulation G and Item 10(e) of Regulation S-K?

Answer: No. Non-GAAP financial measures do not include financial measures that are required to be disclosed by GAAP. Exchange Act Release No. 47226 lists "measures of profit or loss and total assets for each segment required to be disclosed in accordance with GAAP" as examples of such measures. The measure of segment profit or loss and segment total assets under Accounting Standards Codification 280 is the measure reported to the chief operating decision maker for purposes of making decisions about allocating resources to the segment and assessing its performance.

Question 104.02

Does Item 10(e)(1)(ii) of Regulation S-K prohibit the discussion in MD&A of segment information determined in conformity with Accounting Standards Codification 280?

Answer: No. Where a company includes in its MD&A a discussion of segment profitability determined consistent with Accounting Standards Codification 280, which also requires that a footnote to the company's consolidated financial statements provide a reconciliation, the company also should include in the segment discussion in the MD&A a complete discussion of the reconciling items that apply to the particular segment being discussed.

Question 104.03

Is a measure of segment profit/loss or liquidity that is not in conformity with Accounting Standards Codification 280 a non-GAAP financial measure under Regulation G and Item 10(e) of Regulation S-K?

Answer: Yes. Segment measures that are adjusted to include amounts excluded from, or to exclude amounts included in, the measure reported to the chief operating decision maker for purposes of making decisions about allocating resources to the segment and assessing its performance do not comply with Accounting Standards Codification 280. Such measures are, therefore, non-GAAP financial measures and subject to all of the provisions of Regulation G and Item 10(e) of Regulation S-K.

Question 104.04

In the footnote that reconciles the segment measures to the consolidated financial statements, a company may total the profit or loss for the individual segments as part of the Accounting Standards Codification 280 required reconciliation. Would the presentation of the total segment profit or loss measure in any context other than the Accounting Standards Codification 280 required reconciliation in the footnote be the presentation of a non-GAAP financial measure?

Answer: Yes. The presentation of the total segment profit or loss measure in any context other than the Accounting Standards Codification 280 required reconciliation in the footnote would be the presentation of a non-GAAP financial measure because it has no authoritative meaning outside of the Accounting Standards Codification 280 required reconciliation in the footnotes to the company's consolidated financial statements.

Question 104.06

Company X has operations in various foreign countries where the local currency is used to prepare the financial statements which are translated into the reporting currency under the applicable accounting standards. In preparing its MD&A, Company X will explain the reasons for changes in various financial statement captions. A portion of these changes will be attributable to changes in exchange rates between periods used for translation. Company X wants to isolate the effect of exchange rate differences and will present financial information in a constant currency—e.g., assume a constant exchange rate between periods for translation. Would such a presentation be considered a non-GAAP measure under Regulation G and Item 10(e) of Regulation S-K?

Answer: Yes. Company X may comply with the reconciliation requirements of Regulation G and Item 10(e) by presenting the historical amounts and the amounts in constant currency and describing the process for calculating the constant currency amounts and the basis of presentation.

¶ 920 THE SEC IS WATCHING

If you haven't gathered yet from this chapter, the SEC has heightened interest in non-GAAP financial measures and ensuring that their use is limited, where possible, and appropriate. However, even with the overall principles and interpretations outlined by the SEC, there are still plenty of entities that push the bounds and are put in the position of having to respond to an SEC comment letter.

While comment letters have been on a downward trend in the past few years, the SEC has remained focused on these non-GAAP financial measures. The article "As Comment Letters Decrease, SEC Keeps Focus on Non-GAAP Accounting" (April 9, 2020), published on Intelligize, notes the following:

> Comment letters issued in 2019 declined 22.5% from the year before. It marked the third straight year of double-digit percentage decreases. That doesn't mean the SEC has taken a step back on all issues, however. To the contrary, it appears to have kept its focus on the use of non-GAAP financial measures.

> To be sure, the number of comment letters issued on non-GAAP topics has declined, down some 19% in the last 12 months versus the year-earlier period. But comment letters related to non-GAAP measures climbed as a share of the whole in the same time frame. That suggests the agency is prioritizing that particular topic. Moreover, thorny issues like non-GAAP metrics in MD&A disclosure take on average 31 days to resolve (much longer than, say, the 22-day average for general filing comments) and receive a follow-up question from the staff more often than all but one other topic that we track (assets). Don't expect a promise to fix non-GAAP metrics in future filings to suffice under this increased scrutiny.

> If you've been following along lately with the Commission's agenda, the emphasis on non-GAAP metrics won't come as a surprise. Enforcement actions show a similar focus on non-GAAP measures, for instance. And as we have flagged, a joint statement late last year from Clayton, SEC Chief

Accountant Sagar Teotia and Division of Corporation Finance Director William Hinman mentioned that companies' audit committees should pay particularly close attention to alternative accounting measures: "We encourage audit committees to be actively engaged in the review and presentation of non-GAAP measures and metrics to understand how management uses them to evaluate performance," they said.

So while the volume of comments has been on a decline, the relative proportion of those comments related to non-GAAP financial measures has risen. This is supported by two of the Big 4 accountings (PwC and EY) as well. In both of their annual publications related to SEC comment letter trends, the firms note non-GAAP financial measures are the most frequent SEC comment letter topic.

In PwC's publication ("US SEC Comment Letter Trends") published on March 12, 2021, the firm notes the SEC has several focus areas as it relates to non-GAAP measures. Refer to the following Exhibit for an excerpt from this publication.

Exhibit 12: PwC Comment Letter Trends

Non-GAAP Financial Measures

Non-GAAP financial measures result in frequent comments regarding compliance with Item 10(e) of Regulation S-K and the related compliance and disclosure interpretations, sometimes resulting in requests to remove or substantially modify non-GAAP metrics. Focus areas have included:
- The presentation with equal or greater prominence of the most directly comparable GAAP financial measure;
- The reconciliation to the most comparable GAAP financial measure;
- The appropriateness of adjustments to eliminate or smooth items identified as non-recurring, infrequent, or unusual;
- The use of individually tailored accounting principles; and
- The disclosure of why management believes the non-GAAP presentation provides useful information to investors regarding the financial condition or results of operations of the registrant.

The key takeaways from EY's similar publication ("Highlights of Trends in 2021 SEC Comment Letters," published on September 23, 2021) are very similar. In its publication, the firm notes the following with respect to non-GAAP financial measures.

The SEC staff continues to focus on whether non-GAAP financial measures reported by registrants comply with its compliance and disclosure interpretations (C&DIs) on this topic, including whether certain performance indicators should have been identified as non-GAAP measures and whether identified non-GAAP measures are presented with the most directly comparable GAAP financial measure at the appropriate prominence level. In addition, the SEC staff has continued to challenge whether a registrant was presenting a non-GAAP measure that employs an individually tailored accounting principle that may be misleading. For example, the SEC staff recently has challenged non-GAAP measures with the word "revenue" in the title, as discussed below. Most of the SEC staff comments have focused on registrants' use of non-GAAP measures in earnings releases and SEC filings. However, the SEC staff also reviews non-GAAP measures registrants use to communicate elsewhere (e.g., on their websites, in investor presentations).

Over the last year, the SEC staff emphasized the importance to investors of revenue determined in accordance with US GAAP and said more companies are inappropriately presenting non-GAAP measures with the word "revenue" in the title. For example, presenting a measure entitled "gross revenue" before discounts or other incentives that reduce revenue under US GAAP would not be appropriate. However, the staff said a registrant could present such a measure and call it "billings" if it is consistent with amounts invoiced to customers. In that case, the non-GAAP rules wouldn't apply because the metric would be considered a key performance indicator.

As you'll note from the preceding excerpts, non-GAAP financial measures aren't going away, and their importance is increasing with the regulators.

¶ 921 ILLUSTRATIVE EXAMPLES: SEC COMMENT LETTERS

Both of the firms' comment letter publications mentioned in the previous section of this chapter also provide excerpts from actual SEC comments (identifying entity information removed, though). However, in this final section of this chapter we'll review a few actual comment letters from the SEC as well as provide the responses from the respective entity to help provide a more comprehensive appreciation of the facts and circumstances. Note that all of the information provided is publicly available on the SEC.gov website, and some of the information, for presentation purposes, has been omitted.

Peloton Interactive, Inc.

The first comment letter example comes from Peloton Interactive, Inc. In this example, the entity received a comment letter from the SEC related to a Form 8-K that it filed on February 4, 2021. In response to the 8-K, the SEC noted the following:

> Form 8-K Furnished on February 4, 2021
>
> Exhibit 99.1
>
> Key Operating Metrics and Non-GAAP Financial Measures, page 14
>
> 2. Please revise to present your GAAP financial statements prior to your reconciliations of non-GAAP measures to avoid giving undue prominence to the non-GAAP data in accordance with Item 10(e)(1)(i)(A) of Regulation S-K. We also note similar disclosures in your 10-Q filings.

Subsequent to receipt of this comment letter, the entity provided the following response to the SEC:

> The Company respectfully acknowledges the Staff's comment and advises the Staff that as requested, the Company will present its GAAP financial statements prior to the Company's reconciliations of non-GAAP measures in future filings in accordance with Item 10(e)(1)(i)(A) of Regulation S-K.

In this example, which was fairly straightforward, the SEC required that the entity present its GAAP financial statements prior to the reconciliation of non-GAAP financial measures. The entity responded with an affirmative confirmation that it will do that going forward, and the SEC comment letter process ceased (for that year at least).

Monster Beverage Corp.

Sometimes the SEC comment letter process doesn't go quite as smoothly, and a few rounds of back-and-forth may be necessary. The next comment letter example provides an example of this situation.

> We have reviewed your filing and have the following comment. In our comment, we may ask you to provide us with information so we may better understand your disclosure.
>
> Please respond to this comment within ten business days by providing the requested information or advise us as soon as possible when you will respond. If you do not believe our comment applies to your facts and circumstances, please tell us why in your response.

Form 10-K for the Year Ended December 31, 2019

Management's Discussion and Analysis of Financial Condition and Results of Operations

Non-GAAP Financial Measures, page 48

We refer to your presentation of Gross Sales and note it is not a measure recognized under GAAP. Please help us understand:

- What Gross Sales represents. For example, tell us if this amount represents: the amount invoiced to your customers, the full retail price of your products, or some other value;

- How you considered Item 10(e) of Regulation S-K and Regulation G;

- How you analyze trends in the level of Promotional and Other Allowances, aside from the amount as percentage of gross sales as disclosed in your filing; and

- How Gross Sales is useful to investors given that gross sales may not be realized in the form of cash receipts due to the allowances given to your bottlers/distributors or retail customers.

In its response to the SEC, the entity noted the following:

Gross Sales represents the recognition of deferred revenue and amounts invoiced to customers net of cash discounts and returns. In future filings, beginning with the Company's quarterly report on Form 10-Q for the quarter ended September 30, 2020, anticipated to be filed with the Commission in November 2020, the Company will, where applicable, revise the disclosure as follows:

**Gross Sales represents the recognition of deferred revenue and amounts invoiced to customers net of cash discounts and returns.

The Company has considered both Item 10(e) of Regulation S-K and Regulation G in the Company's presentation of Gross Sales. With respect to Item 10(e) of Regulation S-K, the Company includes: (i) a presentation, with equal or greater prominence, of Net Sales (the most directly comparable GAAP financial measure) beginning on page 44 of the Form 10-K; (ii) a reconciliation of Gross Sales with Net Sales in a table on page 50 of the Form 10-K; and (iii) a footnote on pages 49-50 of the 10-K disclosing why the Company's management believes the presentation of Gross Sales provides useful information to investors regarding the Company's financial condition and results of operations. With respect to Regulation G, the Company includes (i) a presentation of Net Sales, the most directly comparable financial measure calculated and presented in accordance with GAAP, beginning on page 44 of the Form 10-K; and (ii) a reconciliation of Gross Sales with Net Sales in a table on page 50 of the Form 10-K. The Company will continue to ensure that the Company's presentation of Gross Sales complies with all applicable provisions of Item 10(e) of Regulation S-K and Regulation G.

The Company primarily analyzes trends in Promotional and Other Allowances as a percentage of Gross Sales as disclosed on page 49 of the Form 10-K. In addition, the Company analyzes trends on a per unit case volume basis. (Unit case volume is defined on page 50 of the Form 10-K.) For each of the foregoing, the Company compares historical trends from year to year, quarter to quarter, and month to month.

Although Gross Sales may not be realized in the form of cash receipts, we believe that Gross Sales is useful to investors because, as described in the footnote on pages 49-50 of the Form 10-K, Gross Sales allows evaluation of sales performance before the effect of any promotional items, which can mask certain performance issues, such as the timing of certain promotional programs. In addition, the presentation of Gross Sales with a reconciliation to Net Sales discloses the level of promotional spend incurred by the Company. The reconciliation of Gross Sales with Net Sales in a table on page 50 of the Form 10-K provides investors with the information necessary to understand the amount of Gross Sales that will be realized in the form of cash receipts, namely Net Sales.

We appreciate the Staff's time and attention and we hope that the foregoing has been responsive to the Staff's comment. If you have any further questions or need any additional information, please feel free to contact the undersigned at (951) 739-6200 at your convenience.

The fun didn't end there. While the previous example resulted in just one back-and-forth with the SEC, this example resulted in further follow-up from the SEC to the entity's response. Refer below for the SEC's follow-up note shortly thereafter.

We have carefully considered your response to prior comment 1 and your revised disclosures that "gross sales" represent the recognition of deferred revenue and amounts invoiced to customers, net of cash discounts and returns. Based on this clarification, it appears that "gross sales" is more akin to a billings-type metric. Accordingly, please revise the title of this metric so as not to imply that it represents GAAP sales or revenue and comply with the metrics guidance set forth in SEC Release No. 33-10751. Please also clarify for us how the amount of deferred revenue included in Gross Sales is determined. In your response, please include your proposed revisions, including your discussion of this metric in MD&A.

In response to the SEC's follow-up comment, the entity provided the following (Note: certain sections have been omitted for presentation purposes):

In future filings, where applicable, the Company will revise the title of Gross Sales to "Adjusted Billings" so as not to imply that it represents GAAP sales or revenue and to comply with the metrics guidance set forth in SEC Release No. 33-10751.

The amount of deferred revenue included in Gross Sales (to be titled Adjusted Billings in future filings) represents payments received from certain bottlers/distributors at inception of their distribution contracts or at the inception of certain sales/marketing programs and are accounted for as deferred revenue. Amounts received are recognized as revenue ratably over the anticipated life of the respective distribution agreement, generally 20 years, or through completion of the sales/marketing program.

STUDY QUESTIONS

5. Which Regulation includes the SEC rules that prescribe the detailed disclosure requirements applicable to periodic reports (e.g., Form 10-Qs and Form 10-Ks)?

    a. Regulation G

    b. Regulation D

    c. Regulation S-X

    d. Regulation S-K

6. When an entity includes non-GAAP financial measures in its notes to its financial statements, Regulation S-K requires a statement indicating which of the following?

    a. The reasons why the entity believes that presentation of the non-GAAP financial measure provides useful information to investors.

    b. Why the entity believes that the GAAP financial measures are not relevant.

    c. The reasons why the entity should not have to follow GAAP.

    d. Why the entity believes the non-GAAP financial measures provided will not result in an SEC comment letter.

CPE NOTE: When you have completed your study and review of chapters 8 and 9, which comprise Module 3, you may wish to take the Final Exam for this Module. Go to **cchcpelink.com/printcpe** to take this Final Exam online.

¶ 10,100 Answers to Study Questions
¶ 10,101 MODULE 1—CHAPTER 1

1. a. *Incorrect.* This is a correct statement regarding cryptocurrency. An example of a cryptocurrency is Bitcoin.

b. *Incorrect.* This is a correct statement regarding cryptocurrency. An example of a cryptocurrency is Dogecoin.

c. *Correct.* **This is an incorrect statement. Instead, cryptocurrency is not considered a security under U.S. securities law.**

d. *Incorrect.* This is a correct statement regarding cryptocurrency. An example of a cryptocurrency is Litecoin.

2. a. *Incorrect.* This is the accounting for companies that are not investment companies. Note that the AICPA added three new topics in 2022 related to cryptocurrency.

b. *Correct.* **This is the correct accounting for cryptocurrency for investment companies. For these companies, there is subsequent remeasurement of cryptocurrency.**

c. *Incorrect.* This is the accounting for companies that are not investment companies. Note that there was a Presidential Executive order issued in March 2022 to comprehensively consider opportunities for digital currencies.

d. *Incorrect.* This is the accounting for companies that are not investment companies. Cryptocurrency is rapidly growing and globally has over $1.5 trillion in market value.

3. a. *Incorrect.* This was not one of four recent SEC proposals discussed in the chapter. Instead, one of the proposals related to Rule 10b5/Insider Trading.

b. *Incorrect.* This was not one of four recent SEC proposals discussed in the chapter. Instead, one of the proposals related to share repurchases.

c. *Correct.* **This requires companies to disclose the relationship between executive compensation and financial performance (Dodd-Frank Act). Smaller reporting companies would provide scaled disclosures.**

d. *Incorrect.* This was not one of four recent SEC proposals discussed in the chapter. Instead, one of the proposals related to recovery of executive compensation.

4. a. *Incorrect.* This ASC Topic does not address disclosure requirements related to government assistance. Instead, it includes the requirements related to segment reporting.

b. *Incorrect.* This ASC Topic does not address disclosure requirements related to government assistance. Instead, it includes the accounting and reporting requirements related to revenue recognition.

c. *Correct.* **The amendments from ASU 2021-10 are expected to increase transparency in financial reporting by requiring business entities to disclose information about certain types of government assistance they receive.**

d. *Incorrect.* This ASC Topic does not address disclosure requirements related to government assistance. Instead, it includes the accounting and reporting requirements related to leasing transactions.

5. a. *Incorrect.* This ASU provides amendments related to stock compensation and is effective prospectively for fiscal years beginning after December 15, 2021, and interim periods within fiscal years beginning after December 15, 2022.

b. *Correct.* **The amendments are effective for public business entities for fiscal years, including interim periods within those fiscal years, beginning after December 15, 2022. For all other entities they are effective for fiscal years, including interim periods within those fiscal years, beginning after December 15, 2023.**

c. *Incorrect.* This ASU relates to government assistance. It is effective for financial statements issued for annual periods beginning after December 15, 2021, for all entities except not-for-profit entities and employee benefit plans within the scope of Topics 960, 962, and 965 on plan accounting.

d. *Incorrect.* This ASU relates to discount rates as it relates to ASC Topic 326. ASU No. 2022-01 is effective for public business entities for fiscal years beginning after December 15, 2022, and interim periods within those fiscal years.

6. a. *Incorrect.* Instead, ASU 2021-08 provided amendments related to business combinations. The amendments improve comparability after the business combination by providing consistent recognition and measurement guidance for revenue contracts with customers acquired in a business combination and revenue contracts with customers not acquired in a business combination.

b. *Incorrect.* ASU No. 2020-06 is effective for public business entities that meet the definition of a SEC filer, excluding entities eligible to be smaller reporting companies as defined by the SEC, for fiscal years beginning after December 15, 2021, including interim periods within those fiscal years.

c. *Incorrect.* This ASU does not address lease transactions. Note that for the subject ASU, early application is permitted.

d. *Correct.* **Consequently, more convertible debt instruments will be reported as a single liability instrument and more convertible preferred stock as a single equity instrument with no separate accounting for embedded conversion features.**

¶ 10,102 MODULE 1—CHAPTER 2

1. a. *Incorrect.* Social media is not used for phishing attacks.

b. *Correct.* **Phishing is done via email.**

c. *Incorrect.* Vishing is done over the phone.

d. *Incorrect.* Smishing is done using text messaging.

2. a. *Incorrect.* Phishing uses email to obtain personal information or to get you to download malware by clicking on a link.

b. *Correct.* **Ransomware encrypts the information on your computer.**

c. *Incorrect.* Spoofing hides the true origin of an email or website to make it look legitimate.

d. *Incorrect.* Spyware tracks one's information; it doesn't encrypt it.

3. a. *Correct.* **A good security configuration includes applying security patches to ensure the secure configuration of all systems is maintained and creating a system inventory and defining a baseline build for all devices.**

b. *Incorrect.* Incident management consists of establishing an incident response and disaster recovery capability, testing your incident management plans, providing specialist training, and reporting criminal incidents to law enforcement.

c. *Incorrect.* Network security consists of protecting your networks from attack, defending the network perimeter, filtering out unauthorized access and malicious content, and monitoring and testing security controls.

d. *Incorrect.* Monitoring consists of establishing a monitoring strategy and producing supporting policies, continuously monitoring all systems and networks, and analyzing logs for unusual activity that could indicate an attack.

4. a. *Incorrect.* COBIT is commonly used by public companies in the United States.

b. *Incorrect.* ISO 27001 is commonly used internationally.

c. *Correct.* **NIST is used by government agencies and contractors.**

d. *Incorrect.* HITRUST is used in the healthcare industry.

5. a. *Incorrect.* A passphrase containing 16 numbers could be cracked in 1 year.

b. *Incorrect.* A passphrase containing 13 mixed lowercase and uppercase letters could be cracked in 21,000 years.

c. *Incorrect.* A passphrase containing 13 numbers, and mixed lowercase and uppercase letters could be cracked in 6,000 years.

d. *Correct.* **A passphrase containing 11 mixed numbers, upper case letters, lowercase letters, and special symbols would take 71,000 years to crack.**

6. a. *Correct.* **A virtual private network (VPN) is used to create a secure encrypted Internet connection.**

b. *Incorrect.* Firewalls are used to prevent hacking and malware.

c. *Incorrect.* The PCI Security Standards are cybersecurity standards for credit card processing.

d. *Incorrect.* Biometrics are a means of identification.

¶ 10,103 MODULE 1—CHAPTER 3

1. a. *Incorrect.* Data on a blockchain is known as a block.

b. *Incorrect.* A series of blocks is a blockchain.

c. *Correct.* **Diverse computers used to store blocks of data are nodes.**

d. *Incorrect.* The Internet connects nodes, but it is not a node.

2. a. *Correct.* **Consensus occurs when all participants agree to the validity of a transaction.**

b. *Incorrect.* Provenance occurs when participants know where the asset, liability, or transaction came from and how it has changed over time.

c. *Incorrect.* Immutability occurs when recorded transactions cannot be changed.

d. *Incorrect.* Finality is a single shared ledger that provides all participants one place to go to determine the information.

3. a. *Incorrect.* Blocks contain data for valid transactions that are hashed and encoded into the blockchain.

b. *Correct.* **Decentralization is storing data across a peer-to-peer network.**

c. *Incorrect.* Block time is the average time it takes a network to add an additional block to the blockchain.

d. *Incorrect.* The digital signature comes from a combination of a private key and a public key.

4. a. *Incorrect.* A hard fork refers to a radical change to the protocol of a blockchain network that effectively results in two branches.

b. *Incorrect.* Staking is a consensus technique that allows blockchain networks to use less energy while retaining a reasonable level of decentralization on the Internet.

c. *Incorrect.* A sign message is an ID system to prove the ownership of cryptocurrency addresses.

d. *Correct.* **An airdrop occurs when free crypto coins are sent to your wallet.**

5. a. *Incorrect.* The IRS has ruled that virtual currency transactions create taxable events.

b. *Correct.* **The IRS considers virtual currencies to be property.**

c. *Incorrect.* Even though a Texas judge ruled Bitcoins to be a currency, the IRS considers them to be property.

d. *Incorrect.* Virtual currencies are not considered to be securities by the IRS, even though the Securities and Exchange Commission (SEC) considers them to be securities.

6. a. *Incorrect.* Closed virtual currencies have value in online games but not in the real world.

b. *Correct.* **Airline frequent flyer programs are examples of a single flow virtual currency.**

c. *Incorrect.* Convertible virtual currencies can be purchased and sold on the open market.

d. *Incorrect.* There is no such thing as a public virtual currency.

¶ 10,104 MODULE 2—CHAPTER 4

1. a. *Incorrect.* This is the term that is used to indicate that a requirement is presumptively mandatory. The auditor must comply with a presumptively mandatory requirement in all cases in which such a requirement is relevant except in rare circumstances discussed in paragraph .26 of AU-C Section 200.

b. *Incorrect.* This is not the correct term. Note that GAAS uses two categories of professional requirements, identified by specific terms, to describe the degree of responsibility it imposes on auditors.

c. *Correct.* **The auditor must comply with an unconditional requirement in all cases in which such requirement is relevant. In this respect, GAAS uses the word "must" to indicate an unconditional requirement.**

d. *Incorrect.* This is not the correct term. While GAAS uses two categories of professional requirements, for SSAEs and SSARS, the terms used for these categories mean the same.

2. a. *Correct.* **The engagement partner and other key engagement team members should discuss the susceptibility of the entity's financial statements to material misstatement and the application of the applicable financial reporting framework to the entity's facts and circumstances.**

b. *Incorrect.* Risk assessment procedures by themselves do not provide sufficient appropriate audit evidence on which to base the audit opinion.

c. *Incorrect.* Risk assessment procedures should include inquiries of management, analytical procedures, and observation/inspection.

d. *Incorrect.* During planning, the auditor should consider the results of the assessment of the risk of material misstatement due to fraud along with other information gathered in the process of identifying the risks of material misstatements.

3. a. *Incorrect.* In exercising professional judgment about which risks are significant risks, the auditor should consider at least the other risks.

b. *Incorrect.* Note that obtaining an understanding of the entity and its environment, including the entity's internal control, is a continuous, dynamic process of gathering, updating, and analyzing information throughout the audit.

c. *Correct.* **In exercising this judgment, the auditor should exclude the effects of identified controls related to the risk.**

d. *Incorrect.* It's also important to note that an understanding of the entity establishes a frame of reference within which the auditor plans the audit and exercises professional judgment throughout the audit when certain points occur.

4. a. *Correct.* **This section addresses the auditor's responsibility to consider laws and regulations in an audit of financial statements.**

b. *Incorrect.* This section addresses the auditor's responsibility to communicate with those charged with governance in an audit of financial statements.

c. *Incorrect.* This section addresses the auditor's responsibility to appropriately communicate to those charged with governance and management deficiencies in internal control that the auditor has identified in an audit of financial statements.

d. *Incorrect.* This section addresses the auditor's responsibility to plan an audit of financial statements.

5. a. *Incorrect.* This is one of the aspects related to internal control. Note that smaller entities may use less structured means and simpler processes and procedures to achieve their objectives.

b. *Incorrect.* This is one of the aspects related to internal control. Note that the components of internal control may not be clearly distinguished within smaller entities, but their underlying purposes are equally valid.

c. *Incorrect.* This is one of the aspects related to internal control. Note that internal control, no matter how effective, can provide an entity with only reasonable assurance about achieving the entity's financial reporting objectives.

d. *Correct.* **However, note that the way in which internal control is designed, implemented, and maintained varies with an entity's size and complexity.**

6. a. *Incorrect.* This section addresses the auditor's responsibility to consider laws and regulations in an audit of financial statements.

b. *Correct.* **This section explains what constitutes audit evidence in an audit of financial statements and addresses the auditor's responsibility to design and perform audit procedures to obtain sufficient appropriate audit evidence to be able to draw reasonable conclusions on which to base the auditor's opinion.**

c. *Incorrect.* This section applies when the auditor has decided to use audit sampling in performing audit procedures. It addresses the auditor's use of statistical and non-statistical sampling when designing and selecting the audit sample, performing tests of controls and tests of details, and evaluating the results from the sample.

d. *Incorrect.* This section addresses the auditor's responsibility to obtain written representations from management and, when appropriate, those charged with governance in an audit of financial statements.

¶ 10,105 MODULE 2—CHAPTER 5

1. a. *Incorrect.* A public key and a private key are used together to transfer cryptocurrency.

b. *Correct.* **Block explorer is a website or a tool that allows one to browse through blocks, view wallet addresses, network hash rates, transaction data, and other key information on the blockchain.**

c. *Incorrect.* A virtual currency wallet is used to store cryptocurrency.

d. *Incorrect.* Nodes are diverse computers used to store blocks of data.

2. a. *Incorrect.* A hard fork refers to a radical change to the protocol of a blockchain network that effectively results in two branches.

b. *Incorrect.* Staking is a consensus technique that allows blockchain networks to use less energy while retaining a reasonable level of decentralization on the Internet.

c. *Incorrect.* A sign message is an ID system to prove the ownership of cryptocurrency addresses.

d. *Correct.* **An airdrop occurs when free crypto coins are sent to one's wallet.**

3. a. *Incorrect.* The matching principle indicates expenses should be matched against the revenue they generate.

b. *Correct.* **Constructive receipt indicates that revenue is recognized, on a cash basis, when the funds are available to the recipient.**

c. *Incorrect.* The revenue recognition principle indicates that revenue is recognized, on an accrual basis, when the goods or services are provided.

d. *Incorrect.* Periodicity allows accountants to record and report transactions in distinct time periods such as months, quarters, or years.

4. a. *Correct.* **The requirement for an auditor to have adequate technical training and proficiency to perform the audit is in the General Standards.**

b. *Incorrect.* The Standards of Field Work cover planning, supervising, obtaining an understanding of the entity, and obtaining sufficient appropriate audit evidence but do not address training or proficiency.

c. *Incorrect.* The Standards of Reporting address the preparation of the audit report but do not address technical training and proficiency.

d. *Incorrect.* There are no Standards of Training.

5. a. *Incorrect.* Only 68% of all data points are within 1 standard deviation of the mean.

b. *Correct.* **95% of all data points fall within 2 standard deviations of the mean.**

c. *Incorrect.* 99.7% of all data points fall within 3 standard deviations of the mean.

d. *Incorrect.* Over 99.7% of all data points fall within 4 standard deviations of the mean.

6. a. *Correct.* **Vouching starts with the transaction record and verifies there is a corresponding source document.**

b. *Incorrect.* Tracing starts with the source document and verifies there is a transaction posted in the accounting records.

c. *Incorrect.* Data mining is used to identify items to test.

d. *Incorrect.* Controls testing is testing the efficiency of the organization's internal controls.

¶ 10,106 MODULE 2—CHAPTER 6

1. a. *Incorrect.* Robbery and murder are categorized as blue-collar crimes, not white-collar crimes.

b. *Incorrect.* The term *white-collar crime* is attributed to Dr. Edwin Sutherland. Gabriel Tarde was a 19th-century French criminologist who developed the theory of differential reinforcement.

c. *Incorrect.* According to a study by the Association of Certified Fraud Examiners, only 15 percent of such victims make a full recovery.

d. *Correct.* **Court-ordered restitution and voluntary restitution agreements are common punishments for white-collar criminals.**

2. a. *Incorrect.* Gabriel Tarde developed the Theory of Differential Association.

b. *Correct.* **Ronald Akers developed the Social Learning Theory.**

c. *Incorrect.* Edwin Sutherland developed the Theory of Differential Association.

d. *Incorrect.* Donald Cressey developed the Fraud Triangle Theory.

3. a. *Incorrect.* Corruption occurs less frequently than other types of occupational fraud.

b. *Incorrect.* Financial statement fraud is the least frequent type of occupational fraud.

c. *Incorrect.* Tax fraud is not a type of occupational fraud.

d. *Correct.* **Asset misappropriations are the most frequently occurring occupational fraud.**

4. a. *Correct.* **A virtual private network is used to create a secure encrypted Internet connection.**

b. *Incorrect.* Firewalls are used to prevent hacking and malware.

c. *Incorrect.* The PCI Security Standards are cybersecurity standards for credit card processing.

d. *Incorrect.* Biometrics are a means of identification.

5. a. *Incorrect.* Cash larceny is stealing cash that has been recorded in the accounting system either from a register, deposit, or the safe.

b. *Incorrect.* Kiting is done with checks, not with cash.

c. *Correct.* **Skimming is the act of taking the cash before it is recorded in the accounting system.**

d. *Incorrect.* Cash drawer loans involve employees putting personal nonsufficient funds (NSF) checks in their cash drawer in exchange for cash.

6. a. *Incorrect.* A bill and hold scheme is a revenue scheme.

b. *Incorrect.* Lapping is an accounts receivable fraud.

c. *Incorrect.* Cooking the books is financial statement fraud.

d. *Correct.* **Short shipping is a type of inventory fraud.**

¶ 10,107 MODULE 2—CHAPTER 7

1. a. *Incorrect.* This is an area related to the governance component. The governance component of ESG encompasses information about the system of rules, practices, and processes by which an entity is directed and controlled.

b. *Correct.* **Inclusion policies and efforts relate to the social component of ESG. Instead, a component of the governance component relates to entity resiliency.**

c. *Incorrect.* This is an area related to the governance component. Note that the social component encompasses information about an entity's values and business relationships.

d. *Incorrect.* This is an area related to the governance component. Note that the environmental component addresses how an entity is exposed to and manages risks and opportunities related to the environment.

2. a. *Incorrect.* This is an example of an industry factor. Entities in certain industries or geographic locations may need to implement changes to enable their business activities to continue in the event of extreme climate-related events, such as wildfires or flooding.

b. *Incorrect.* This is an example of an industry factor. Note that some entities face uncertainty about future climate regulations.

c. *Correct.* **The regulatory environment related to ESG matters continues to evolve, with a current emphasis on climate change.**

d. *Incorrect.* This is an example of an industry factor. Note that some regulations may create economic disincentives for entities to continue to emit carbon by imposing levies or taxes on high-emission sources.

3. a. *Incorrect.* This section requires the auditor to obtain an understanding of the entity and its environment, including the entity's internal control as it relates to the audit.

b. *Correct.* **Note that the auditor has a responsibility to plan and perform the audit to obtain reasonable assurance about whether the financial statements as a whole are free from material misstatement to enable the auditor to report on whether the financial statements are prepared, in all material respects, in accordance with the applicable financial reporting framework.**

c. *Incorrect.* This section addresses the auditor's responsibility to evaluate the effect of identified misstatements on the audit and the effect of uncorrected misstatements, if any, on the financial statements.

d. *Incorrect.* This section applies when the auditor has decided to use audit sampling in performing audit procedures. It addresses the auditor's use of statistical and non-statistical sampling when designing and selecting the audit sample, performing tests of controls and tests of details, and evaluating the results from the sample.

4. a. *Incorrect.* Preparers of sustainability information often seek (but have not always sought) to increase the credibility of their reported sustainability information to users.

b. *Incorrect.* Entities often prepare (but have not always prepared) separate reports on GHG information. Note that AICPA attestation standards offer some guidance for how to approach these engagements.

c. *Correct.* **For example, sustainability information related to biodiversity is likely to require more extensive procedures on measurement uncertainty and**

the methodologies for capturing and reporting such information than sustainability information related to health and safety or employment practices.

d. *Incorrect.* The characteristics of sustainability information affect the availability of sufficient evidence and the nature of the procedures to be performed.

5. a. *Correct.* **As required by AT-C Section 205, the practitioner should consider materiality for the subject matter when establishing the overall engagement strategy, including the determination of the nature, timing, and extent of procedures; and when evaluating whether uncorrected misstatements are material— individually or in the aggregate.**

b. *Incorrect.* As required by AT-C Section 210, the practitioner should consider materiality when planning and performing the review engagement, including the determination of the nature, timing, and extent of procedures.

c. *Incorrect.* Materiality as a concept relates to both what information is material to users and thus should be included in the sustainability report and to whether an identified misstatement, including an omitted disclosure, would be material to users.

d. *Incorrect.* Assessing the significance of a misstatement of some items of the sustainability information may be more dependent on qualitative than quantitative considerations.

6. a. *Incorrect.* In forming an opinion or conclusion, AT-C Sections 205 and 210 require the practitioner to evaluate his or her conclusion regarding the sufficiency and appropriateness of engagement evidence obtained and whether uncorrected misstatements are material, individually or in the aggregate.

b. *Correct.* **The criteria for sustainability information may not include explicit criteria for the disclosure of measurement uncertainty.**

c. *Incorrect.* Additionally, the consistency of criteria and measurement method(s) used from the prior period should also be considered.

d. *Incorrect.* One should also consider whether the disclosures are informative of matters that affect the use, understanding, and interpretation of the sustainability information in the context of its intended purpose.

¶ 10,108 MODULE 3—CHAPTER 8

1. a. *Correct.* **This is not something that would be disclosed in MD&A. Instead, this would be discussed in the notes to the financial statements.**

b. *Incorrect.* This would be included in the introduction of MD&A. The SEC further notes in Item 303 that MD&A should focus specifically on "material events and uncertainties known to management that are reasonably likely to cause reported financial information not to be necessarily indicative of future operating results or of future financial condition."

c. *Incorrect.* This would be included in the introduction of MD&A. Overall, the SEC notes that MD&A must be "of the financial statements and other statistical data that the registrant believes will enhance a reader's understanding of the registrant's financial condition, cash flows and other changes in financial condition and results of operations."

d. *Incorrect.* This would be included in the introduction of MD&A. This would include those presented by known material trends and uncertainties, on which the company's executives are most focused for both the short and long term, as well as the actions they are taking to address these opportunities, challenges, and risks.

2. a. *Incorrect.* The results of operations area of MD&A should present those transactions/events that are unusual or infrequent, and it should present significant economic changes that materially affected the amount of income reported.

b. *Incorrect.* Critical accounting estimates reflect those types of estimates which involve either a significant level of uncertainty and/or a potential material impact on a company's income statement or balance sheet.

c. *Correct.* However, this section of the MD&A should not simply give a description of the various inflows and outflows of cash.

d. *Incorrect.* This is not one of the three MD&A areas. Instead, the three areas include liquidity and capital resources, results of operations, and critical accounting estimates.

3. a. *Incorrect.* Critical accounting estimates reflect those types of estimates which involve a significant level of uncertainty and/or a potential material impact on a company's income statement or balance sheet.

b. *Incorrect.* The primary goal of the liquidity and capital resources section is to provide additional information and context around a company's ability to meet its short-term obligations as well as the company's plans for using cash both in the short and long-term.

c. *Incorrect.* This is a component of the liquidity and capital resources section of MD&A. The SEC notes that in addition to explaining how the cash requirements identified in MD&A fit into a company's overall business plan, the company should focus on the resources available to satisfy those cash requirements.

d. *Correct.* In addition to these points, it should be reserved for discussions about known trends or uncertainties that may have had a positive or negative impact on income from continuing operations.

4. a. *Correct.* This is an incorrect statement. Registrants should address the underlying reasons for changes in the price versus volume mix. For example, if sales declined because the volume of goods sold decreased by 20 percent, but this was offset by a 10 percent increase in price, the discussion in MD&A should not stop once it identifies the price and volume components.

b. *Incorrect.* This is a correct statement. In fact, the discussion and analysis of segments may be integrated with the discussion of the consolidated amounts to avoid unnecessary duplication.

c. *Incorrect.* This is a correct statement. The discussion and analysis should be comprehensive. All components of a company's results of operations, including those that may not be allocated to the segments in determining the segmental profit or loss should be discussed.

d. *Incorrect.* This is a correct statement. A discussion of the nature and impact of significant tax rate reconciling items should also be considered.

5. a. *Incorrect.* These are incorrect terms with respect to critical accounting estimates. The discussion of critical accounting estimates in the MD&A section should "supplement, not duplicate, the description of accounting policies that are already disclosed in the notes to the financial statements" and "provide greater insight into the quality and variability of information regarding financial condition and operating performance."

b. *Incorrect.* While critical accounting estimates involve estimation uncertainty, they are not limited to those where there is simply a "likely" impact. Instead, there is a different type of impact involved.

¶10,108

c. *Incorrect.* While critical accounting estimates involve a potential material impact, they are not limited to those that simply involve judgment. There is another term that is more appropriate.

d. *Correct.* **Companies are required to provide qualitative and quantitative information necessary to understand the estimation uncertainty and the impact the critical accounting estimate has had or is reasonably likely to have on financial condition or results of operations to the extent the information is material and reasonably available.**

6. a. *Correct.* **In other words, MD&A would focus on material changes in liquidity and capital resources, results of operations, and critical accounting estimates from the most recent 10-K.**

b. *Incorrect.* This is the incorrect term. Instead, another type of change is more applicable with respect to the previous annual period.

c. *Incorrect.* This is the incorrect term. You should note that for the annual period, companies need to disclose information about liquidity and capital resources, results of operations, and critical accounting estimates.

d. *Incorrect.* This is the incorrect term. The interim reporting requirements for MD&A are also included within Item 303 of Regulation S-K.

¶ 10,109 MODULE 3—CHAPTER 9

1. a. *Incorrect.* Diluted EPS is not a type of non-GAAP financial measure. Diluted EPS is a calculation used to assess the quality of a company's EPS if all convertible securities were exercised.

b. *Incorrect.* Cash flows from operating activities is not a type of non-GAAP financial measure. Cash flow from operations is a section of an entity's cash flow statement that represents the amount of cash a company generates (or consumes) from its primary operations.

c. *Incorrect.* Net income is not a type of non-GAAP financial measure. Instead, a non-GAAP financial measure adjusts the most directly comparable GAAP measure reported on the audited financial statements by excluding items the company believes are not good indicators of its performance.

d. *Correct.* **This is a type of non-GAAP financial measure. Free cash flow is an important measurement since it shows how efficient a company is at generating cash.**

2. a. *Correct.* **Number of subscribers is a type of nonfinancial key performance indicator. Another example of a nonfinancial key performance indicator is number of employees.**

b. *Incorrect.* This is not a nonfinancial key performance indicator. Instead, this is an example of a financial key performance indicator.

c. *Incorrect.* This is not a nonfinancial key performance indicator. Note that key performance indicators can often be bucketed between financial and nonfinancial.

d. *Incorrect.* Sales per square foot is not a nonfinancial key performance indicator. Instead, this is an example of a financial key performance indicator.

3. a. *Incorrect.* One of the overarching principles with respect to non-GAAP financial measures is that they cannot be misleading. In other words, they can't be used in a way which seemingly shows an entity is doing better than its counterpart that is not using the same non-GAAP financial measures (if it's not the case).

b. *Incorrect.* The U.S. Public Company Accounting Oversight Board (PCAOB) is a private-sector, non-profit corporation, created by the Sarbanes-Oxley Act of 2002, to oversee the auditors of public companies in order to protect the interests of investors and further the public interest.

c. *Incorrect.* The International Accounting Standards Board (IASB) is an independent, private-sector body that develops and approves International Financial Reporting Standards (IFRSs).

d. *Correct.* **The FASB further noted that "the challenge lies in the potential for investors to misunderstand performance if they selectively use highly customized or tailored non-GAAP-based figures."**

4. a. *Correct.* **Regulation G, and many other non-GAAP financial measures regulations, came about as a direct result of the Sarbanes-Oxley Act of 2002. Regulation G, in fact, was just one of several new/revised regulations as the SEC took on the task of reigning in the rampant use of non-GAAP financial measures.**

b. *Incorrect.* Regulation D relates to the rules governing the limited offer and sale of securities without registration under the Securities Act of 1933.

c. *Incorrect.* Regulation S-X relates to the form and content of and requirements for financial statements.

d. *Incorrect.* Regulation S-K does not relate to earnings calls or investor presentations but rather to reporting requirements.

5. a. *Incorrect.* Regulation G identifies what are not non-GAAP financial measures.

b. *Incorrect.* Regulation D relates to the rules governing the limited offer and sale of securities without registration under the Securities Act of 1933.

c. *Incorrect.* Regulation S-X relates to the form and content of and requirements for financial statements.

d. *Correct.* **Regulation S-K also requires that an entity disclose the reasons the entity believes that presentation of the non-GAAP financial measure provides useful information to investors regarding the registrant's financial condition and results of operations.**

6. a. *Correct.* **Additionally, the entity also needs to provide a presentation, with equal or greater prominence, of the most directly comparable financial measure calculated and presented in accordance with GAAP.**

b. *Incorrect.* This is not a required disclosure by Regulation S-K. Note that both Regulation G and Regulation S-K require a comparable GAAP presentation along with an appropriate of reconciliation.

c. *Incorrect.* This is not a required disclosure by Regulation S-K. Regulation S-K includes the SEC rules that prescribe the detailed disclosure requirements applicable to registration statements, periodic reports.

d. *Incorrect.* This is not a required disclosure by Regulation S-K. As long as non-GAAP financial measures are properly presented, properly disclosed, and respective regulations are followed, then these measures can be perfectly acceptable and provide certain insights into an entity's performance.

¶10,109

Index

References are to paragraph (¶) numbers.

¶ 10,200 Glossary

Accounting: The process of documenting and recording a company's business transactions.

Accounts payable: Amounts due to vendors for products and services received.

Accounts receivable: Amounts due from customers for products or services provided.

AICPA: American Institute of Certified Public Accountants.

Airdrop: Occurs when one has free crypto coins sent to their wallet. They did not purchase or earn the coins.

Automated controls: Controls are controls that are built into computer software. Automated controls can be either preventive or detective.

Balance sheet: Summarizes a company's assets, liabilities, and shareholders' equity at a specific point in time.

Bank reconciliation: The process of matching the balances in an entity's accounting records for a cash account to the corresponding information on a bank statement.

Bitcoin: A type of virtual currency.

Block time: The average time it takes the network to add an additional block to the blockchain.

Blockchains: Lists of records held on diverse computers (nodes) that are used to record and verify data.

Boilerplate: Any text, such as a financial statement disclosure, that is/can be reused more than once in a new context without any substantial changes to the original.

Business combination: A transaction or other event in which an acquirer obtains control of one or more businesses. Transactions sometimes referred to as *true mergers* or *mergers of equals* also are business combinations.

Chart of accounts: A list of all accounts used in a business.

Closed virtual currencies: Virtual currencies used in a closed community, most commonly multiplayer online games. The currency is fictional and has no value outside the game.

Computer crime: An illegal act conducted using a computer or electronic device.

Computer forensics: Procedures applied to computers and electronic equipment to gather evidence that can be used in a court of law.

Computer virus: Usually hidden in a computer program and performs functions such as copying or deleting data files. A computer virus creates copies of itself that it inserts in data files or other programs.

Computer worm: A type of malware that transmits itself over networks and the Internet to infect more computers with the malware.

Consensus: All participants agree to the validity of the transaction.

Constant currency: When certain exchange rates are used to eliminate the effect of significant fluctuations when calculating financial performance numbers.

Control activities: Activities such as approvals, segregation of duties, reconciliations, reviews, procedures, etc., that ensure that processes are followed and that the opportunities for errors or fraud have been minimized.

Control environment: Often referred to as the "tone at the top," it is the ethical values of the organization and relies on the strength of corporate governance.

Control risk: The risk that a control does not prevent or detect a material misstatement in an account balance.

CPA: Certified Public Accountant.

Critical accounting estimates: Those types of estimates which involve either a significant level of uncertainty and/or a potential material impact on a company's income statement or balance sheet.

Cryptocurrency: A digital currency using cryptography to secure transactions and to control the creation of new currency units. Cryptocurrency is medium of exchange that is built on distributed ledger technology.

Current liabilities: Liabilities expected to be paid in cash within 12 months or the accounting cycle of a business. The 12-month period is almost always used.

Data breach: The release or taking of data from a secure source to an unsecured third-party location (computer).

Data mining: A process that uses mathematical algorithms to detect hidden patterns in data.

Debt covenant: A condition (or conditions) in a loan agreement that requires the borrower to meet certain conditions or to not take certain action.

Decentralization: Storing data across a peer-to-peer network.

Detective controls: Policies and procedures that are put in place to help find fraud of errors that have already occurred. Detective controls are put in place so that corrections can be made.

Diagrams or graphs: Representations of quantified measurements and factual information or may be representative of soft narrative information.

EBIT: Earnings before interest and taxes.

EBITDA: Earnings before interest, taxes, depreciation, and amortization.

Embezzlement: Theft of money or property by an employee or fiduciary from their employer.

Entity-level controls: Internal controls designed to provide reasonable assurance that the entity's objectives are met. Entity-level controls relate to the whole organization.

ESG: Environmental, social, and corporate governance, an approach to evaluating the extent to which a corporation works on behalf of social goals that go beyond the role of a corporation to maximize profits on behalf of the corporation's shareholders.

Factual narrative: Nonnumerical information that is supported by events that have occurred and is objectively determinable.

Fair value: The price that would be received to sell an asset or paid to transfer a liability in an orderly transaction between market participants at the measurement date.

Financial Accounting Standards Board (FASB): A private, non-profit organization standard-setting body whose primary purpose is to establish and improve generally accepted accounting principles (GAAP) within the United States in the public's interest.

Financial statement fraud: Fraud designed to "cook the books" and present false information on the financial statements.

Firewall: Hardware or software designed to prevent malware from being installed on a computer and to prevent unauthorized access to a computer system.

Fixed assets: Assets that are used to generate revenue or operate the business. Fixed assets are generally held as long-term assets and are not quickly converted into cash.

Fraud: A deception deliberately practiced in order to secure unfair or unlawful gain.

Fraud auditor: An accountant especially skilled in auditing who is generally engaged in auditing with a view toward fraud discovery, documentation, and prevention.

Fraud triangle: The theory developed by Dr. Donald Cressey explaining why individuals commit occupational fraud.

Free cash flow: Cash from operations minus capital expenditures.

Generally accepted accounting principles (GAAP): The accounting principles and standards accepted by consensus among professional accountants.

Ghost employee: A phantom employee that exists only on the books.

Going concern: A term for a company that has the resources needed in order to continue to operate indefinitely.

Hacker: Someone attempting to gain access to a computer for malicious or illegal purposes.

Hard fork: Refers to a radical change to the protocol of a blockchain network that effectively results in two branches, one that follows the previous protocol and one that follows the new version. In a hard fork, holders of tokens in the original blockchain will be granted tokens in the new fork as well, but miners must choose which blockchain to continue verifying. A hard fork can occur in any blockchain, and not only Bitcoin (where hard forks have created Bitcoin Cash and Bitcoin SV, among several others, for example).

I-9: A form used to document an employee's legal right to work in the United States.

Identifying information: Information such as a name, phone number, address, or Social Security number that can be used to identify an individual.

Identity theft: Broadly defined as the use of one person's identity or personally identifying information by another person without his or her permission. Identity theft is a type of fraud and can be committed against an individual or organization.

Immutability: Recorded transactions cannot be changed. If an error occurs, a new transaction must be input to reverse the error.

Impairment: An other than temporary decline in value of an asset where the market value of the asset is lower than the book value of the asset.

Inquiry: Consists of seeking information of knowledgeable persons within or outside the entity.

Internal control: A process effected by those charged with governance, management, and other personnel that is designed to provide reasonable assurance about the achievement of the entity's objectives with regard to the reliability of financial reporting, effectiveness and efficiency of operations, and compliance with applicable laws and regulations.

Item 303: A section of Regulation S-K that prescribes the reporting requirements related to Management's Discussion and Analysis (MD&A).

Key performance indicator (KPI): Evaluates the success of an organization or of a particular activity in which it engages.

Lease: A contract, or part of a contract, that conveys the right to control the use of identified property, plant, or equipment (an identified asset) for a period of time in exchange for consideration.

Liquidity: A company's ability to convert an asset or a security into cash.

Malware: Software that is placed on computers or cell phones to hijack the computers, steal data, or encrypt the data for ransom.

Management's Discussion and Analysis (MD&A): A section within a company's annual report or quarterly filing where executives analyze the company's performance.

Manual controls: Controls that are that are done by individuals. Manual controls can be either preventive or detective.

Matching principle: Principle that requires companies to match expenses with the revenue they generate. The matching principle is important for accrual-based accounting.

Materiality: A concept or convention within auditing and accounting relating to the importance/significance of an amount, transaction, or discrepancy.

Means of identification: Any type of information that can identify a particular individual, such as Social Security numbers, credit card numbers, or the like.

Misappropriation: Obtaining something of value or avoiding an obligation by deception or false statements; a type of fraud.

Money laundering: Taking funds from an illegal source, hiding the source of funds, and making the funds available for use without legal restrictions or penalties.

Non-GAAP financial measure: A numerical measure of a registrant's historical or future financial performance, financial position, or cash flow that excludes amounts, or is subject to adjustments that have the effect of excluding amounts, that are included in the most directly comparable measure calculated and presented in accordance with GAAP in the statement of comprehensive income, balance sheet, or statement of cash flows of the issuer; or includes amounts, or is subject to adjustments that have the effect of including amounts, that are excluded from the most directly comparable GAAP measure so calculated and presented.

Occupational fraud: Fraud occurring in the workplace or relating to employment.

Periodicity assumption: Assumption that allows accountants to post transactions in time periods, even if the transaction extends beyond the end of the period. Accountants usually use months, quarters, and years to report accounting information.

Pharming: A virus or malicious software is secretly loaded onto the victim's computer and hijacks the web browser.

Phishing: Is a technique used by fraudsters to obtain personal information for purposes of identity theft. This theft can include sending illegitimate emails asking for personal information.

Predication of fraud: Circumstances, when taken as a whole, will lead a reasonably prudent professional to believe a fraud is occurring, has occurred, or will occur.

Preventive controls: Policies and procedures that are put in place to help prevent errors or fraud from occurring.

Process-level controls: Internal controls designed to provide reasonable assurance that the entity's processes are followed, applications are working, and transactions are properly completed and recorded. Process-level controls relate to a single activity.

Prominence: The quality, state, or fact of being prominent or conspicuous.

Quantified information: Numerical information including statistics, which may be produced internally or obtained externally (such as from other organizations outside its organizational boundary but within its operational boundary).

Reasonable assurance: The level of confidence that the financial statements are not materially misstated that an auditor, exercising professional skill and care, is expected to attain from an audit.

Regulation G: Provides the general rules regarding disclosure of non-GAAP financial measures.

Regulation S-K: Provides the standard instructions for filing forms under the Securities Act of 1933, Securities Exchange Act of 1934, and Energy Policy and Conservation Act of 1975.

Reference rate reform: The global transition away from referencing the London Interbank Offered Rate (LIBOR) and other interbank offered rates (IBORs), toward new reference rates that are more reliable and robust.

Risk assessment: An assessment conducted to determine where key controls need to be in the processes of the organization. Controls should be put in place in high-risk areas, but it is necessary to consider the cost/benefit of each control because excessive controls can reduce an organization's efficiency.

Rootkits: Software tools that modify the operating system to hide malware from the computer users. Some rootkits contain code that prevents the malware from being removed from the computer.

Sign messages: Sign messages, wallet signing, and digital signatures are digital ways to verify documents and digital messages. Sign messages is a kind of ID system to prove the ownership of Bitcoin or a cryptocurrency address. Without revealing your private keys, you can prove the ownership by sharing your wallet signature.

Skimming: Removal of cash from a victim entity prior to its entry in an accounting system.

Soft narrative: Nonnumerical information that is subjective.

Spoofing: Term used to describe fraudulent email activity in which the sender's address or other parts of the email header are altered to appear as though the email originated from a different source.

Staking or farming: A "proof of stake" is a consensus technique that allows blockchain networks to use less energy while retaining a reasonable level of decentralization on the internet.

Substantial doubt: In management's judgment, it is probable that the client will not continue as a going concern.

U.S. Securities and Exchange Commission (SEC): Protects investors by enforcing U.S. securities laws, taking action against wrongdoers, and overseeing U.S. securities markets and firms to ensure that investors are treated fairly and honestly.

Virtual currency: A currency that only exists in cyberspace. There is no physical or tangible item to represent the currency.

¶ 10,300 Final Exam Instructions

To complete your Final Exam go to **cchcpelink.com/printcpe**, click on the title of the exam you wish to complete and add it to your shopping cart (you will need to register with CCH CPELink if you have not already). Click **Proceed to Checkout** and enter your credit card information. Click **Place Order** to complete your purchase of the final exam. The final exam will be available in **My Dashboard** under **My Account**.

This Final Exam is divided into three Modules. There is a grading fee for each Final Exam submission.

Online Processing Fee:	Recommended CPE:
$144.00 for Module 1	6 hours for Module 1
$144.00 for Module 2	6 hours for Module 2
$96.00 for Module 3	4 hours for Module 3
$384.00 for all three Modules	16 hours for all three Modules

Instructions for purchasing your CPE Tests and accessing them after purchase are provided on the **cchcpelink.com/printcpe** website. **Please note, manual grading is no longer available for Top Accounting and Auditing Issues. All answer sheets must be submitted online for grading and processing.**

Recommended CPE credit is based on a 50-minute hour. Because CPE requirements vary from state to state and among different licensing agencies, please contact your CPE governing body for information on your CPE requirements and the applicability of a particular course for your requirements

---

Expiration Date: September 30, 2024

Evaluation: To help us provide you with the best possible products, please take a moment to fill out the course Evaluation located after your Final Exam.

Wolters Kluwer, CCH is registered with the National Association of State Boards of Accountancy (NASBA) as a sponsor of continuing professional education on the National Registry of CPE Sponsors. State boards of accountancy have final authority on the acceptance of individual courses for CPE credit. Complaints regarding registered sponsors may be submitted to the National Registry of CPE Sponsors through its website: www.learningmarket.org.

Additional copies of this course may be downloaded from **cchcpelink.com/printcpe**. Printed copies of the course are available for $8.00 by calling 1-800-344-3734 (ask for product 10024493-0010).

¶ 10,301 FINAL EXAM QUESTIONS: MODULE 1

1. Which of the following identifies a medium of exchange that is built on distributed ledger technology?

    a. Blockchain

    b. Soft fork

    c. Cryptocurrency

    d. Smart contract

2. Which organization added three new topics in 2022 to its agenda with respect to cryptocurrency?

    a. FASB

    b. AICPA

    c. SEC

    d. PCAOB

3. The requirement that companies disclose the relationship between executive compensation and financial performance is a result of which of the following Congressional Acts?

    a. Dodd-Frank Act

    b. Sarbanes-Oxley Act

    c. Tax Cuts and Jobs Act

    d. SECURE Act

4. One of the recent Securities and Exchange Commission (SEC) proposals discussed requires a company to provide more detailed and more frequent disclosures about purchases of which of the following?

    a. Debt

    b. Intangible assets

    c. Cryptocurrency

    d. Its equity securities

5. Which Accounting Standards Update (ASU) eliminates the troubled debt restructuring (TDR) recognition and measurement guidance and requires that an entity evaluate whether the modification represents a new loan or a continuation of an existing loan?

    a. ASU 2021-09

    b. ASU 2021-10

    c. ASU 2022-01

    d. ASU 2022-02

6. ASU 2021-09 allows _____ that are not public business entities to make the risk-free rate election by class of underlying asset, rather than at the entity-wide level.

    a. Lessees

    b. Lessors

    c. Both lessees and lessors

    d. Either lessees or lessors

7. ASU 2021-08 requires that entities apply which of the following ASC Topics to recognize and measure contract assets and contract liabilities in a business combination?

    a. ASC Topic 350

    b. ASC Topic 606

    c. ASC Topic 805

    d. ASC Topic 958

8. ASU 2021-05 amends the lease classification requirements for lessors to align them with practice under which of the following ASC Topics?

    a. ASC Topic 350

    b. ASC Topic 530

    c. ASC Topic 606

    d. ASC Topic 840

9. ASU 2021-02 introduces a new practical expedient that simplifies the application of the guidance about identifying performance obligations for which of the following?

    a. Not-for-profits

    b. Investment companies

    c. Franchisors

    d. Financial service entities

10. ASU 2020-06 related to the accounting for convertible instruments and contracts in an entity's own equity is effective for SEC filers for fiscal years beginning after which of the following dates?

    a. December 15, 2021

    b. December 15, 2022

    c. December 15, 2023

    d. December 15, 2024

11. The PCI Data Security Standard v4.0 must be implemented by which of the following dates?

    a. March 31, 2022

    b. March 31, 2023

    c. March 31, 2024

    d. March 31, 2025

12. Which of the following is *not* an example of router security for employees working from home?

    a. Changing the default SSID

    b. Using WPA3 security

    c. Using a universal plug-and-play

    d. Using ethernet connections instead of Wi-Fi

13. Which of the following is *not* one of the five components of the NIST framework?

    a. Identify

    b. Opportunity

    c. Detect

    d. Recover

14. Which of the following would be considered part of the Internet of things (IoT)?

    a. Cloud computing

    b. Websites

    c. Cars

    d. Laptops

15. The Internet Crime Complaint Center reported _____ in cyber fraud losses in 2021.

    a. $2.7 billion

    b. $3.5 billion

    c. $4.2 billion

    d. $6.9 billion

16. Which of the following countries reported the largest number of cyber fraud victims in 2021?

    a. United States

    b. Mexico

    c. Japan

    d. Canada

17. Which percentage of data breaches is caused by insiders?

    a. 62 percent

    b. 11 percent

    c. 25 percent

    d. 2 percent

18. Using the Internet to connect with remote servers to access software or data is known as which of the following?

    a. Cloud computing

    b. Virtual private network

    c. Firewall

    d. Proxies

19. Which of the following is *not* a key cybersecurity internal control when employees are working from home?

    a. Employee training

    b. Multifactor authentication

    c. SOC for cybersecurity

    d. Antivirus software

20. Which of the following is *not* a cost-effective cybersecurity for small businesses?

    a. IT department personnel monitoring the IT system 24/7

    b. Conducting regular phishing and vishing tests

    c. Using external hard drives for data storage

    d. Having a guest network

21. Which of the following statements is incorrect with respect to blockchain technology?

    a. Data is stored on computer nodes.

    b. Public blockchains are "open source" and can be used by anyone.

    c. Private blockchains are maintained on closed or private networks.

    d. Blockchains cannot be hacked or compromised.

22. Which type of virtual currency wallet is the safest from online hacking?

    a. Paper

    b. Desktop

    c. Mobile

    d. Web

23. The _____ has issued recommended recording crypto asset transactions as long-lived intangible assets.

    a. IASB

    b. AICPA

    c. FASB

    d. ASB

24. Which of the following identifies a way that businesses could use blockchains?

    a. Voter registration and to verify votes

    b. Tracking smart contracts

    c. Tracking criminal records

    d. Police and criminal records

25. Which of the following would *not* be a viable use of a blockchain for auditors?

    a. Storing and managing audit evidence

    b. Verification of the care, custody, and control of audit evidence

    c. Verification of the date audit evidence was obtained

    d. Gathering audit evidence

26. Which of the following is *not* a type of blockchain?

    a. Public blockchain

    b. Permissioned blockchain

    c. Enhanced blockchain

    d. Consortium blockchain

27. Blockchains can be used to track all of the following, *except?*

    a. Tangible assets

    b. Digital assets

    c. Accounting transactions

    d. Human assets

28. New technologies that facilitate business and financial transactions include all of the following, *except?*

    a. Barter

    b. Mobile applications

    c. ATMs

    d. Cryptocurrencies

29. Which of the following is *not* a new technology that is changing the way we do business?

    a. Artificial intelligence

    b. Regulations

    c. Biometrics

    d. Social Media

30. Which of the following is a type of fraud?

    a. Cryptojacking

    b. Air drops

    c. Staking

    d. Provenance

¶ 10,302 FINAL EXAM QUESTIONS: MODULE 2

1. Which of the following terms is used within generally accepted auditing standards (GAAS) to indicate that a requirement is relevant except in rare circumstances?

    a. Must

    b. Unconditional

    c. May

    d. Should

2. Which Statement on Auditing Standards delays the effective dates of SAS Nos. 134–140, and the amendments to other SASs made by SAS Nos. 134–140?

    a. SAS No. 141

    b. SAS No. 142

    c. SAS No. 143

    d. SAS No. 144

3. Which of the following is a process designed to provide reasonable assurance about the achievement of the entity's objectives regarding the reliability of financial reporting, effectiveness and efficiency of operations, and compliance with applicable laws and regulations?

    a. Due diligence

    b. Safeguarding

    c. Internal control

    d. Stewardship

4. The risk assessment procedures should include each of the following, *except?*

    a. Inquiries of management

    b. Tests of controls

    c. Analytical procedures

    d. Observation and inspection

5. The understanding of the entity establishes a frame of reference within which the auditor plans the audit and exercises _____ throughout the audit when certain points occur.

    a. Professional judgment

    b. Sampling

    c. Tests of controls

    d. Due diligence

6. Which of the following is *not* one of the five components of internal control?

    a. Control environment

    b. Risk assessment process

    c. Procure to pay

    d. Control activities

7. Which of the following AU-C Sections provides requirements that relate to modifications to the opinion in the independent auditor's report?

    a. AU-C Section 250

    b. AU-C Section 310

    c. AU-C Section 470

    d. AU-C Section 705

8. The first section of the auditor's report should include the auditor's opinion and have which of the following headings?

    a. Introduction

    b. Opinion

    c. Disclaimer

    d. Foreword

9. In July 2020, the AICPA Auditing Standards Board (ASB) issued Statement on Auditing Standards (SAS) No. 142 related to which of the following?

    a. Audit evidence

    b. Going concern

    c. Fair value assertions

    d. Statistical sampling

10. When substantial doubt exists with respect to going concern, disclosure in the financial statement notes is _____.

    a. Encouraged

    b. Not required

    c. Optional

    d. Required

11. Which of the following is the basis for internal control testing?

    a. Impairment analysis

    b. Hypothesis testing

    c. Correlations

    d. Trend analysis

12. Which of the following types of data distribution would normally consist of yes/no or true/false data?

    a. Normal distribution

    b. Random distribution

    c. Selection distribution

    d. Binomial distribution

13. Which type of data analytics allows auditors to look at an entity's past performance?

    a. Descriptive analytics

    b. Diagnostic analytics

    c. Predictive analytics

    d. Ratio analytics

14. Which of the following allows practitioners to take a subset of a population and test it, and then extrapolate the characteristics of the sample to the whole population?

    a. Regression analysis

    b. Sampling

    c. Risk assessment

    d. Valuation

15. Which of the following identifies the correct formula for the audit risk model?

    a. $IR = CR \times DR \times AR$

    b. $CR = AR \times IR \times DR$

    c. $AR = IR \times CR \times DR$

    d. $DR = CR \times AR \times IR$

16. The risk that the sample supports the conclusion that the recorded account balance is materially misstated when it is not materially misstated is known as the risk of which of the following?

    a. Incorrect acceptance

    b. Incorrect rejection

    c. Assessing control risk too low

    d. Assessing control risk too high

17. Which of the following is *not* one of the five steps in the revenue recognition model?

    a. Identify the contract(s) with a customer.

    b. Identify revenue transactions.

    c. Identify the performance obligations in the contract.

    d. Determine the transaction price.

18. Which of the following is *not* a required procedure with respect to revenue recognition?

    a. Identify the contract(s) with the customer.

    b. Identify the performance obligations in the customer contract(s).

    c. Determine the transaction price.

    d. Determine when the payment was received.

19. Which of the following is *not* an indicator of an impairment?

    a. Loss of assets

    b. Decline in market value

    c. Obsolescence due to new technological changes

    d. Decline in performance

20. Which of the following is the most complex type of analytical procedure auditors use?

    a. Ratio analysis

    b. Regression analysis

    c. Trend analysis

    d. Complex analysis

21. Which of the following is *not* an element of fraud?

   a. The act

   b. Concealment

   c. Conversion

   d. Rationalization

22. Which of the following types of payroll frauds uses fictitious employees?

   a. Slow work for overtime

   b. Vacation abuse

   c. Ghost employees

   d. Falsification of hours worked

23. Which of the following is *not* part of the fraud triangle?

   a. Rationalization

   b. Concealment

   c. Opportunity

   d. Pressure

24. The fraud triangle theory was developed by which of the following?

   a. Gabriel Tarde

   b. Edwin Sutherland

   c. Ronald Akers

   d. Donald Cressey

25. Which fraud scheme involves stealing payments from one customer and covering the theft with payments stolen from other customers?

   a. Skimming

   b. Lapping

   c. Billing fraud

   d. Graft

26. Which of the following would *not* normally be involved in a skimming scheme?

   a. Business owners

   b. Employees

   c. Managers

   d. Customers

27. Which statement is true regarding the reliability of audit evidence?

   a. Audit evidence obtained by inference is more reliable than audit evidence obtained directly.

   b. Audit evidence in documentary form is more reliable than oral audit evidence.

   c. Audit evidence in a photocopy is more reliable than an original document.

   d. Audit evidence from independent sources is less reliable than evidence from a source within the entity.

28. Which theory indicates that people are most likely to imitate the actions of their superiors?

    a. Theory of Differential Association

    b. Social Learning Theory

    c. Theory of Differential Reinforcement

    d. Fraud Triangle Theory

29. Which theory postulates that fraudsters will commit a crime if they think the potential benefits of the crime outweigh the risk of punishment?

    a. Social learning theory

    b. Theory of differential association

    c. Fraud triangle theory

    d. Cognitive dissonance theory

30. Improperly recording hours worked is a type of _____ fraud.

    a. Financial statement

    b. Payroll

    c. Inventory

    d. Cyber

31. The environmental component addresses how an entity is exposed to and manages risks and opportunities related to each of the following, *except?*

    a. Climate-related matters

    b. Natural resource scarcity

    c. Pollution

    d. Fair labor practices

32. The social component encompasses information about an entity's values and business relationships and addresses issues such as which of the following?

    a. Product quality and safety

    b. Executive compensation

    c. Critical event responsiveness

    d. Entity resiliency

33. Which of the following is *not* a likely area an auditor needs to know about management's policies and procedures that are unique to climate-related matters?

    a. Capturing information about climate-related matters that may affect the entity's financial statements

    b. Independence considerations for accepting an attestation engagement on climate matters

    c. Assessing the risks of material misstatement of the financial statements resulting from climate-related matters

    d. Appropriately evaluating climate-related matters to determine whether they may need to be reflected in the entity's financial statements

34. When applying current accounting standards, entities _____ consider climate-related changes in their business and operating environment when those changes have a material effect on the financial statements.

    a. May

    b. Can

    c. Should not

    d. Must

35. Examples of _____ factors include the degree of competitiveness within the industry, customer preferences, supplier relationships, and technological developments.

    a. Regulatory

    b. Entity

    c. Industry

    d. Market

36. Management may need to consider entity-specific factors such as _____ or the effects on the entity of shifting consumer preferences for environmentally friendly alternatives.

    a. Legal factors

    b. Technological developments

    c. Investor activism

    d. Climate

37. Which of the following AU-C Sections requires an auditor to identify and assess the risks of material misstatement in the financial statements through understanding the entity and its environment, including the entity's internal control?

    a. AU-C Section 315

    b. AU-C Section 320

    c. AU-C Section 330

    d. AU-C Section 350

38. Many of the estimates affected by climate-related matters may have a _____ degree of estimation uncertainty.

    a. Low

    b. High

    c. Moderate

    d. De minimis

39. Each of the following are examples of climate-related matters that could raise substantial doubt about an entity's ability to continue as a going concern, *except?*

    a. An entity's need to obtain an opinion of its climate-related disclosures during an attestation engagement

    b. The disruption of business and the uncertainty created by operating in a geographic location that has a history of being highly susceptible to extreme weather events

    c. Increased compliance costs related to enacted emissions regulations

    d. Significant litigation claims by a city vulnerable to sea level rise

40. Which type of the following types of narrative represents subjective nonnumerical information?

    a. Stringent

    b. Hard

    c. Soft

    d. Descriptive

¶ 10,303 FINAL EXAM QUESTIONS: MODULE 3

1. Which of the following provides the reporting requirements with respect to MD&A?

    a. Regulation S-K

    b. ASC Topic 205

    c. Sarbanes-Oxley Act

    d. Regulation G

2. The SEC notes in Item 303 that MD&A should focus specifically on _____ events and uncertainties known to management that are _____ to cause reported financial information not to be necessarily indicative of future operating results or of future financial condition.

    a. Probable / Certain

    b. Material / Reasonably Likely

    c. Probable / Reasonably Likely

    d. Material / Certain

3. Information about a company's ability to generate and obtain adequate amounts of cash to meet its requirements and its plans for cash in the short-term should be disclosed in what section of MD&A?

    a. Critical accounting estimates

    b. Liquidity and capital resources

    c. Results of operations

    d. Cash flow from operating activities

4. Which of the following terms refers to a company's ability to convert an asset or a security into cash?

    a. Flexibility

    b. Elasticity

    c. Convertibility

    d. Liquidity

5. The results of operations area of MD&A should present those transactions/events that are _____, and it should present significant economic changes that materially affected the amount of income reported.

    a. Unusual/infrequent

    b. Negative

    c. Positive

    d. Noteworthy

6. The SEC's Financial Reporting Manual notes that the results of operations may not always be prepared on a consistent basis. When this occurs, the SEC notes companies may need to consider whether they need to supplement the discussion based upon _____ financial information.

    a. Pro forma

    b. Forecasted

    c. Restated

    d. Estimated

7. Which of the following is likely *not* an example of a critical accounting estimate?

   a. Inventory markdown

   b. Vendor allowances

   c. Amortization method of finite-lived intangibles

   d. Client incentives related to revenue recognition

8. Which of the following is *not* one of the four areas noted by the SEC to accomplish the objective of enhancing MD&A?

   a. Focus on materiality

   b. Focus on free cash flow

   c. Focus on analysis

   d. Focus on material trends and uncertainties

9. The SEC notes that the effectiveness of MD&A _____ with the accumulation of unnecessary detail or duplicative or uninformative disclosure that obscures material information.

   a. Slightly increases

   b. Increases

   c. Stays the same

   d. Decreases

10. Where a company's financial statements reflect material restructuring or impairment charges, or a decline in the profitability of a plant or other business activity, MD&A should also, where material, analyze the reasons underlying these matters, such as an inability to realize previously projected economies of scale, a failure to renew or secure key customer contracts, or a failure to keep downtime at acceptable levels due to aging equipment. This is an example of focusing on which of the following?

   a. Materiality

   b. Analysis

   c. Judgment

   d. Trends

11. A(n) _____ financial measure is a numerical measure of a registrant's historical or future financial performance, financial position, or cash flow that excludes amounts that are included in the most directly comparable measure calculated and presented in accordance with GAAP.

   a. Non-GAAP

   b. Adjusted

   c. Synthetic

   d. IFRS

12. EBIT and EBITDA are examples of which of the following?

   a. GAAP financial measures

   b. Non-GAAP financial measures

   c. Both GAAP and non-GAAP financial measures

   d. Neither GAAP nor non-GAAP financial measures

13. Free cash flow is an example of which of the following?

    a. GAAP financial measure

    b. Non-GAAP financial measure

    c. Both GAAP and non-GAAP financial measure

    d. Neither GAAP nor non-GAAP financial measure

14. Which of the following identifies the type of currency used to eliminate the effect of these significant fluctuations when calculating financial performance numbers?

    a. Functional currency

    b. Legal currency

    c. Balanced currency

    d. Constant currency

15. One of the overarching principles with respect to non-GAAP financial measures is that they cannot be which of the following?

    a. Presented

    b. Misleading

    c. Communicated

    d. Justified

16. Which of the following disclosures is within the scope of Regulation G?

    a. Disclosure of material information that includes a non-GAAP financial measure

    b. Disclosure of amounts of expected indebtedness

    c. Disclosure of estimated revenues or expenses of a new product line

    d. Disclosure of amounts of repayments that have been planned or decided upon but not yet made

17. Regulation G requires a quantitative reconciliation for historical non-GAAP measures presented unless which of the following applies?

    a. The non-GAAP measures are well known and used by the entity's peer group.

    b. The entity receives pre-clearance from the FASB to not include the reconciliation.

    c. The activity involves unreasonable efforts, and the reasons thereof are properly disclosed.

    d. The entity is a non-accelerated SEC filer.

18. Regulation S-K requires that an issuer, when including a non-GAAP financial measure in a filing with the SEC, must include a presentation, with equal or greater _____, of the most directly comparable financial measure or measures calculated and presented in accordance with GAAP.

    a. Importance

    b. Prominence

    c. Distinction

    d. Position

19. According to SEC interpretations, certain adjustments, although not explicitly prohibited, _____ result in a non-GAAP measure that is misleading.

    a. Should not

    b. Cannot

    c. Will not

    d. Can

20. According to the SEC, entities _____ provide income tax effects on its non-GAAP measures depending on the _____ of the measures.

    a. Should not, nature

    b. Should, nature

    c. Should not, materiality

    d. Should, materiality

¶ 10,400 Answer Sheets

¶ 10,401 Top Accounting and Auditing Issues for 2023 CPE Course: MODULE 1

Go to **cchcpelink.com/printcpe** to complete your Final Exam online for instant results.

A $144.00 processing fee will be charged for each user submitting Module 1 to **cchcpelink.com/printcpe** online for grading.

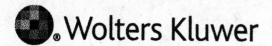
Wolters Kluwer

Module 1: Answer Sheet

Please answer the questions by indicating the appropriate letter next to the corresponding number.

1. _____	10. _____	19. _____	28. _____
2. _____	11. _____	20. _____	29. _____
3. _____	12. _____	21. _____	30. _____
4. _____	13. _____	22. _____	
5. _____	14. _____	23. _____	
6. _____	15. _____	24. _____	
7. _____	16. _____	25. _____	
8. _____	17. _____	26. _____	
9. _____	18. _____	27. _____	

Please complete the Evaluation Form (located after the Module 3 Answer Sheet). Thank you.

¶ 10,402 Top Accounting and Auditing Issues for 2023 CPE Course: MODULE 2

Go to **cchcpelink.com/printcpe** to complete your Final Exam online for instant results.

A $144.00 processing fee will be charged for each user submitting Module 2 to **cchcpelink.com/printcpe** for online grading.

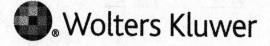

Module 2: Answer Sheet

Please answer the questions by indicating the appropriate letter next to the corresponding number.

1. ___	11. ___	21. ___	31. ___
2. ___	12. ___	22. ___	32. ___
3. ___	13. ___	23. ___	33. ___
4. ___	14. ___	24. ___	34. ___
5. ___	15. ___	25. ___	35. ___
6. ___	16. ___	26. ___	36. ___
7. ___	17. ___	27. ___	37. ___
8. ___	18. ___	28. ___	38. ___
9. ___	19. ___	29. ___	39. ___
10. ___	20. ___	30. ___	40. ___

Please complete the Evaluation Form (located after the Module 3 Answer Sheet). Thank you.

¶ 10,403 Top Accounting and Auditing Issues for 2023 CPE Course: MODULE 3

Go to **cchcpelink.com/printcpe** to complete your Final Exam online for instant results.

A $96.00 processing fee will be charged for each user submitting Module 3 to **cchcpe-link.com/printcpe** online for grading.

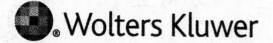

Module 3: Answer Sheet

Please answer the questions by indicating the appropriate letter next to the corresponding number.

1. _____ 6. _____ 11. _____ 16. _____

2. _____ 7. _____ 12. _____ 17. _____

3. _____ 8. _____ 13. _____ 18. _____

4. _____ 9. _____ 14. _____ 19. _____

5. _____ 10. _____ 15. _____ 20. _____

**Please complete the Evaluation Form (located after the Module 3 Answer Sheet).
Thank you.**

¶ 10,500 Top Accounting and Auditing Issues for 2023 CPE Course: Evaluation Form
(10024493-0010)

Please take a few moments to fill out and submit this evaluation to Wolters Kluwer so that we can better provide you with the type of self-study programs you want and need. Thank you.

About This Program

1. Please circle the number that best reflects the extent of your agreement with the following statements:

		Strongly Agree				Strongly Disagree
a.	The Course objectives were met.	5	4	3	2	1
b.	This Course was comprehensive and organized.	5	4	3	2	1
c.	The content was current and technically accurate.	5	4	3	2	1
d.	This Course content was relevant and contributed to achievement of the learning objectives.	5	4	3	2	1
e.	The prerequisite requirements were appropriate.	5	4	3	2	1
f.	This Course was a valuable learning experience.	5	4	3	2	1
g.	The Course completion time was appropriate.	5	4	3	2	1

2. What do you consider to be the strong points of this Course?

3. What improvements can we make to this Course?

THANK YOU FOR TAKING THE TIME TO COMPLETE THIS SURVEY!

—